C++/C#
PROGRAMMER'S GUIDE TO
WINDOWS 2000®

ISBN 0-13-040947-2

90000

9 780130 409478

PRENTICE HALL SERIES ON MICROSOFT® TECHNOLOGIES

C++/C#

PROGRAMMER'S GUIDE TO WINDOWS 2000®

Ronald D. Reeves

Prentice Hall PTR, Upper Saddle River, NJ 07458
www.phptr.com

CARROLL COLLEGE LIBRARY
Waukesha, Wisconsin 53186

Editorial/Production Supervision: Kathleen M. Caren
Acquisitions Editor: Mike Meehan
Development Editor: Ralph Moore
Cover Design Director: Jerry Votta
Manufacturing Manager: Maura Zaldivar
Series Design: Maureen Eide
Marketing Manager: Debby Van Dijk
Art Director: Gail Cocker-Bogusz

© 2002 by PrenticeHall PTR
Prentice-Hall, Inc.
Upper Saddle River, New Jersey 07458

Prentice Hall books are widely used by corporations and government agencies for
training, marketing, and resale. The publisher offers discounts on this book when
ordered in bulk quantities. For more information, contact:
Corporate Sales Department,
Prentice Hall PTR
One Lake Street
Upper Saddle River, NJ 07458
Phone: 800-382-3419; FAX: 201-236-7141
E-mail (Internet): corpsales@prenhall.com

All rights reserved. No part of this book may be reproduced, in any form
or by any means, without permission in writing from the publisher.

Printed in the United States of America

10   9   8   7   6   5   4   3   2   1

ISBN 0-13-040947-2

Pearson Education Limited (UK)
Pearson Education Australia Pty Ltd
Prentice Hall Canada Ltd
Pearson Educación de Mexico, S.A. de C.V.
Pearson Education Japan KK
Pearson Education China Ltd
Pearson Education Asia Pte Ltd
Prentice Hall, Upper Saddle River, New Jersey

CONTENTS

▼ THREE .NET Framework   47

FOREWORD

Visual Studio.NET represents a significant step forward in the continuing evolution of software application development environments. The .NET Framework represents our greatest step forward to date, in using the rich semantics of classes and object-oriented design in communication, and control of the powerful Windows 2000 Operating System. A very powerful synergy is formed between the developer, the compiler, the .NET Framework base classes, the Common Language Runtime (CLR), and the Windows 2000 Operating System. A great deal of the cognitive load is taken off the developer, by the encapsulating of the Windows 2000 Operating System Win32 APIs by the .NET Framework base classes. The intelligent collaboration between the base classes, and the CLR automates and controls many functions involved in Windows 2000 application development and execution.

Over the past 7 years, Dr. Ron Reeves has been a consultant and trainer for UCI Software Technical Training. As a trainer, Ron will consistently go the extra mile to make sure his students clearly understand the material and at the same time make the learning experience enjoyable. As an author, he demonstrates yet another remarkable talent. He is an excellent and gifted writer. As a reader of this book you will like what he has to contribute.

In this first-class book, Ron has borrowed on his 40 plus years of computer system design and implementation to discuss this revolutionary approach to creating software applications. He takes a bottom-up approach to explaining how this whole new architecture fits together. First, he covers the Windows 2000 Operating System architecture and what major components are in it. The next chapter then reviews how the Win32 APIs are used to develop an application to run under Windows 2000. Of course this is the unmanaged mode of Visual C++ and is the default for the compiler. Then he covers the architecture of the .NET Framework and the significant components involved in it. He shows the relationship of this framework to the Win32 APIs of Windows 2000. He then steps on up to the Visual C++ compiler, and how it is structured to work in the new environment. The last chapter then covers the new C# compiler and how it is structured to work in the new environment. The book also points out how we are continuing to develop more and smarter META layers of software between the developer and the under lying hardware engine. It shows how these META layers affects the developer's cognitive understanding of the structure.

Andrew Scoppa
UCI software Technical Training

PREFACE

Windows 2000 is a large and important system, and it is the core of a more embracing architecture Microsoft calls Windows DNA 2000. In this context DNA stands for Distributed interNet Applications, and represents Microsoft's vision for building distributed systems. This type of architecture is focused on developing the new "digital nervous system" for enterprises. In this context, the "digital nervous system" is the corporate, digital equivalent of the human nervous system: an information system that can provide a well-integrated flow of information at the right time, to the right place in an organization. Such systems can be programmed at many levels, from the lowest level of device drivers giving access to privileged instructions, to very high levels using powerful software application development tools. This book is aimed at Windows 2000 application programming, using C++/C# and the Visual Studio.NET development environment. The C++/C# and Visual Studio.NET discussions and examples are based upon the BETA 1Win32 programming required for Windows 2000. The book should prove suitable for programmers migrating to Windows 2000 from other environments, such as UNIX and mainframes, as well as for programmers moving up from earlier versions of Windows. A large part of the book addresses issues of what components actually make up the .NET Framework and the Windows 2000 Operating System. One must realize, there are numerous constraints among all the components, and one needs to try to understand, from the beginning, how they fit into the whole .NET Framework and the Windows 2000 Operating System.

Learning such complex technology can be quite a challenge. The documentation is vast, equivalent to tens of thousands of printed pages, and it is changing all the time. You can subscribe to various Internet discussion groups, and you will receive hundreds of emails every day. There are many, many books on different parts of this technology. But, how do you grasp the whole picture? This book aims to be holistic, to provide a practical guide for the C++/C# programmer. It is not a substitute for documentation or more specialized books, including "bibles" of various sorts that help you learn different APIs. Rather, the book provides a tutorial, giving you all the basic information you need to create working Windows 2000 application systems. The book and companion CD has many example programs in both C++ and C# to aid you in gaining an understanding of how the whole environment fits together.

Chapter 1 is an introduction showing an architectural overview of Windows 2000. It shows an overall block diagram of Windows 2000 and then discusses in general some of the key components of Windows 2000. The chapter also contains a general description of the different versions of Windows 2000.

Chapter 2 covers the most essential fundamentals of Windows 2000 programming for C++/C# programmers. We start off with an architectural overview of Windows 2000. There is enough detail to enable an experienced C++ programmer new to Windows 2000 to get an understanding of Windows 2000. This chapter also covers the concepts of processes, threads, jobs, and the handling of errors and exceptional conditions. The software priority structure is also covered in this chapter. The chapter explains the use of Win32 APIs for programming without the use of the .NET Framework base classes. We will see however, that the .NET Framework base classes almost completely encapsulate these Win32 APIs for application development. As a C++ programmer you can still, in native mode, work with the Win32 APIs if you should choose to do so. You can also mix native mode and managed code mode in your application components. C# works, as we will see, in managed code mode only. There are keywords, however, to let the C# code have sections of native mode code. Visual Studio.NET, as we will see in Chapter 4, has one standard approach to handling errors and exceptions. These topics bear directly on the issues of being able to create scalable and robust applications discussed above. The recently published book, *Win32 System Services—The Heart of Windows 98 and Windows 2000*, by Ron Reeves and Marshall Brain, covers in detail the use of Win32 APIs for application development.

Chapter 3 covers the most essential features of the new .NET Framework primarily from an architectural point of view. This material is the *raison d'être* for the book. It is expected that the .NET Framework will become absolutely central to modern Windows application architecture and programming development. Hence, it is important for you to understand the basics. This chapter will give you the background for the discussions in Chapters 4 and 5 on Visual C++ and C#. COM+ will continue to play an important role in the development of multiple-tier application systems. For COM+ details, there are many other books on the subject, including Robert Oberg's book, *Understanding and Programming COM+—A Practical Guide to Windows 2000 DNA*.

Chapter 4 covers the Visual C++ 7.0 compiler and what is involved in using the compiler to create applications. The discussion is primarily based upon the use of C++ in a managed code mode, because that is the only mode that uses the Common Language Runtime (CLR) component. This mode picks up all the advantages of the new management features of the CLR. It discusses in detail the Managed Extensions for C++ that enables the programmer to take advantage of the .NET Framework architecture. The chapter covers the considerations of using the compiler in applications, as opposed to just a language syntax discussion.

Chapter 5 covers the C# compiler and what is involved in using the compiler to create applications. Windows 2000 and .NET Framework is expected to rely heavily on C# for enterprise level system development. Also, this new approach to distributed processing using C# does not require the System Register for any of its activity—just a language syntax discussion.

The appendices cover in detail the supporting material for the chapters. In some cases, a given appendix will be as big as a chapter. All the Win32 APIs and the .NET Framework base classes are listed in the appendices, along with software priority charts, and so on.

Introduction

*I*n the next few sections we will establish the main Windows 2000 Operating System capabilities for the fundamentals involved in programming for Windows 2000. There are obviously many more sections that could be covered, but we deemed these to be most important for understanding the programming of Windows 2000. This fundamental knowledge, along with the other topics covered in this book, will enable you to program the many Windows 2000 services. Included in the Windows 2000 services are base services, component services, data access services, graphics and multimedia services, management services, messaging and collaboration services, networking services, security, tools and languages, user interface services, and Web services. The topics covered in the overall book should put into perspective these Windows 2000 services, and provide a kind of roadmap for how to program these capabilities. With this understanding, we will go into the Visual Studio.NET software development environment and show you how to implement applications under this new development environment. We will show you how this seamless new development environment lets you control and harness the power of the Windows 2000 engine.

One of the key architectural features of a sophisticated operating system, which enables it to handle many activities concurrently, is the software priority scheme. Usually, this is one of the first things I try to figure out when I want to start developing application programs using the Operating System (OS). The OS also uses a hardware priority scheme, but we will not cover that in this book. The next thing that I like to understand is the interface communication capabilities APIs (Application Programming Interface) that are available to me for controlling and communicating with the OS. Of course, rolled into this scheme of things is how the OS partitions work and allocate resources to the various application software activities, especially memory allocation. The software synchronizing mechanism, available to control application and system resource allocations, is closely related to the software priority scheme. In a pseudo real-time OS like Windows 2000 it is very important to be able to synchronize the various events relative to thread priorities. We will cover these aspects in detail as we proceed through the various sections. These fundamentals work the same across all Windows 2000 platforms. The Windows 2000 platform consists of four products as follows:

- Windows 2000 Professional
- Windows 2000 Server
- Windows 2000 Advanced Server
- Windows 2000 Data Center

Microsoft has done an excellent job, in that the Win32 API family of Windows 2000 programming interfaces is the standard programming interface for all Windows 2000 platforms. The Win32 APIs are the interface communication capabilities (APIs) that I mentioned earlier, which allow the programmer to control and communicate with the various capabilities of Windows 2000. Microsoft has also provided a rich set of libraries, the Windows Foundation Classes (WFC). The .NET Framework wraps the Windows 2000 and provides a very rich semantic interface for our use of the Windows 2000 Operating System capabilities. The Visual C++ compiler, and the C# compiler and associated tools of the Integrated Development Environment (IDE), allows program development, execution, and debug within this IDE. This environment gives the programmer a simpler but powerful tool, for developing application software using the Windows 2000 APIs and associated services. If one is programming using either the WinForm or the Web Services APIs that wrap the Win32 APIs, they significantly reduce the software footprint the application programmer needs to worry about to create their applications. The Microsoft Foundation Class (MFC) library and the Active Template Library (ATL) are also available to the application developer. These libraries simplify the creation of COM+ components, Graphical User Interfaces (GUI), database interfaces, and other aspects of application development. Interestingly enough, ATL is integrated into MFC and allows the best of both worlds for GUI and small efficient software component development.

As we proceed, we will use both the C++ compiler and the C# compiler, and use them with the associated tools of the new Visual Studio.Net Integrated Development Environment (Visual Studio.Net is the next release after Visual Studio 6.0). We are using Visual Studio.Net BETA 1 so there will be some changes by the time of the final release. However, the software development environment does not affect the fundamentals of the Windows 2000 OS, which is what we will cover in the first few chapters of the book. We are covering the fundamentals from the standpoint of API calls and using them for your application. Visual Studio.Net does introduce another framework that wraps the Windows 2000 OS; this is the .NET Framework. We will cover this new framework after we cover Windows 2000. This framework is middleware that sets between your application and the Windows 2000 OS.

Windows 2000 Operating System Architecture

Figure 1–1 shows the overall view of the major blocks in the Windows 2000 Operating System. As the block diagram shows, applications are kept separate from the operating system itself. The operating-system code runs in a privileged processor mode known as the *kernel* and has access to system data and hardware. Applications run in a nonprivileged processor mode known as *user mode* and have limited access to system data and hardware through a set of tightly controlled APIs. One of the design goals of the Windows 2000 operating system was to keep the base operating system as small and efficient as possible. This was accomplished by allowing only those functions that could not reasonably be performed elsewhere to remain in the base operating system. The functionality that was pushed out of the kernel ended up in a set of nonprivileged servers know as the *protected subsystems*. The protected subsystems provide the traditional operating system support to applications through a feature-rich set of APIs.

Executive

The kernel-mode portion of the Windows 2000 operating system is called the *Executive* and, except for a user interface, is a complete operating system unto itself. The Executive is never modified or recompiled by the system administrator. The Executive is actually a family of software components that provide basic operating-system services to the protected subsystems and to each other. The Executive components, as shown in Figure 1–1, include:

- I/O Manager
- Object Manager
- Security Reference Monitor
- Process Manager
- Local Procedure Call Facility
- Virtual Memory Manager
- Window Manager
- Graphics Device Interface
- Graphics Device Drivers

The Executive components are completely independent of one another and communicate through carefully controlled interfaces. This module design allows existing Executive components to be removed and replaced with ones

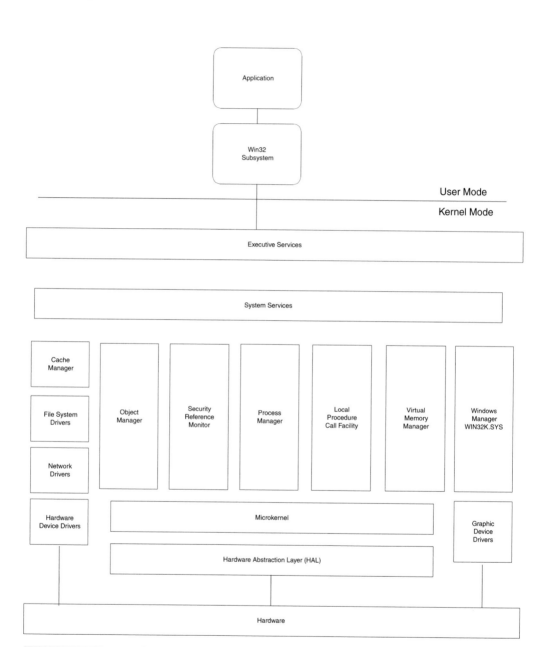

Figure 1–1   *Windows 2000 Block Diagram.*

that implement new technologies or features. As long as the integrity of the existing interface is maintained, the operating system runs as before. The top layer of the Executive is called the *System Services*, which are the interface between user-mode protected subsystems and kernel mode. Each Executive component has a set of APIs. These APIs that are exported to user space are collectively called "System Services," as shown in Figure 1–1. As we'll see later, Local Procedure Call (LPC) facility communication to these System Service APIs are handled via the LPC.

Appendix D shows a complete listing of all APIs without their associated parameters. There are 1,939 Win32 API functions, which are shown in alphabetical order. There are 95 categories of Win32 functions, which these 1,939 functions are distributed over. By looking at the category of functionality you are interested in programming, you can see the list of possible Win32 APIs available for your use. Also the functionality should give you an idea which Executive component is involved in supplying the needed functionality. This gives you an idea of what we meant earlier when we said a feature-rich set of APIs are available for your use.

Protected Subsystems

The protected subsystems are *user-mode* servers that are started when Windows 2000 is started. There are two types of protected subsystems: integral and environment. An *integral subsystem* is a server that performs an important operating system function, such as security. An *environment subsystem* is a server that provides support to applications written for or native to different operating system environments, such as OS/2. The Windows 2000 currently ships with three environment subsystems: the Win32 subsystem, the POSIX subsystem, and the OS/2 subsystem.

The Win32 (or 32-bit Windows) subsystem is the native subsystem of Windows 2000. It provides the most capabilities and efficiencies to its applications and is the subsystem of choice for new software development. The POSIX and OS/2 subsystems provide compatibility environments for their respective applications and are not as feature-rich as the Win32 subsystem.

Local Procedure Call Facility

Applications and environment subsystem have a client-server relationship. That is, the client (an application) makes calls to the environment server (a subsystem) to satisfy a request for some types of system services. To allow for a client-server relationship between applications and the environment subsystem, Windows 2000 provides a communication mechanism between them. The Executive implements a message-passing facility called a *Local Procedure Call* (LPC) facility. It works very much like the Remote Procedure Call (RPC) facility used for networked processing. However, the LPC facility is optimized for two processes running on the same computer.

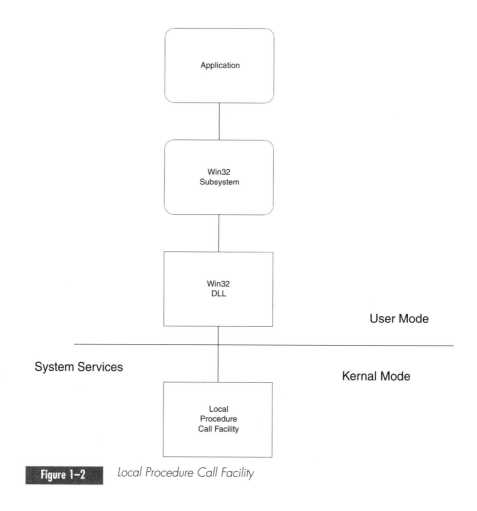

Figure 1–2   *Local Procedure Call Facility*

Applications communicate with environment subsystems by passing messages via the LPC facility. The message-passing process is hidden from the client applications by function stubs (nonexecutable placeholders used by calls from the server environment) provided in the form of special dynamic-link libraries (DLLs). When an application makes an application program interface (API) call to the environment subsystem, the stub in the client (application) process packages the parameters for the call and sends them to a server (subsystem) process that implements the call (see Figure 1–2). It is the LPC facility that allows the stub procedure to pass the data to the server process and wait for a response. For example, consider how this process works in the Win32 subsystem. When a Win32 application is loaded to run, it is linked to a DLL that contains stubs for all of the functions in the Win32

APIs. When the application calls a Win32 function (in this example, the **CreateWindow** Win32 function) the call is processed as follows:

1. The **CreateWindow()** stub function in the DLL is called by the client Win32 application.

2. The stub function constructs a message that contains all the data needed to create a window and sends the message to the Win32 server process (that is, the Win32 subsystem).

3. The Win32 subsystem receives the message and calls the real **CreateWindow()** function. The window is created.

4. The Win32 subsystem sends a message containing the results of the **CreateWindow()** function back to the stub function in the DLL.

5. The stub function unpacks the server message from the subsystem and returns the results to the client Win32 application.

From the application's perspective, the **CreateWindow()** function in the DLL created the window. The application does not know that the work was actually performed by the Win32 server process (the Win32 subsystem), that a message was sent to make it happen, or even that the Win32 server process exists. It does not know that the subsystem called one or more Executive system servers to support its call to **CreateWindow**. Key to this functionality is the operating system environment for applications. This is covered in some detail in the next chapter.

Processes, Threads, and Jobs in Windows 2000

*L*et's look at the basic programming environment for an executable application program. This basic programming environment is called a process for a given executable. Jobs, which are new with Windows 2000, can be viewed as a container of processes. It gives us a common point of control over a related set of executables (processes). A job object allows groups of processes to be managed as a unit. Job objects are namable, securable, sharable objects that control attributes of the processes associated with them. Operations performed on the job object affect all processes associated with the job object. In some cases only a single executable may be in a Job, just to gain the additional control available, with the Job container, over the executable.

A Win32 based application consists of one or more processes. A process, in the simplest terms, is an executing program. One or more threads run in the context of the process. A thread is the basic unit to which the operating system allocates processor time (unit of work). A thread can execute any part of the process code, including parts currently being executed by another thread. A fiber is a unit of execution that must be manually scheduled by the application. Fibers run in the context of the threads that schedule them. Fibers were added to Windows 2000 to make porting UNIX applications to Windows easier. Fibers should be typically avoided, and normal Windows 2000 threads used. We will not be covering fibers in this book. Each process provides the resources needed to execute a program. A process has a virtual address space, executable code, data, object handles, environment variables, a base priority, and minimum and maximum working set sizes. Each process is started with a single thread, often called the primary thread, but additional threads can be created from any of its threads. All threads of a process share its virtual address space and system resources. In addition, each thread maintains exception handlers, a scheduling priority, and a set of structures the system will use to save the thread context until it is scheduled. The thread context includes the thread's set of machine registers, the kernel stack, a thread environment block, and a user stack in the address space of the thread's process. Windows 2000 supports preemptive multitasking, which creates the effect of simultaneous execution of multiple threads from multiple processes. On a multiprocessor computer, Windows 2000 can simultaneously execute as many threads as there are processors on the computer. There isn't anything special you need to do to take advantage of this multiple CPU thread processing.

Appendix A shows the Process, Thread, and Job APIs available for utilization in programming your application. This is the platform software development kit (SDK) Win32 APIs for the Process, Threads, and Job objects. There are similar-named APIs in MFC (Microsoft Foundation Classes) that are used to perform these functions. In most cases, the MFC API has a similar name as the SDK name, but typically has a reduced parameter set. Often, the MFC API call will pick up other SDK APIs, such that only one call is necessary to perform a multifunction SDK API sequence. We will not be covering the MFC Framework but will cover the new .NET WinForm instead. However, the MFC Framework, as well as the ATL class library, is still available to be used. At this point, I would like to show the **CreateProcess** Win32 API since this is one of the more important ones that gets the whole programming activity started. We will just show its form and then in a later programming example we will show the C++ call to set up the Process and its primary thread. The following is an example of a SDK API call that is not wrapped for example by the MFC. When you see a call with :: in front of it, you know that it is a direct call to the SDK API such as **::CreateProcess**(........). I have not listed the parameter definitions in most of the API discussions, so that we may follow the behavioral logic easier. Only with some of the APIs have I included the parameters and their definitions. I have put the APIs in **BOLD** so they stand out in the discussion. All APIs are available online under the Visual C++ Help file and the MSDN Library. When one looks at the APIs, and the extensive parameters available, one can start to get a feel for the rich semantics available for dialoguing with Windows 2000. In Appendix F we list the data types supported by the Microsoft Win32 APIs that are used to define function return values, function and message parameters, and structure members. This appendix also defines the size and meaning of these elements. As you can see, they have predefined quite a few of the HANDLES and POINTER types that one needs to develop an application.

Object Categories

The system provides three categories of objects: user, graphics device interface (GDI), and kernel. The system uses user objects to support window management, GDI objects to support graphics, and kernel objects to support memory management, process execution, and interprocess communications (IPC). See Appendix C for a list of these objects and information about creating and using a specific object. In general, the Win32 APIs distribute across these objects to allow us to create, use, and delete the various system objects.

Processes

CREATING AND TERMINATING PROCESSES

Each process that you will create belongs to one of the following priority classes:

    IDLE_PRIORITY_CLASS
    BELOW_NORMAL_PRIORITY_CLASS
    NORMAL_PRIORITY_CLASS
    ABOVE_NORMAL_PRIORITY_CLASS
    HIGH_PRIORITY_CLASS
    REALTIME_PRIORITY_CLASS

Note   The BELOW_NORMAL_PRIORITY_CLASS and ABOVE_NORMAL_PRIORITY_CLASS are new for Windows 2000.

By default, the priority class of a process is NORMAL_PRIORITY_CLASS. Use the **CreateProcess** function to specify the priority class of a child process when you create it. If the calling process is IDLE_PRIORITY_CLASS or BELOW_NORMAL_CLASS, the new process will inherit this class. Use the **GetPriorityClass** function to determine the current priority class of a process, and the **SetPriorityClass** function to change the priority class of a process.

Processes that monitor the system, such as screen savers or applications that periodically update a display, should use IDLE_PRIORITY_CLASS. This prevents the threads of this process, which do not have high priority, from interfering with higher priority threads. Use HIGH_PRIORITY_CLASS with care. If a thread runs at the highest priority level for extended periods, other threads in the system will not get processor time. If several threads are set at high priority at the same time, the threads lose their effectiveness. The high-priority class should be reserved for threads that must respond to time-critical events. If your application performs one task that requires the high-priority class while the rest of its tasks are normal priority, use **SetPriorityClass** to raise the priority class of the application temporarily; then reduce it after the time-critical task has been completed. Another strategy is to create a high-priority process that has all of its threads blocked most of the time, awakening threads only when critical tasks are needed. The important point is that a high-priority thread should execute for a brief time, only when it has time-critical work to perform. You should almost never use REALTIME_PRIORITY_CLASS, because this interrupts system threads that manage mouse input, keyboard input, and background disk flushing. This class can be appropriate for applications that "talk" directly to hardware or that perform brief tasks that should have limited interruptions.

CreateProcess is one of the key APIs for constructing your application. The API call is shown with the many parameters, and an explanation of the parameters is given. The priority for the process is specified in dwCreationFlags parameter. This is used to set the base priority for individual threads. Thread priorities are specified relative to the process in which they are contained. Appendix B shows the complete assignment possibilities for priorities of threads and their associated process priority.

```
BOOL CreateProcess (
    LPCTSTR                 lpApplicationName,
    LPTSTR                  lpCommandLine, // command line string
    LPSECURITY_ATTRIBUTE    SlpProcessAttributes,
    LPSECURITY_ATTRIBUTE    SlpThreadAttributes,
    BOOL                    bInheritHandles, // handle inheritance option
    DWORD                   dwCreationFlags, // creation flags
    LPVOID                  lpEnvironment,    // new environment block
    LPCTSTR                 lpCurrentDirectory,
    LPSTARTUPINFO           lpStartupInfo,
    LPPROCESS_INFORMATION   lpProcessInformation);
Parameters
```

lpApplicationName
[in] Pointer to a null-terminated string that specifies the module to execute. The string can specify the full path and file name of the module to execute or it can specify a partial name. In the case of a partial name, the function uses the current drive and current directory to complete the specification. The function will not use the search path. The lpApplicationName parameter can be NULL. In that case, the module name must be the first white space-delimited token in the lpCommandLine string. If you are using a long file name that contains a space, use quoted

strings to indicate where the file name ends and the arguments begin; otherwise, the file name is ambiguous. For example, consider the string "c:\program files\sub dir\program name". This string can be interpreted in a number of ways. The system tries to interpret the possibilities in the following order:

c:\program.exe files\sub dir\program name
c:\program files\sub.exe dir\program name
c:\program files\sub dir\program.exe name
c:\program files\sub dir\program name.exe

lpCommandLine

[in] Pointer to a null-terminated string that specifies the command line to execute. The system adds a null character to the command line, trimming the string, if necessary, to indicate which file was actually used. The lpCommandLine parameter can be NULL. In that case, the function uses the string pointed to by lpApplicationName as the command line. If both lpApplicationName and lpCommandLine are non-NULL, *lpApplicationName specifies the module to execute, and *lpCommandLine specifies the command line. The new process can use GetCommandLine to retrieve the entire command line. If lpApplicationName is NULL, the first white-space delimited token of the command line specifies the module name. If you are using a long name that contains a space, use quoted strings to indicate where the first name ends and the arguments begin.

lpProcessAttributes

[in] Pointer to a SECURITY_ATTRIBUTES structure that determines whether the returned handle can be inherited by child processes. If lpProcessAttributes is NULL, the handle cannot be inherited. If the ipProcessAttributes is NULL, the process gets a default security descriptor.

lpThreadAttributes

[in] Pointer to a SECURITY_ATTRIBUTES structure that determines whether the returned handle can be inherited by child processes. If lpThreadAttributes is NULL, the handle cannot be inherited. If lpThreadAttribute is NULL, the thread gets a default security descriptor.

bInheritHandles

[in] Indicates whether the new process inherits handles from the calling process. If TRUE, each inheritable open handle in the calling process is inherited by the new process. Inherited handles have the same value and access privileges as the original handles.

dwCreationFlags

[in] Specifies additional flags that control the priority class and the creation of the process. The following creating flags can be specified in any combination, except as noted.

Value	Meaning
CREATE_BREAKAWAY_FROM_JOB	The child processes of a process associated with a job are not associated with the job. If the calling process is not associated with a job, this flag has no effect. If the calling process is associated with a job, the job must set the JOB_OBJEC_LIMIT_BREAKAWAY_OK limit or CreateProcess will fail.

Note   There are many more flags for various possible setting.

The dwCreationFlags parameter also controls the new process's priority class, which is used to determine the scheduling priorities of the process's threads. If none of the following priority class flags is specified, the priority class defaults to NORMAL_PRIORITY_CLASS unless the priority class of the creating process is IDLE_PRIORITY_CLASS or BELOW_NORMAL_PRIORITY_CLASS. In this case, the child process receives the default priority class of the calling process. You can specify one of the following values:

Priority	Meaning
ABOVE_NORMAL_PRIORITY_CLASS	Indicates a process that has priority higher than NORMAL_PRIORITY_CLASS but lower than HIGH_PRIORITY_CLASS.
BELOW_NORMAL_PRIORITY_CLASS	Indicates a process that has priority higher than IDLE_PRIORITY_CLASS but lower than NORMAL_PRIORITY_CLASS.
HIGH_PRIORITY_CLASS	Indicates a process that performs time-critical tasks. The threads of a high-priority class preempt the threads of normal-priority or idle-priority class processes. An example is the Task List, which must respond quickly when called by the user, regardless of the load on the system. Use extreme care when using the high-priority class, because a CPU bound application with a high-priority class can use nearly all available machine cycles.
IDLE_PRIORITY_CLASS	Indicates a process whose threads run only when the system is idle and are preempted by the threads of any process running in a higher priority class. An example is a screen saver. The idle priority class is inherited by child processes.

NORMAL_PRIORITY_CLASS	Indicates a normal process with no special scheduling needs.
REALTIME_PRIORITY_CLASS	Indicates a process that has the highest possible priority. The threads of a real-time priority class process preempt the threads of all other processes, including operating system processes performing important tasks. For example, a real-time process that executes for more than a very brief interval can cause disk caches not to flush or cause the mouse to be unresponsive.

lpEnvironment
> [in] Pointer to an environment block for the new process. If this parameter is NULL, the new process uses the environment of the calling process. An environment block consists of a null-terminated block of null-terminated strings. Each string is in the form:
>
> > name=value
>
> Because the equal sign is used as a separator, it must not be used in the name of an environment variable.

lpCurrentDirectory
> [in] Pointer to a null-terminated string that specifies the current drive and directory for the child process. The string must be a full path and file name that includes a drive letter. If this parameter is NULL, the new process will have the same current drive and directory as the calling process. This option is provided primarily for shells that need to start an application and specify its initial drive and working directory.

lpStartupInfo
> [in] Pointer to a STARTUPINFO structure that specifies how the main window for the new process should appear.

lpProcessInformation
> [out] Pointer to a PROCESS_INFORMATION structure that receives identification information about the new process.

Return Values
> If the function succeeds, the return value is nonzero.
> If the function fails, the return value is zero. To get extended error information, call GetLastError.

Note   There is additional information on this **CreateProcess** function in the remarks section of the API description in the Windows 2000 documentation.

Terminating A Process

The **ExitProcess** function ends a process and all its threads. This function does not return a value.

> void **ExitProcess**(UINT uExitCode);

uExitCode [in] – Specifies the exit code for the process, and for all threads that are terminated as a result of this call. Use the **GetExitCodeProcess** function to retrieve the process's exit value. Use the **GetExitCodeThread** function to retrieve a thread's exit value.

   ExitProcess is the preferred method of ending a process. This function provides a clean process shutdown. This includes calling the entry-point function of all attached dynamic-link (DLLs) with a value indicating that the process is detaching from the DLL. If a process terminates by calling **TerminateProcess**, the DLLs that the process is attached to are not notified of the process termination. After all attached DLLs have executed any process termination value, this function terminates the current process.

   Terminating a process causes the following:

1. All of the object handles opened by the process are closed.
2. All of the threads in the process terminate their execution.
3. The state of the process object becomes signaled, satisfying any threads that had been waiting for the process to terminate.
4. The states of all threads of the process become signaled, satisfying any threads that had been waiting for the threads to terminate.
5. The termination status of the process changes from STILL_ACTIVE to the exit value of the process.

   Terminating a process does not cause child processes to be terminated. Terminating a process does not necessarily remove the process object from the operating system. A process object is deleted when the last handle to the process is closed. The **ExitProcess**, **ExitThread**, **CreateThread**, **CreateRemoteThread** functions and a process that is starting (as the result of a call by **CreateProcess**) are serialized between each other within a process. Only one of these events can happen in an address space at a time. This means the following restrictions hold:

1. During process startup and DLL initialization routines, new threads can be created, but they do not begin execution until DLL initialization is done for the process.
2. Only one thread in a process can be in a DLL initialization or detach routine at a time.
3. If any process is in its DLL initialization or detach routine, **ExitProcess** does not return.

Warning: The **TerminateProcess** function should be used only in extreme circumstances, since it does not allow threads to clean up or save data and does not notify DLLs. If you need to have a process terminate another process, the following steps provide a better solution:

1. Have both processes call the **RegisterWindowMessage** function to create a private message.

2. One process can terminate the other process by broadcasting the private message using the **BroadcastSystemMessage** function as follows:

BroadcastSystemMessage(

BSF_IGNORECURRENTTASK, // do not send message to this process
BSM_APPLICATIONS,   // broadcast only to applications
                                        // private message, message
                                        // registered in previous step
wParam,   // message-specific value
lParm);   // message-specific value

The process receiving the private message calls **ExitProcess** to terminate its execution.

Note   When the system is terminating a process, it does not terminate any child processes that the process created.

PROCESS USE OF MUTEXES, SEMAPHORES, AND EVENTS

The section on Thread Synchronization covers these objects in some detail. Processes can share mutexes (short for mutual exclusion), semaphores, and events. Processes can coordinate their activities by sharing objects, as threads do. The mechanisms for sharing are inheritance, where the new process receives copies of the creating parent's handles. Those handles marked for inheritance when they were created will be passed on.

Other methods involve calling functions to create a second handle to an existing object. Which function you call depends on what information you already have. Call **DuplicateHandle** if you have handles to both the source and destination processes. If you have the name of the object only, call one of the Open functions. Two programs could agree in advance on the name of the object they share. One could pass the name to the other through shared memory, DDEML (DDE Management Library), or a pipe.

BOOL **DuplicateHandle**(
        HANDLE hSourceProcess, // process that owns the original object
        HANDLE hSource, // handle to the original object

```
    HANDLE hTargetProcess,  // process that wants a copy of the handle
    LPHANDLE lphTarget,      // place to store duplicated handle
    DWORD fdwAccess,         // requested access privileges
    BOOL bInherit,      // may the duplicate handle be inherited
    DWORD   fdwOptions);     // optional actions
```

HANDLE **OpenMutex(**

```
    DWORD   fdwAccess,    // requested access privileges
    BOOL    bInherit,     // TRUE if children may inherit this handle
    LPTSTR  lpszName);    // name of the mutex
```

HANDLE **OpenSemaphore(**

```
    DWORD   fdwAccess,    // requested access privileges
    BOOL    bInherit,     // TRUE if children may inherit this handle
    LPTSTR  lpszName);    // name of the semaphore
```

HANDLE **OpenEvent(**

```
    DWORD   fdwAccess,    // requested access privileges
    BOOL    bInherit,     // TRUE if children may inherit this handle
    LPTSTR  lpszName);    // name of the event
```

Note   The LPTSTR variable type is a generic text type that compiles differently depending on whether an application uses Unicode or ASCII strings.

Mutexes, semaphores, and events persist in memory until all the processes that own them end or until all the object's handles have been closed with **CloseHandle**.

```
    BOOL CloseHandle( hObject);
```

PROCESS SECURITY AND ACCESS RIGHTS

Windows 2000 security enables you to control access to process objects. You can specify a security descriptor for a process when you call the **CreateProcess**, **CreateProcessAsUser**, or **CreateProcessWithLogonW** function. To retrieve a process's security descriptor, call the **GetSecurityInfo** function. To change a process's security descriptor, call the **SetSecurityInfo** function. The handle returned by the **CreateProcess** function has PROCESS_ALL_ACCESS access to the process object. When you call the **OpenProcess** function, the system checks the requested access rights against the DACL (discretionary access-control list) in the security descriptor. When you call the **GetCurrentProcess** function, Windows 2000 returns a pseudo handle with the maximum access that the DACL allows to the caller.

The valid access rights for process objects include DELETE, READ_CONTROL, SYNCHRONIZE, WRITE_DAC, and WRITE_OWNER standard access rights, in addition to the following process-specific access rights.

Value	Meaning
PROCESS_ALL_ACCESS	Specifies all possible access rights for a process object.
PROCESS_CREATE_PROCESS	Required to create a process.
PROCESS_CREATE_THREAD	Required to create a thread.
PROCESS_DUP_HANDLE	Required to duplicate a handle.
PROCESS_QUERY_INFORMATION	Required to retrieve certain information about a process, such as its priority class.
PROCESS_SET_QUOTA	Required to set memory limits.
PROCESS_SET_INFORMATION	Required to set certain information about a process, such as its priority class.
PROCESS_TERMINATE	Required to terminate a process.
PROCESS_VM_OPERATION	Required to perform an operation on the address space of a process.
PROCESS_VM_READ	Required to read memory in a process.
PROCESS_VM_WRITE	Required to write to memory in a process.
SYNCHRONIZE	A standard right required to wait for the process to terminate.

Threads

CREATING AND TERMINATING THREADS

CreateThread is another key API for constructing your application. The API call is shown with the parameters, and an explanation of the parameters is given. Remember, the thread is the unit of work that is scheduled by the Windows 2000 kernel. The Micro Kernel schedules ready threads for processor time based upon their dynamic priority, a number from 1 to 31, which represents the importance of the task (see Appendix B). The highest priority thread always runs on the processor, even if this requires that a lower-priority thread be interrupted. The **SetThreadPriority** API, which we will show, is used to set up the thread base priority (see Appendix B). There is also a **CreateRemoteThread** API function that creates a thread that runs in the virtual address space of another process. Each thread has its own set of CPU registers and a stack.

```
HANDLE CreateThread (
    LPSECURITY_ATTRIBUTES lpThreadAttributes,
    DWORD                     dwStackSize,
    LPTHREAD_START_ROUTINE    lpStartAddress,
    LPVOID                    lpParameter,
    DWORD                     dwCreationFlags,
    LPDWORD                   lpThreadId);
```

Parameters

lpThreadAttributes

Ignored. Must be NULL.

dwStackSize

Ignored. The default stack size for a thread is determined by the linker setting /STACK.

lpStartAddress

Long pointer to the application-defined function of type LPTHREAD_START_ROUTINE to be executed by the thread and represents the starting address of the thread.

lpParameter

Long pointer to a single 32-bit parameter value passed to the thread.

dwCreationFlags

Specifies flags that control the creation of the thread.

Value	Description
CREATE_SUSPENDED	The thread is created in a suspended state, and will not run until the ResumeThread function is called. If 0, the thread runs immediately after creation.

lpThreadId

Long pointer to a 32-bit variable that receives the thread identifier. If this parameter is NULL, the thread identifier is not returned.

The **CreateThread** function covered above creates a new thread for a process. The creating thread must specify the starting address of the code that the new thread is to execute. Typically, the starting address is the name of a function defined in the program code. This function takes a single parameter and returns a DWORD value. A process can have multiple threads simultaneously executing the same function. The following example demonstrates how to create a new thread that executes the locally defined function, ThreadFunc.

```
#include <windows.h>
#include <conio.h>

DWORD WINAPI ThreadFunc( LPVOID lpParam)
{
    char szMsg[80];
```

```
        wsprintf(szMsg, "Paramter = %d.", *(DWORD)lpParam);
        MessageBox(NULL, szMsg, "ThreadFunc", MB_OK);
        return 0;
}
VOID main(VOID)
{
    DWORD dwThreadId;
    DWORD dwThrdParam = 1;
    HANDLE hThread;
    char szMsg[80];

    hThread = CreateThread(
        NULL,        // no security attributes
        0,                                  // use default stack size
        ThreadFunc,                         // thread function
        &dwThrdParam,                       // argument to thread function
        0,                                  // use default creation flags
        &dwThreadId);                       // returns the thread identifier

    // Check the return value for success.

    if(hThread == NULL)
      {
          wsprintf(szMsg, "CreateThread failed.");
          MessageBox(NULL, szMsg, "main", MB_OK);
}
else
{
          _getch();
          CloseHandle(hThread);
}
}
```

For simplicity, this example passes a point to a DWORD value as an argument to the thread function. This could be a pointer to any type of data or structure, or it could be omitted altogether by passing a NULL pointer and deleting the references to the parameter in ThreadFunc. It is risky to pass the address of a local variable if the creating thread exits before the new thread, because the pointer becomes invalid. Instead, either pass a pointer to dynamically allocated memory or make the creating thread wait for the new thread to terminate. Data can also be passed from the creating thread to the new thread using global variables. With global variables, it is usually necessary to synchronize access by multiple threads.

In processes where a thread might create multiple threads to execute the same code, it is inconvenient to use global variables. For example, a process that enables the user to open several files at the same time can create a new thread for each file, with each of the threads executing the same thread function. The creating thread can pass the unique information (such as the file name) required by each instance of the thread as an argument. You cannot use a single global variable for this purpose, but you could use a dynamically allocated string buffer.

You can also create a thread by calling the **CreateRemoteThread** function. This function is used by debugger processes to create a thread that runs in the address space of the process being debugged.

Terminating a Thread

A thread executes until one of the following events occurs:

- The thread calls the ExitThread function.
- Any thread of the process calls the ExitProcess function.
- The thread function returns.
- Any thread calls the TerminateThread function with a handle to the thread.
- Any thread calls the TerminateProcess function with a handle to the process.

The **GetExitCodeThread** function returns the termination status of a thread. While a thread is executing, its termination status is STILL_ACTIVE. When a thread terminates, its termination status changes from STILL_ACTIVE to the exit code. The exit code is either the value specified in the call to **ExitThread**, **ExitProcess**, **TerminateThread**, or **TerminateProcess**, or the value returned by the thread function. When a thread terminates, the state of the thread object changes to signaled, releasing any other threads that had been waiting for the thread to terminate.

If a thread is terminated by **ExitThread**, the system calls the entry-point function of each attached DLL with a value indicating that the thread is detaching from the DLL (unless you call the **DisableThreadLibraryCalls** function). If a thread is terminated by **ExitProcess**, the DLL entry-point functions are involved once, to indicate that the process is detaching. DLLs are not notified when a thread is terminated by **TerminateThread** or **TerminateProcess**.

Note

The **TerminateThread** and **TerminateProcess** functions should be used only in extreme circumstances, since they do not allow threads to clean up, do not notify DLLs, and do not free the initial stack. The following steps provide a better solution:

- Create an event object using the CreateEvent function.
- Create the threads.

- Each thread monitors the event state by calling the WaitForSingleObject function. Use a wait time-out interval of zero.
- Each thread terminates its own execution when the event is set to the signaled state (WaitForSingleObject returns WAIT_OBJECT_0).

SUSPENDING THREAD EXECUTION

A thread can suspend and resume the execution of another thread using the **SuspendThread** and **ResumeThread** functions. While a thread is suspended, it is not scheduled for time on the processor. The **SuspendThread** function is not particularly useful for synchronization because it does not control the point in the code at which the thread's execution is suspended. However, you might want to suspend a thread in a situation where you are waiting for user input that could cancel the work the thread is performing. If the user input cancels the work, have the thread exit; otherwise, call ResumeThread.

If a thread is created in a suspended state (with CREATE_SUSPENDED flag), it does not begin to execute until another thread calls **ResumeThread** with a handle to the suspended thread. This can be useful for initializing the thread's state before it begins to execute. Suspending a thread at creation can be useful for one-time synchronization, because this ensures that the suspended thread will execute the starting point of its code when you call **ResumeThread**.

A thread can temporarily yield its execution for a specified interval by calling the **Sleep** or **SleepEx** functions. This is useful particularly in cases where the thread responds to user interaction, because it can delay execution long enough to allow users to observe the results of their actions. During the sleep interval, the thread is not scheduled for time on the processor. The **SwitchToThread** function is similar to **Sleep** and **SleepEx**, except that you cannot specify the interval. **SwitchToThread** allows the thread to give up its time slice.

Another useful thread API is **GetThreadTimes**. The **GetThreadTimes** function obtains timing information for a thread. It returns the thread creation time, how much time the thread has been executing in kernel mode, and how much time the thread has been executing in user mode. These times do not include time spent executing system thread or waiting in a suspended or blocked state. If the thread has exited, **GetThreadTimes** returns the thread exit time.

THREAD STACK SIZE AND THREAD LOCAL STORAGE

Each new thread receives its own stack space, consisting of both committed and reserve memory. By default, each thread uses 1 MB of reserved memory, and one page (the x86 is 4 KB) of committed memory. The system will commit one page block from the reserved stack memory as needed, until the stack cannot grow any farther. To specify a different default stack size, use the STACKSIZE statement in the module definition (.DEF) file. To increase the amount of stack space, which is to be initially committed for a thread, specify the value in the dwStackSize parameter of the **CreateThread** function. This value is rounded to the nearest page and used to set the initial size of the committed memory. The call to **CreateThread** will fail if there is not enough memory to commit the number of bytes you request. If the dwStackSize value is smaller than the default size, the new thread uses the same size as the thread that created it. The stack is freed when the thread terminates.

All threads of a process share the virtual address space and the global variables of that process. The local variables of a thread function are local to each thread that runs the function. However, the static or global variables used by that function have the same value for all threads. With thread local storage (TLS), you can create a unique copy of a variable for each thread. Using TLS, one thread allocates an index that can be used by any thread of the process to retrieve its unique copy. Use the following steps to implement TLS:

- Use the **TlsAlloc** function during process or dynamic-link library (DLL) initialization to allocate a TLS index.
- For each thread that needs to use the TLS index, allocate dynamic storage, then use the **TlsSetValue** function to associate the index with a pointer to the dynamic storage.
- When you need a thread to access its storage, specify the TLS index in a call to the **TlsGetValue** function to retrieve the pointer.
- When each thread no longer needs the dynamic storage that it has associated with a TLS index, it must free the index. When all threads have finished using a TLS index, use the **TlsFree** function to free the index.

The constant TLS_MINIMUM_AVAILABLE defines the minimum number of TLS indexes available in each process. This minimum is guaranteed to be at least 64 for all systems.

In Windows 2000 there is a limit of 1088 TLS indexes per process. In Windows NT 4.0 and earlier there is a limit of 64 TLS indexes per process.

It is ideal to use TLS in a DLL. Perform the initial TLS operations in the DllMain function in the context of the process or thread attaching to the DLL. When a new process attaches to the DLL, call **TlsAlloc** in the entry-point function to allocate a TLS index for that process. Then store the TLS index in a global variable that is private to each attached process. When a new thread attaches to the DLL, allocate dynamic memory for that thread in the entry-point function, and use **TlsSetValue** with the TLS index from **TlsAlloc** to save private data to the index. Then you can use the TLS index in a call to **TlsGetValue** to access the private data for the calling thread from within any function in the DLL. When a process detaches from the DLL, call **TlsFree**.

The following is an example of using TLS. TLS enables multiple threads of the same process to use an index allocated by the **TlsAlloc** function to store and retrieve a value that is local to the thread. In this example, an index is allocated when the process starts. When each thread starts, it allocates a block of dynamic memory and stores a pointer to this memory by using the TLS index. The TLS index is used by the locally defined CommonFunc function to access the data local to the calling thread. Before each thread terminates, it reases its dynamic memory.

```
#include <stdio.h>
#include <windows.h>

#define THREADCOUNT 4
DWORD dwTlsIndex;

VOID ErrorExit(LPTSTR);

VOID CommonFunct(VOID)
{
LPVOID lpvData;

// Retrieve a data pointer for the current thread.

    LpvData = TlsGetValue(dwTlsIndex);
    if((lpvData == 0) && (GetLastDerror() != 0))
            ErrorExit("TlsGetValue error");

// Use the data stored for the current thread.
    Prtintf("common: thread %d: lpvData=%lx\n",
                GetCurrentThreadID(), lpvData);
    Sleep(5000);
}

DWORD WINAPI ThreadFunc(VOID)
{
        LPVOID lpvData;

// Initialize the TLS index for this thread.

        LpvData = (LPVOID) LocalAlloc (LPTR, 256);
        if(!TlsSetValue(dwTlsIndex, lpvData))
                ErrorExit("TlsSetValue error");

        Printf("thread %d: lpvData=%1x\n", GetCurrentThreadID(), lpvData);

        CommonFunc();
```

```
// Release the dynamic memory before the thread returns.

    lpvData = TlsGetValue(dwTlsIndex);
    if(lpvData != 0)
            LocalFree((HLOCAL) lpvData);
    return 0;
}

DWORD main(VOID)
{
    DWORD           IDThread;
    HANDLE          hThread[THREADCOUNT];
    int             i;

// Allocate a TLS index.

    if((dwTlsIndex = TlsAlloc()) == -1)
            ErrorExit("TlsAlloc failed");

// Create multiple threads.

    for(i = 0; i< THREADCOUNT; i++)
    {
    hThread[i] = CreateThread(NULL,       // no security attributes
                            0,          // use default stack size
                            LPTHREAD_START_ROUTINE  ThreadFunc,
                            NULL,
                            0,
                            &IDThread);

// Check the return value for success.

    if(hThread[i] == NULL)
            ErrorExit("CreateThread error\n");
}

    for(i=0; i<THREADOUNT; i++)
            WaitForSingleObject(hThread[i], INFINITE);
    return 0;
}

VOID ErrorExit(LPTSTR lpszMessage)
{
        fprintf(stderr, "%s\n", lpszMessage);
        ExitProcess(0);
}
```

THREAD SYNCHRONIZATION

When you work with threads, you must be able to coordinate their actions. Coordination requires ensuring that certain actions happen in a specific order. The Win32 APIs contains functions to make threads wait for signals from objects, such as files and processes. Besides these functions there are ones to create threads and modify their scheduling priority. Win32 also supports synchronization objects, such as mutexes and semaphores.

Functions that wait for an object to reach its signaled state illustrate how synchronization objects are used. There are also a set of generic waiting commands that allow you to wait for processes, threads, mutexes, semaphores, events, and a few other objects to reach their signaled states. The following command waits for one object to turn on its signal:

DWORD **WaitForSingleObject**(HANDLE hObject,   // object to wait for
DWORD dwMilliseconds);// maximum wait time

WaitForSingleObject will allow a thread to suspend itself until signaled by a specific object. With this command, a thread may state how long it is willing to wait for the object. Set the interval to INFINITE to wait indefinitely. **WaitForSingleObject** returns 0 and execution resumes if the object is already available, or if it reaches its signal state within the designated time. The function returns WAIT_TIMEOUT if the interval passes, and the object is still not signaled.

NOTE   If you set the interval to INFINITE, and if for any reason the object never reaches a signaled state, the thread will never resume. If two threads establish a reciprocal infinite wait, they will deadlock.

WaitForMultipleObjects is used to make a thread wait for several objects at once. You can make this function return as soon as one or more of the objects becomes available. It can also be set to make it wait until all requested objects reach their signaled states. A program might set up an array of objects, and then wait to respond when anyone of interest signals.

DWORD **WaitForMultipleObjects**(
     DWORD   dwNumObjects,   // number of objects to wait for
     LPHANDLE   lpHandles,   // array of object handles
     BOOL   bWaitAll,   // TRUE, wait all, FALSE, wait any
     DWORD   dwMilliseconds);   // maximum waiting period

As before, a return value of WAIT_TIMEOUT indicates that the interval passed with no objects being signaled. If bWaitAll is FALSE, a flag from any one element indicates which element of the lpHandles array has become signaled. This is a successful return value, which indicates the element. (The first element is 0, the second is 1, and so on.) If bWaitAll is TRUE, there is no response until all flags (all threads) have completed.

There are two extended versions of the wait functions. These add an alert status that allows a thread to resume if an asynchronous read or write command happens to end during the wait.

```
DWORD WaitForSingleObjectEx(
    HANDLE      hObject,          // object to wait for
    DWORD       dwMilliseconds,   // maximum time to wait
    BOOL        bAlertable);      // TRUE end wait I/O completes
```

```
DWORD WaitForMultipleObjectEx(
    DWORD       dwNumObjects,     // number of objects to wait for
    LPHANDLE    lpHandles,        // array of object handles
    BOOL        bWaitAll,         // TRUE wait all; FALSE wait any
    DWORD       dwMilliseconds,   // maximum waiting period
    BOOL        bAlertable);      // TRUE end wait if I/O complete
```

When successful, wait commands usually modify the awaited object in some way. For instance, when a thread waits for and acquires a mutex, the wait function restores the mutex to its unsignaled state. Other threads will then know the mutex is in use. The wait commands in semaphores decrease the counter of a semaphore, and reset some kinds of events. The specified object state is not modified by the wait commands until all objects are simultaneously signaled. A mutex can be signaled for instance, but the thread does not receive ownership immediately. It is required to wait until the other objects are also signaled; therefore, the wait function cannot modify the object. The mutex may come under the ownership of another thread while waiting. This will further delay the completion of the wait condition. You have to create an object before you can wait for it. We usually start with mutexes and semaphores since they have parallel API commands to create the objects, acquire or release them, get handles to them, and destroy them.

MUTEX AND SEMAPHORE CREATION

The mutex and semaphore creation functions need to be told some initial conditions for the object, what access privileges you want, and an optional name for the object.

```
HANDLE CreateMutex(
    LPSECURITY_ATTRIBUTES   lpsa,   // optional security attributes
```

```
    BOOL         bInitialOwner          // TRUE creator wants ownership
    LPTSTR       lpszMutexName);

HANDLE CreateSemaphore(
    LPSECURITY_ATTRIBUTES    lpsa,    // optional security attributes
    LONG         lInitialCount          // initial count
    LONG         lMaxCount              // maximum count-limits # thread
    LPTSTR       lpszSemName);
```

The names are optional; they are useful for identification purposes when several different processes want handles to the same object. If the security descriptor is NULL, the returned handle will possess all access privileges and will not be inherited by child processes. A thread both creates and acquires a mutex at once, by setting the bInitialOwner flag to TRUE. The new mutex remains unsignaled until the thread releases it. Only one thread at a time may acquire a mutex. A semaphore remains signaled until its acquisition count reaches iMaxCount. If more threads try to wait for the semaphore, they will be suspended until some other thread decreases the acquisition count.

ACQUIRING MUTEXES, SEMAPHORES, AND RELEASING

Threads interact with a semaphore or mutex by acquiring and releasing them. To acquire either object, a thread calls **WaitForSingleObject** (or one of its variants). When a thread finishes, it releases the object with one of these functions:

```
BOOL ReleaseMutex(HANDLE hMutex);
BOOL ReleaseSemaphore(
     HANDLE  hSemaphore,
     LONG    lRelease,  // amount to increment counter on release
                        // (usually 1)
     LPLONG  lplPrevious);      // variable receive previous count
```

Releasing a mutex or a semaphore increments its counter. Whenever the counter rises above 0, the object assumes its signaled state, and the system checks to see whether any other threads are waiting for it. Only a thread that already owns a mutex can release it. With a semaphore, however, any thread can call **ReleaseSemaphore** to adjust the acquisition counter by any amount up to its maximum value. As your program runs, changing the semaphore counter by arbitrary amounts lets you vary the number of threads that may own it. **CreateSemaphore** allows you to set the counter for a new semaphore to something other than its maximum value. You might, for example, create it with an initial count of 0 to block all threads while your program initializes, and then raise the counter with **ReleaseSemaphore**.

Note   Remember to release synchronization objects. If you forget to release a mutex, for example, any threads that wait for it without specifying a maximum interval will deadlock; they will not be released.

Each wait that a thread does must be matched with a release. A thread may wait for the same object more than once without blocking. This is true of mutexes, semaphores, and critical sections.

EVENTS

The object a program creates when it requires a mechanism for alerting threads if some action occurs is an event. A manual reset event, one of the simplest, turns its signal on and off in response to the two commands **SetEvent** (signal on) and **ResetEvent** (signal off). When the signal is on, all threads that wait for the event will receive it. When the signal is off, all threads that wait for the event become blocked. Manual reset events only change their state when some thread explicitly sets or resets them. You might use a manual reset event to allow a thread, for instance, to execute after the user enters certain information. Here are the basic commands for working with events:

```
HANDLE CreateEvent(
    LPSECURITY_ATTRIBUTES       lpsa,      // security privileges
    BOOL            bManualReset,    // TRUE event reset manually
    BOOL            bInitialState,   // TRUE create signaled state
    LPTSTR          lpszEventName);

HANDLE SetEvent( HANDLE hEvent );

HANDLE ResetEvent( HANDLE hEvent );
```

CreateEvent allows the new event to arrive in the world already signaled by setting the bInitialState parameter. The **SetEvent** and **ResetEvent** functions return TRUE or FALSE to indicate success or failure. **CreateEvent** lets you create an automatic reset event instead of a manual reset event by using the bManualReset parameter. An automatic reset event returns to its unsignaled state immediately after a **SetEvent** command. **ResetEvent** would not be used for an automatic reset event. An automatic reset event always releases only a single thread on each signal before resetting. Where one master thread prepares data for other working threads, an automatic reset event would be useful. When the master thread has a new data set ready, it sets the event and a single working thread is released. The other threads continue to wait in line for more assignments.

Besides setting and resetting events, you can pulse events.

> BOOL **PulseEvent**(hEvent);

A pulse turns the signal on for a very short time and then turns it back off. Pulsing a manual event allows all waiting threads to pass and then resets the event. Pulsing an automatic event lets one waiting thread pass and then resets the event. Setting an automatic event causes the event to leave its signal on until some threads starts waiting for it. As soon as one thread passes, the event resets itself.

CRITICAL SECTION OBJECTS

Critical Section Objects provide synchronization similar to that provided by mutex objects, except that **Critical Section Objects** can be used only by the threads of a single process. Event, mutex, and semaphore objects can also be used in a single-process application, but **Critical Section Objects** provide a slightly faster, more efficient mechanism for mutual-exclusion synchronization. Like a mutex object, a **Critical Section Object** can be owned by only one thread at a time, which makes it useful for protecting a shared resource from simultaneous access. There is no guarantee about the order in which threads will obtain ownership of the **Critical Section Object**, however, the system will be fair to all threads.

The process is responsible for allocating the memory used by a **Critical Section Object**. Typically, this is done by simply declaring a variable of type CRITICAL_SECTION. Before the threads of the process can use it, initialize the **Critical Section Object** by using the **InitializeCriticalSection** or **InitializeCriticalSectionAndSpinCount** function. A thread uses the **EnterCriticalSection** or **TryEnterCriticalSection** function to request ownership of a **Critical Section Object**. It uses the **LeaveCriticalSection** function to release ownership of a **Critical Section Object**. If the **Critical Section Object** is currently owned by another thread, **EnterCriticalSection** waits indefinitely for ownership. In contrast, when a mutex object is used for mutual exclusion, the wait functions accept a specified time-out interval. The **TryEnterCriticalSection** function attempts to enter a **Critical Section Object** without blocking the calling thread.

Once a thread owns a **Critical Section Object**, it can make additional calls to **EnterCriticalSection** or **TryEnterCriticalSection** without blocking its execution. This prevents a thread from deadlocking itself while waiting for a **Critical Section Object** that it already owns. To release its ownership, the thread must call **LeaveCriticalSection** once for each time that it enters the **Critical Section Object**. A thread uses the **InitializeCriticalSection AndSpinCount** or **SetCriticalSectionSpinCount** function to specify a spin count for the **Critical Section Object**. The following call is used for a spinlock setting with a critical section.

```
BOOL InitializeCriticalSectionAndSpinCount(
        PCRITICAL_SECTION      cs,
        DWORD                  dwSpinCount);
```

The first parameter is the address of the critical section structure. In the second parameter you pass the number of times you want the spinloop to function before making the thread wait. On single-process systems, the spin count is ignored and the **Critical Section Object** spin count is set to 0 operation, the calling thread avoids the wait operation. Any thread of the process can use the **DeleteCriticalSection** function to release the system resources that were allocated when the critical section was initialized. After this function has been called, the **Critical Section Object** can no longer be used for synchronization. When a **Critical Section Object** is owned, the only other threads affected are those waiting for ownership in a call to **EnterCriticalSection**. Threads that are not waiting are free to continue running.

THREAD PRIORITIES

Each thread is assigned a scheduling priority. The priority levels range from zero (lowest priority) to 31 (highest priority). Only the zero-page thread can have a priority of zero. The zero-page thread is a system thread. The priority of each thread is determined by the following criteria:

- The priority class of its process
- The priority level of the thread within the priority class of its process

The priority class and priority level are combined to form the *base priority* of a thread. We cover this in more detail later in the paragraph. As we mentioned under the discussion on processes, each process belongs to one of the following priority classes:

```
IDLE_PRIORITY_CLASS
BELOW_NORMAL_PRIORITY_CLASS
NORMAL_PRIORITY_CLASS
ABOVE_NORMAL_PRIORITY_CLASS
HIGH_PRIORITY_CLASS
REALTIME_PRIORITY_CLASS
```

Note   BELOW_NORMAL_PRIORITY_CLASS and ABOVE_NORMAL_PRIORITY_CLASS are new for Windows 2000.

By default, the priority class of a process is NORMAL_PRIORITY_CLASS if not otherwise specified in **CreateProcess**. Within a process, the following are priority levels that can be set for threads:

THREAD_PRIORITY_IDLE
THREAD_PRIORITY_LOWEST
THREAD_PRIORITY_BELOW_NORMAL
THREAD_PRIORITY_NORMAL
THREAD_PRIORITY_ABOVE_NORMAL
THREAD_PRIORITY_HIGHEST
THREAD_PRIORITY_TIME_CRITICAL

By default, the priority class of a thread is THREAD_PRIORITY_NORMAL if not otherwise specified in **CreateThread**. This means that the thread priority is the same as the process priority class. As we show below, after you create a thread, you can use the **SetThreadPriority** function to adjust its priority relative to other threads in the process.

A typical strategy is to use THREAD_PRIORITY_ABOVE_NORMAL or THREAD_PRIORITY_HIGHEST for the process's input thread, to ensure that the application is responsive to the user. Background threads, particularly those that are processor intensive, can be set to THREAD_PRIORITY_BELOW_NORMAL or THREAD_PRIORITY_LOWEST, to ensure that they can be pre-empted when necessary. However, if you have a thread waiting for another thread with a lower priority to complete some task, be sure to block the execution of the waiting high-priority thread. To do this, use a wait function, critical section, or the **Sleep** function, **SleepEx**, or **SwitchToThread** function. This is preferable to having the thread execute a loop. Otherwise, the process may become deadlocked, because the thread with lower priority is never scheduled. To determine the current priority level of a thread, use the **GetThreadPriority** function.

The **SetThreadPriority** API function sets the priority value for the specified thread. This value, together with the priority class of the thread's process, determines the thread's base priority level (see Appendix B).

```
BOOL SetThreadPriority(
    HANDLE   hThread    // handle returned from the CreateThread API
    int      nPriority  // thread priority level
);
Parameters
hThread
```
[in] Handle to the thread whose priority value is to be set. The handle must have the THREAD_SET_INFORMATION access right associated with it.

nPriority

[in] Specifies the priority value for the thread. This parameter can be one of the following values:

Priority	Meaning
THREAD_PRIORITY_ABOVE_NORMAL	Indicates 1 point above normal priority for the priority class.
THREAD_PRIORITY_BELOW_NORMAL	Indicates 1 point below normal priority for the priority class.
THREAD_PRIORITY_HIGHEST	Indicates 2 points above normal priority for the priority class.
THREAD_PRIORITY_IDLE	Indicates a base priority level of 1 for IDLE_PRIORITY_CLASS, BELOW_NORMAL_PRIORITY_CLASS, NORMAL_PRIORITY_CLASS, ABOVE_NORMAL_PRIORITY_CLASS, or HIGH_PRIORITY_CLASS processes, and a base priority level of 16 for REALTIME_PRIORITY_CLASS processes.
THREAD_PRIORITY_LOWEST	Indicates 2 points below normal priority for the priority class.
THREAD_PRIORITY_NORMAL	Indicates normal priority for the priority class.
THREAD_PRIORITY_TIME_CRITICAL	Indicates a base priority level of 15 for IDLE_PRIORITY_CLASS, BELOW_NORMAL_PRIORITY_CLASS, NORMAL_PRIORITY_CLASS, ABOVE_NORMAL_PRIORITY_CLASS, or HIGH_PRIORITY_CLASS processes, and a Base priority level of 31 for REALTIME_PRIORITY_CLASS processes.

Every thread has a base priority level determined by the thread's priority value and the priority class of its process. See Appendix B for this scheme. The system uses the base priority level of all executable threads to determine which thread gets the next slice of CPU time. Threads are scheduled in a round-robin fashion at each priority level, and only when there are no executable threads at a higher level does scheduling of threads at a lower level take place. For example, specifying THREAD_PRIORITY_HIGHEST in a call to **SetThreadPriority** for a thread of an IDLE_PRIORITY_CLASS process sets the thread's base priority level to 6. All threads initially start at THREAD_PRIORITY_NORMAL. One can use the **GetPriorityClass** function to get the priority value of a thread.

We would use the priority class of a process to differentiate between applications that are time critical and those that have normal or below nomal scheduling requirements. We would then use thread priority values to differentiate the relative priorities of the tasks (threads) of a process. For example, a thread that handles input for a window could have a higher priority level than a thread that performs intensive calculations for the CPU. When manipulating priorities, be careful to ensure that a high-priority thread does not consume all of the available CPU time. A thread with a base priority level above 11 interferes with the normal operation of the Windows 2000 operating system. Using REALTIME-PRIORITY_CLASS may cause disk caches to not flush, hang the mouse, and so on.

THREAD MULTITASKING

Based on the priority assignments we discussed above, the operating system divides the available processor time among the processes or threads that need it. The system is designed for preemptive multitasking; it allocates a process *time slice* to each thread it executes. The currently executing thread is suspended when its time slice elapses, allowing another thread to run. When the system switches from one thread to another, it saves the context of the preempted thread and restores the saved context of the next thread in the queue. The length of the time slice depends on the operating system and the processor. Because each time slice is small (approximately 20 milliseconds), multiple threads appear to be executing at the same time. This is actually the case on multiprocessor systems, where the executable threads are distributed among the available processors.

Windows 2000 uses a symmetric multiprocessing (SMP) model to schedule threads on multiple processors. With this model, any thread can be assigned to any processor. Therefore, scheduling threads on a computer with multiple processors is similar to scheduling threads on a computer with a single processor. However, the scheduler has a pool of processors, so that it can schedule threads to run simultaneously. Scheduling is still determined by thread priority. However, on a multiprocessor computer, you can also affect scheduling by setting thread affinity and thread ideal processor.

Thread affinity forces a thread to run on a specific subset of processors. Use the **SetProcessAffinityMask** function to specify thread affinity for all threads of the process. To set the thread affinity for a single thread, use the **SetThreadAffinityMask** function. The thread affinity must be a subset of the process affinity. You can obtain the current process affinity by calling the **GetProcessAffinityMask** function. Setting thread affinity should generally be avoided, because it can interfere with the OS scheduler's ability to schedule threads effectively across processors. This can decrease the performance gains produced by parallel processing. An appropriate use of thread affinity is testing each processor.

When you specify a thread ideal processor, the scheduler runs the thread on the specified processor when possible. Use the **SetThreadIdealProcessor** function to specify a preferred processor for a thread. This does not guarantee that the ideal processor will be chosen, but provides a useful hint to the scheduler.

THREAD POOLING

Windows 2000 has some new thread pooling functions that make thread general management easier. There are many applications that create threads that spend a great deal of time in the sleeping state waiting for an event to occur. Other threads may enter a sleeping state only to be awakened periodically to poll for a change or update status information. Thread pooling enables you to use threads more efficiently by providing your application with a pool of worker threads that are managed by the system. At least on thread monitors the status of all wait operations are queued to the thread pool. When a wait operation has completed, a worked thread from the thread pool executes the corresponding callback function.

You can also queue work items that are not related to a wait operation to the thread pool. To request that a work item be handled by a thread in the thread pool, call the **QueueUserWorkItem** function. This function takes a parameter to the function that will be called by the thread selected from the thread pool. There is no way to cancel a work item after it has been queued. Timer-queue-timers and registered wait operations also use the thread pool. Their callback functions are queued to the thread pool. You can also use the **BinIoCompletionCallback** function to post asynchronous I/O operations. On completion of the I/O, the callback is executed by a thread pool thread.

The thread pool is created the first time you call **QueueUserWorkItem** or **BindIoCompletionCallback**, or when a timer-queue-timer or registered wait operation queues a callback function. The number of threads that can be created in the thread pool is limited only by available memory. Each thread uses the default stack size and runs at the default priority. There are two types of worker threads in the thread pool: I/O and non-I/O. An I/O worker thread is a thread that waits in a state that can be alerted. Work items are queued to I/O worker threads as asynchronous procedure calls (APCs). You should queue a work item to an I/O worker thread if it will be executed in a thread that waits in an alert state.

A non-I/O worker thread waits on I/O completion ports. Using non-I/O worker threads is more efficient than I/O worker threads. Therefore, you should use non-I/O worker threads whenever possible. Both I/O and non-I/O worker threads do not exit if there are pending asynchronous I/O requests. Both types of threads can be used by work items that initiate asynchronous I/O completion requests. However, avoid posting asynchronous I/O completion requests in non-I/O worker threads if they could take a long time to complete. To use thread pooling, the work item and all the functions they call must be thread-pool safe. A safe function does not assume that thread executing it is a dedicated or persistent thread. In general, you should avoid thread local storage and queuing asynchronous calls that require a persistent thread, such as the **RegNotifyChangeKeyValue** function. However, such functions can be queued to a persistent worker thread using **QueueUserWorkItem** with the WT_EXECUTEINPERSISTENTTHREAD option.

THREAD SECURITY AND ACCESS RIGHTS

Windows 2000 security enables you to control access to thread objects. You can specify a security descriptor for a thread when you call the **CreateProcess**, **CreateProcessAsUser**, **CreateProcessWithLogonW**, **CreateThread**, or **CreateRemoteThread** function. To retrieve a thread's security descriptor, call the **GetSecurityInfo** function. To change a thread's security descriptor, call the **SetSecurityInfo** function. The handle returned by the **CreateThread function** has THREAD_ALL_ACCESS access to the thread object. When you call the **GetCurrentThread** function, the system returns a pseudohandle with the maximum access that the thread's security descriptor allows the caller.

The valid access rights for thread objects include the DELETE, READ_CONTROL, SYNCHRONIZE, WRITE_DAC, and WRITE_OWNER standard access right, in addition to the following thread-specific access rights.

Value	Meaning
SYNCHRONIZE	A standard right required to wait for the thread to exit.
THREAD_ALL_ACCESS	Specifies all possible access rights for a thread object.
THREAD_DIRECT_IMPERSONATION	Required for a server thread that impersonates a client.
THREAD_GET_CONTEXT	Required to read the context of a thread using GetThreadContext.
THREAD_IMPERSONATE	Required to use a thread's security information directly without calling it by using a communication mechanism that provides impersonation services.
THREAD_QUERY_INFORMATION	Required to read certain information from the thread object.
THREAD_SET_CONTEXT	Required to write the context of a thread.
THREAD_SET_INFORMATION	Required to set certain information in the thread object.
THREAD_SET_THREAD_TOKEN	Required to set the impersonation token for a thread.
THREAD_SUSPEND_RESUME	Required to suspend or resume a thread.
THREAD_TERMINATE	Required to terminate a thread.

You can request the ACCESS_SYSTEM_SECURITY access right to a thread object if you want to read or write the object's SACL (system access-control list).

To access an object's SACL:

- Call the **AdjustTokenPrivileges** function to enable the SE_SECURI-TY-NAME privilege.
- Request the ACCESS_SYSTEM_SECURITY access right when you open a handle to the object.
- Get or set the object's SACL by using a function such as **GetSecurityInfo** or **SetSecurityInfo**.
- Call **AdjustTokenPrivileges** to disable the SE_SECURITY_NAME privilege.

A SACL enables administrators to log attempts to access a secured object. Each ACE (access-control entry) specifies the types of access attempts by a specified trustee that causes the system to generate a record in the security event log. An ACE in a SACL can generate audit records when an access attempt fails, when it succeeds, or both. The security descriptor for a securable object contains the SACL.

Jobs

As we have seen above, the process is the environment that one or more threads perform some software functions. We also saw that the primary thread, or any other thread, in a process could create child processes that are associated with the parent process. We could not in the past control these processes as a collection, and it was very difficult to manage the processes (parent and children). There was no easy way to control, monitor, and allocate resources to the various processes. In Windows 2000, a new job kernel object is available that lets you group together processes and place restrictions on the processes that you could not do before. You can think of this collection as a container of processes. Because of this added process management capability you may want to consider creating jobs that only contain one process. In Appendix A we show the APIs associated with the job kernel object.

A job object allows groups of processes to be managed as a unit. Job objects are namable, securable, sharable objects that control attributes of the processes associated with them. Operations performed on the job object affect all processes associated with the job object. To create a job object, use the **CreateJobObject** function. When the job is created, there are no associated processes. To associate a process with a job, use the **AssignProcessToJobObject** function. After you associate a process with a job, the association cannot be broken. By default, processes created by a process associated with a job (child processes) are associated with the job. If the job has the extended limit JOB_OBJECT_LIMIT_BREAKAWAY_OK and the process was created with the CREATE_BREAKAWAY_FROM_JOB flag, its child processes are not associated with the job. If the job has the extended limit JOB_OBJECT_LIMIT_SILENT_BREAKAWAY_OK, no child processes are associated with the job.

A job can enforce limits on each associated process, such as the working set size, process priority, end-of-job time limit, and so on. To set the limits for a job object, use the **SetInformationJobObject** function. If a process associated with a job attempts to increase its working set size or process priority, the function calls are silently ignored. The job object also records basic accounting information for all its associated processes, including those that have terminated. To retrieve this accounting information, use the **QueryInformationJobObject** function. To terminate all processes currently associated with a job object, use the **TerminateJobObject function**. To close a job object handle, use the **CloseHandle** function. The job object is destroyed when its last handle has been closed. If there are running processes still associated with the job when it is destroyed, they will continue to run even after the job is destroyed.

CREATING, OPENING, AND TERMINATING JOBS

As we mentioned above, the CreateJobObject and OpenJobObject functions create or open a job object. The TerminateJobObject function terminates all processes currently associated with the job. The following are the detailed API calls for these three functions:

```
HANDLE CreateJobObject(
        LPSECURITY_ATTRIBUTES     lpJobAttributes,     // SD
        LPCTSTR                   lpName);             // job name
```

Parameters
  lpJobAttributes
    [in] Pointer to a SECURITY_ATTRIBUTES structure that specifies the security descriptor for the job object and determines whether child processes can inherit the returned handle. If lpJobAttributes is NULL, the job object gets a default security descriptor and the handle cannot be inherited.
  lpName
    [in] Pointer to a null-terminated string specifying the name of the job. The name is limited to MAX_PATH characters. Name comparison is case-sensitive. If lpName is NULL, the job is created without a name. If lpName matches the name of an existing even, semaphore, mutex, waitable timer, or file-mapping object, the function fails and the GetLastError function returns ERROR_INVALID_HANDLE. This occurs because these functions share the same name space.

If the function succeeds, the return value is a handle to the job object. The handle has JOB_OBJECT_ALL_ACCESS access to the job object. If the object existed before the function call, the function returns a handle to the existing job object and **GetLastError** returns ERROR_ALREADY_EXISTS. If the function fails, the return value is NULL. When a job is created, its accounting information is initialized to zero, all limits are inactive, and there are no associated processes. To close a job object handle, use the **CloseHandle** function. The job is destroyed when its last handle has been closed. If there are running processes still associated with the job when it is destroyed, they will continue to run even after the job is destroyed.

HANDLE **OpenJobObject**(
      DWORD   dwDesiredAccess,   // access right
      BOOL   bInheritHandles,   // inheritance state
      LPCTSTR   lpName);   // job name

Parameters
    dwDesiredAccess
        [in] Specifies the desired access mode to the job object. This parameter can be one or more of the following values.

Value	Meaning
MAXIMUM_ALLOWED	Specifies maximum access rights to the job object that are valid for the caller.
JOB_OBJECT_ASSIGN_PROCESS	Specifies the assign process access right to the object. Allows processes to be assigned to the job.
JOB_OBJECT_SET_ATTRIBUTES	Specifies the set attribute access right to the object. Allows job object attributes to be set.
JOB_OBJECT_QUERY	Specifies the query access right to the object. Allows job object attributes and accounting information to be queried.
JOB_OBJECT_TERMINATE	Specifies the terminate access right to the object. Allows termination of all processes in the job object.
JOB_OBJECT_SET_SECURITY_ATTRIBUTES	Specifies the security attributes access right to the object. Allows security limitations on all processes in the job object to be set.
JOB_OBJECT_ALL_ACCESS	Specifies the full access right to the job object.

bInheritHandles
  [in] Specifies whether the returned handle is inherited when a new process is created. If this parameter is TRUE, the new process inherits the handle.
lpName
  [in] Pointer to a null-terminated string specifying the name of the job to be opened. Name comparisons are case-sensitive.

If the function succeeds, the return value is a handle to the job. The handle provides the requested access to the job. If the function fails, the return value is NULL. To get extended error information, call **CallLastError**. To associate a process with a job, use the **AssignProcessToJobObject** function.

BOOL **TerminateJobObject**(
  HANDLE   hJob,   // handle to job
  UINT   uExitCode);

Parameters
  hJob
    [in] Handle to the job whose processes will be terminated. The CreateJobObject or OpenJobObject function returns this handle. This handle must have the JOB_OBJECT_TERMINATE access right.
  uExitCode
    [in] Specifies the exit code for the processes and threads terminated as a result of this call.

If the function succeeds, the return value is nonzero. If the function fails the return value is zero. To get extended error information, call **GetLastError**. It is not possible for any of the processes associated with the job to postpone or handle the termination. It is as if **TerminateProcess** were called for each process associated with the job.

ACQUIRING JOB STATUS INFORMATION

As we mentioned above, the **QueryInformationJobObject** function retrieves limit and job state information from the job objects.

BOOL **QueryInformationJobObject**(
  HANDLE   hJob,   // handle to job
  JOBOBJECTINFOCLASS JobObjectInfoClass,   // information class
  LPVOID   lpJobObjectInfo,   // limit information
  DWORD   cbJobObjectInfoLength,   // limit size
  LPDWORD   lpReturnLength);   // data written

Parameters

hJob

[in] Handle to the job whose information is being queried. The **CreateJobObject** or **OpenJobObject** function returns this handle. The handle must have the JOB_OBJECT_QUERY access right associated with it. If this value is NULL and the calling process is associated with a job, the job associated with the calling process is used.

JobObjectInfoClass

[in] Specifies the information class for limits to be queried. This parameter can be one of the following values. Note that the meaning of any parameter is a structure.

Value	Meaning
JobObjectBasicAccountingInformation	The lpJobObjectInfo parameter is a pointer to a JOBOBJECT_BASIC_ACCOUNTING_IN-FORMATION structure.
JobObjectBasicAndIoAccountingInformation	The lpJobObjectInfo parameter is a pointer to a JOBOBJECT_BASIC_AND_IO_ACCOUNT-ING_INFORMAT structure.
JobObjectBasicLimitInformation	The lpJobObjectInfo parameter is a pointer to a JOBOBJECT_BASIC_LIMIT_INFORMA-TION structure.
JobObjectBasicProcessIdList	The lpJobObjectInfo parameter is a pointer to a JOBOBJECT_BASIC_PROCESS_ID_LIST structure.
JobObjectBasicUIRestrictions	The lpJobObjectInfo parameter is a pointer to a JOBOBJECT_BASIC_UI_RESTRICTIONS structure.
JobObjectExtendedLimitInformation	The lpJobObjectInfo parameter is a pointer to a JOBOBJECT_EXTENDED_LIMIT_INFOR-MATION structure.
JobObjectSecurityLimitInformation	The lpJobObjectInfo parameter is a pointer to a JOBOBJECT_SECURITY_LIMIT_INFOR-MATION structure.

lpJobObjectInfo

[out] Receives the limit information. The format of this data depends on the value of the JobObjectInfoClass parameter.

cbJobObjectInfoLength
>   [in] Specifies the count, in bytes, of the job information being queried.
>
> lpReturnLength
>   [out] Pointer to a variable that receives the length of data written to the structure pointed to by the lpJobObjectInfo parameter. If you do not want to receive this information, specify NULL.

If the function succeeds, the return value is nonzero. If the function fails, the return value is zero. To get extended error information, call **GetLastError**. You can use the **QueryInformationJobObject** to object the current limits, modify them, then use the **SetInformationJobObject** function to set new limits. We will cover **SetInformationJobObject** in the following paragraph.

MANAGING JOB'S PROCESSES

You can use the **SetInformationJobObject** function to set several limits in a single call. If you want to establish the limits one at a time or change a subset of the limits, call the **QueryInformationJobObject** function to obtain the current limits, modify these limits, and then call **SetInformation-JobObject**.

```
BOOL SetInformationJobObject(
    HANDLE              hJob,                  // handle to job
    JOBOBJECTINFOCLASS  JobObjectInfoClass,    // information class
    LPVOID              lpJobObjectInfo,       // limit information
    DWORD               cbJobObjectInfoLength); // size information
```

Parameters
>   hJob
>   [in] Handle to the job whose limits are being set. The **CreateJobObject** or **OpenJobObject** function returns this handle. The handle must have the JOB_OBJECT_SET_ATTRIBUTES access right associated with it.
>
> JobObjectInfoClas
>   [in] Specifies the information class for limits to be set. This parameter can be one of the following values.

Value	Meaning
JobObjectAssociateCompletionPortInformation	The lpJobObjectInfo parameter is a pointer to a JOBOBJECT_ASSOCI-ATE_COMPLETION_PORT structure.
JobObjectBasicLimitInformation	The lpJobObjectInfo parameter is a pointer to a JOBOBJECT_BASIC_LIMIT_INFOR-MATION structure.

JobObjectBasicUIRestrictions	The lpJobObjectInfo parameter is a pointer to a JOBOBJECT_BASIC_UI_RESTRIC-TIONS structure.
JobObjectEndOfJobTimeInformation	The lpJobObjectInfo parameter is a pointer to a JOBOBJECT_END_OF_JOB_TIME_IN-FORMATION structure.
JobObjectExtendedLimitInformation	The lpJobObjectInfo parameter is a pointer to a JOBOBJECT_EXTEND-ED_LIMIT_INFORMATION structure.
JobObjectSecurityLimitInformation	The lpJobObjectInfo parameter is a pointer to a JOBOBJECT_SECURI-TY_LIMIT_INFORMATION structure. The hJob handle must have the JOB_OBJECT_SET_SECURITY_ATTRI-BUTES access right associated with it.

lpJobObjectInfo
[in] Specifies the limits to be set for the job. The format of this data depends on the value of JobObjectInfoClass.
cbJobObjectInfoLength
[in] Specifies the count, in bytes, of the job information being set.

If the function succeeds, the return value is nonzero. If the function fails, the return value is zero. To get the extended error information, call **GetLastError**.

I/O COMPLETION PORT AND JOB NOTIFICATION

Job objects use the signaled and non-signaled state of the job to give its status. One can use the WaitForSingleObject, for example, to trap the change of state of a job object. If all the allotted CPU time has been used up by the job, Windows terminates all the processes in the job and signals the job object. You can then use SetInformationJobObject covered above to grant more CPU time to the job.

If you want more sophisticated reporting on the job, such as when there is process creation or termination, an I/O completion port kernel object should be created and associated with the job. The JobObject AssociateCompletionPortInformation above in the **SetInformation JobObject** is the parameter used to form this association. You would use code like the following:

JOBOBJECT_ASSOCIATE_COMPLETION_PORT   ioport;
ioport.CompletionKey = 3;   // a value unique to identify the job
ioport.CompletionPort = hCompPort // handle of a completion port to receive
                                   // notification.

SetInformationJobObject(hJob, JobObjectAssociateCompletionPort
Information, &ioport, sizeof(ioport));

I/O COMPLETION PORTS

I/O completion ports are used with asynchronous I/O. The **CreateIoCompletionPort** function associates an I/O completion with one or more file handles. When an asynchronous I/O operation started on a file handle associated with a completion port is completed, an I/O completion packet is queued to the port. This can be used to combine the synchronization point for multiple file handles into a single object.

A thread uses the **GetQueuedCompletionStatus** function to wait for a completion packet to be queued to the completion port, rather than waiting directly for the asynchronous I/O to complete. Threads that block their execution on a completion port are released in last-in-first-out (LIFO) order. This means that when a completion packet is queued to the completion port, the system releases the last thread to block its execution on the port. When a thread calls **GetQueuedCompletionStatus**, it is associated with the specified completion port until it exits, specifies a different completion port, or frees the completion port. A thread can be associated with at most one completion port.

The most important property of a completion port is the concurrency value. The concurrency value of a completion port is specified when the completion port is created. This value limits the number of runnable threads associated with the completion port. When the total number of runnable threads associated with the completion port reaches the concurrency value, the system blocks the execution of any subsequent threads that specify the completion port until the number of runnable threads associated with the completion port drops below the concurrency value. The most efficient scenario occurs when there are completion packets waiting in the queue, but no wait can be satisfied because the port has reached its concurrency limit. In this case, when a running thread calls **GetQueuedCompletionStatus**, it will immediately pick up the queued completion packet. No context switches will occur, because the running thread is continually picking up completion packets and the other threads are unable to run.

The best value to pick for the concurrency value is the number of CPUs on the machine. If your transaction required a lengthy computation, a larger concurrency value will allow more threads to run. Each transaction will take longer to complete, but more transactions will be processed at the same time. The **PostQueuedCompletionStatus** function allows an application to queue its own special-purpose I/O completion packets to the completion port without starting an asynchronous I/O operation. This is useful for notifying worker threads of external events.

The completion port is freed when there are no more references to it. The completion port handle and every file handle associated with the completion port reference the completion port. All the handles must be closed to free the completion port. To close the port handle, call the function. In the next chapter we will start to look at .NET Framework.

.NET Framework

Introduction

At the beginning of the 1960s when I started programming the logic device we called a computer, I entered strings of binary "1" and "0" corresponding to a front panel switch setting. Then in 1962 I attended my first high-level language programming course, called the Assembler. The input to the Assembler program was strings of alphanumeric characters. Now, I entered my program and data at a keyboard-type device. Of course, supporting the Assembler was an editor-type program that handled the collecting and displaying of the program I was creating. When these alphanumeric strings were run through the Assembler, it then created the strings of binary "1" and "0" that would be executed by the computer hardware logic. A program called a Linker was created so that multiple module outputs from the Assembler could be integrated into one larger program to be run by the computer hardware.

Since day one, there has been this desire to create programs using our English sentence constructs. At about this time the language software system developers realized they could write a program, which converted more English-like commands into input commands for the Assembler. Thus was born a piece of software we called a Compiler (the first FORTRAN and COBOL Compilers actually came out in the late '50s). Of course, now we had two META software layers above the binary bit patterns needed by the computer hardware. The Assembler for all intents and purposes did a straight convert from the alphanumeric string to the binary bit string. The Compiler program code is another matter.

The Compiler program, since it handled much more sophisticated alphanumeric string constructs, was a much more intelligent program. It would perform optimization for creating the best Assembly language input statement sequence. The Compiler then became a very active partner with the programmer, generating perhaps 20 to 30 percent extra assembly language statements. This was due to its functions of converting, optimizing, and error checking. During this same period we were continuing to develop a more sophisticated program, called an Operating System (OS). This OS was now controlling the computer hardware, and had its own set of system commands, now called Application Programmer Interface (API), that the programmer could use to control the OS. We now had three levels of META software levels above the binary bit patterns needed by the computer hardware.

Another key development at about this time was that we realized we could make a computer hardware function, called a priority interrupt representing some physical world event, available to the programmer. The associated software interrupt handler then ran the program logic necessary to handle the event. It wasn't long before we extended this concept to OS software priority interrupts for internal application software execution control by the programmer. These priority schemes allowed us to created OS functionality that would preempt a currently executing program when a software or hardware of higher priority became active. The OS then switched machine context to work on this higher priority software program. The machine context was all the information needed to change back to the program that was interrupted. Primarily it consisted of all the machine hardware register information for that point in the currently executing program.

Then in the early 1980s, another META layer of software appeared, called Object Methodology (we actually started seeing it more in the late '80s). Here we encapsulated the Compiler language into classes, which the programmer worked with. Thus, the programmer was removed one more level from the Computer hardware. However, this methodology, once mastered, did make the programmer communication with the OS simpler. The footprint size of the OS APIs was reduced significantly and the resulting program listings were smaller. Microsoft came out with two significant libraries of classes called Microsoft Foundation Classes (MFC) and Active Template Library (ATL), which, once mastered, again simplified the programmer's input to the OS. All of this abstraction still taxed our cognitive abilities to remember all the program statement constructs and the resulting behavior. This was further compounded by the use of different Compiler languages by different programmers and the lack of any real compatibility between the languages.

Of course, the one common element was the OS, such as the current Windows 2000. The OS APIs (Win32 API) have remained relative stable for a long time, with a gradual evolution of additional functions being added. The system software developers had already started to develop software engines, much like an OS, for particular aspects of application software development. These were such things as ADO, ASP, OLE-DB, SQL, etc. Now, the interconnectivity of the different engines also was starting to tax the cognitive ability of the application software developer. It was obvious we needed another significant shift in the application programmer paradigm. The shift that was needed was not just an evolutionary change, however, but a revolutionary one. As we will see, as we go through the remaining parts of this book, that is exactly what Microsoft has done with the .NET Framework software.

Cognitively, we humans think in terms of objects, not APIs. Although APIs have served us well, as the complexity of computer software systems kept growing, something much closer to our cognitive model was needed. This was both to understand the META software layers, and to let us write our software in an object fashion. Of course, the Object Orientated Programming model came upon the screen as the first major shift in our programming paradigm in perhaps 25 years. However, we were still communicating with the operating system via the APIs. Also we needed to grow on the foundation that has worked well for us up to this point: the Win32 APIs for controlling the application development and use of the Windows Operating System.

As you bore in on the .NET Framework, you will see that we are now working with objects (classes) for our understanding and development of Windows 2000 software. These classes completely encapsulate the Windows 2000 Win32 APIs, and, therefore, the complete Windows 2000 Operating System. Typically, we will not need to go down to the Win32 API level; however, there are hooks (unmanaged code) keywords available for us to use pointers and go straight to the Win32 APIs. So the .NET Framework has us working much more akin to our natural cognitive model in creating and understanding complex software on top of the Windows 2000 Operating System. Our cognitive challenge now is to understand the over 2000 classes that are available to us, and all the associated behavior. This has to be done in such a manner that we not only can use these classes, but derive from them and create even more classes for our applications.

With the advent of Visual Studio.NET and .NET Framework, Microsoft has raised the bar of abstraction between the programmer and the underlying computer hardware. We have shifted to a more intelligent corroboration between various Compiler languages and the new middleware .NET Framework. This should reduce the complexity the programmer has to handle. I think a lot of this will depend on just how well Microsoft has thought out the cognitive relationships (interfaces) between the programmer and the .NET Framework development tools. It will also depend on just how well the programmer can correlate his actions with the resulting computer behavior.

This .NET Framework middleware integrates into a cohesive whole the various engines (ADO, ASP, XML, etc.) and provides a set of .NET Framework Base Classes to interface with them. Two major functional software application development areas, ASP.NET and Windows Forms (WinForms), are on top of this set. Today, this pretty much represents the two major application software development areas, that is, Web-based application and Windows-based applications. Under the .NET Framework base classes is another very intelligent layer, the Common Language Runtime (CLR). Its role is very much into the hardware management via the OS, of such things as memory management, life cycling monitoring, as well as providing a language Common Type System (CTS). The CLR handles such things as automatic garage collection to eliminate problems like memory leaks. Figure 3–1 shows the major META levels that the programmer is at the top of. It looks like there is approximately five major META layers between the programmer and the "0" and "1" I used to work with. Sometimes I miss the simpler days of programming with just my trusted Assembler. But, as I am well aware, the complexity of today's applications have long left that arena. It's truly great that so many fine minds can now get at the power of the computer and its operating system and create great new applications. This is what these META levels have done for software engineering and domain application software development.

Therefore, with .NET Framework we now have six intelligent active agents cooperating to create and execute the computer program. They are the programmer, the compiler, the .NET Framework base classes, the CLR, the Win32 APIs, and the Windows 2000 OS. Therefore, we are looking at a synergetic relationship that will result in a much better computer program creation and execution. Cognitively, of course, while as the interface is simpler, a much heavier load is put upon the programmer. Although with the help of these other agents, the logical error rate of the programmer hopefully will be reduced. With the additional META levels of active agents, much more emphasis is placed upon smarter debuggers and much better error

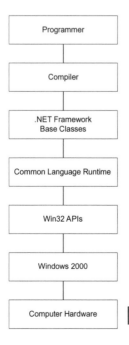

Figure 3–1   *META Levels*

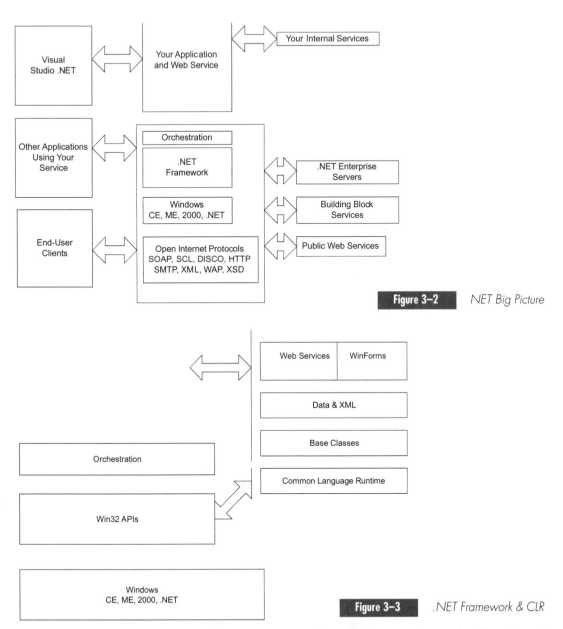

Figure 3-2   .NET Big Picture

Figure 3-3   .NET Framework & CLR

reporting. We will see, as we go through the creation and debugging of programs under the .NET Framework, that these areas have also become much smarter and more helpful to the programmer. Figure 3–2 shows the .NET Framework big picture. You can see it encapsulates the whole Windows 2000 Operating System and the Internet communication protocols. Figure 3–3 shows how the Common Language Runtime (CLR) sets under the .Net Framework classes to interface to the Windows 2000 Operating System.

.NET Framework Base Classes

You don't have to design all your .NET types from the ground up. The .NET framework includes classes, interfaces, and value types that help expedite and optimize the development process and give you access to system functionality. To facilitate interoperability between languages, the .NET Framework types are CLS compliant and can be used from any language compiler that targets the Common Language Runtime. The .NET Framework includes types that encapsulate data structures, perform I/O, give you access to information about a loaded class, and provide a way to invoke .NET Framework security checks, as well as classes that encapsulate exception and other helpful functionality, such as data access, server controls, and rich GUI generation. These types are designed to be the foundation on which .NET applications, components, and controls are built.

The .NET Framework provides both abstract base classes and class implementations derived from those base classes. You can use these derived classes "as is" or derive your own classes from them. Also provided are interfaces and default implementations of those interfaces. To get the interface's functionality, you can either implement the interface yourself or you can use or derive a class from one of the runtime-based classes that implements the interface. .NET Framework types are named using a dot-syntax naming scheme that connotes a naming hierarchy. This technique is used to logically group related classes together so that they can be searched and referenced more easily. For example, the **System.Reflection.FieldInfo** class is related to other classes that also use a **System.Reflection.x** naming pattern. All classes named with a **System.Reflection** prefix can be used to discover information about types at runtime. The part of the name up to the last dot (e.g., **System.Reflection**) is often referred to as the namespace name and the last part (e.g., **FieldInfo**) as the class name. The use of naming patterns to group related classes into namespaces is a useful way to build and document class libraries. This naming syntax has no effect on visibility, member access, inheritance, or binding. A namespace may be partitioned across multiple assemblies (not to be confused with the software assembler MASM) and a single assembly (sometimes called a component) may contain classes from multiple namespaces. It is the assembly that provides the formal structure for visibility and versioning in the runtime. We will be looking at assemblies in detail in subsequent sections; however, an assembly for managed code is the primary unit for deployment. The root namespace for the types in the .NET Framework is the System namespace. This namespace includes classes that represent the base data types used by all applications: Object (the root of the inheritance hierarchy), Byte, Char, Array, Int32, String, etc. Many of these types correspond to the primitive data types that your language compiler uses. When you write code using .NET Framework types, you can, if you wish, use your language's corresponding type when a runtime-based type is expected. The following Table 3–1 lists some of the .NET Framework types, briefly describes each type, and indicates the corresponding type in C#, and the Managed Extensions for C++.

Along with the base data types, there are approximately 94 classes directly in the System namespace along with 8 Interfaces, 25 structures, 4 delegates, and 6 enumerations. There are 83 namespaces of which 81 is **System.xxx**; the other two are **Microsoft.ComServices** and **Microsoft.Win32**. In the .NET Framework namespaces, there are approximately 2,042 classes, 272 interfaces, 435 enumerations, 148 delegates, and 88 structures already predefined for use in application design. Notice that this contrasts to 95 categories of Win32 APIs as shown in Appendix E from Chapter 2. Notice also that we are dealing not with APIs, but with classes,

Table 3–1

Type	Class Name	Description	C# Data Type	Extensions C++ type
Integer	Byte	An 8-bit unsigned integer	byte	char
	Sbyte	An 8-bit signed integer	sbyte	signed char
	Int16	A 16-bit signed integer	short	short
	Int32	A 32-bit signed integer	int	int or long
	Int64	A 64-bit signed integer	long	__int64
	Uint16	A 16-bit unsigned integer	ushort	unsigned short
	Uint32	A 32-bit unsigned integer	uint	unsigned int or unsigned long
	Uint64	A 64-bit unsigned integer	ulong	unsigned __int64
Floating Point	Single	Single-precision (32-bit) floating-point number	float	float
	Double	Double-precision (64-bit) floating-point number	double	double
Other	Object	The base type of the class hierarchy	object	Object*
	Char	A Unicode character (a 16-bit character)	char	__wchar_t
	String	An immutable, fixed length string of Unicode characters	string	String*
	Decimal	A 96-bit decimal value	decimal	Decimal
Logical	Boolean	A Boolean value (true or false)	bool	bool

which provide a much richer semantic content for the developer. There are already more classes defined than the approximately 1,939 Win32 APIs. These namespaces encapsulate the Win32 APIs and, therefore, the Windows 2000 Operating System. The following list shows some of the major categories of namespace functionality that is covered, and some namespaces in each category. In Appendix G we list in more detail all of the .NET Framework namespaces.

1. Data

   System.Data

   System.XML

2. Component Model:

   System.CodeDOM

   System.ComponentModel

   System.Core

3. Configuration

   System.Configuration

4. Framework Services

   System.Diagnostics

   System.DirectoryServices

   System.ServiceProcess

   System.Messaging

   System.Timers

5. Globalization

   System.Globalization

   System.Resources

6. Net

   System.Net

7. Programming Basics

   System.Collection

   System.IO

   System.Text

   System.Threading

8. Reflection

   System.Reflection

9. Rich Client-Side GUI

System.Drawing

System.Winforms

10. Runtime Infrastructure Services

System.Runtime.InteropServices

System.Runtime.Remoting

System.Runtime.Serialization

11. .NET Framework Security

System.Security

12. Web Services

System.Web

For example, suppose we wanted to use the ADO.NET object model. First, we would put the Import construct at the top of the page in the ASP.NET page. You have to tell ASP.NET that you want to use a particular namespace.

<%@ Import Namespace="**System.Data.ADO**" %>

This makes available the **System.Data**, **System.Data.ADO**, **System.Data.SQL**, **System.Data.XML**, and **System.Data.SQLTypes** namespaces for use in these ASP.NET pages. As you can tell by looking in Appendix G at the classes associated with these namespaces, there is a lot of already defined functionality available for the developer.

Common Type System

The Common Type System (CTS) describes the types supported by the runtime and specifies how those types can interact with each other and how they are persisted in metadata. A type defines allowable values and the operations supported by those values. The types in the runtime's type system include classes, interfaces, and value types. Types can have methods that describe the operations on the type, as well as other members such as fields, properties, and events.

The type system is an important part of the runtime's support for cross-language integration because it provides the rules that language compilers follow with respect to defining, referencing, using, and storing types. The fact that types are created and used consistently by language compilers supplies the basis for ensuring that objects written in different languages can interact with each other. As we are seeing, the .NET Framework is built on the type system that the runtime defines. It supplies built-in primitive types, as well as other types that you can use or derive from when building your component or application.

CLASSES

Let's define a bit more about these classes that are found in each .NET Framework **System** namespace. Since you are familiar with object-oriented programming, you know that a class defines the operations the object can perform (methods, events, or properties) and defines variables that hold the state of the object (fields). A class generally includes both definition and implementation, but a class can have one or more members that have no implementation. Class members that have no implementation are abstract members. A class that has one or more abstract members is itself abstract and cannot be instantiated. Some language compilers that target the runtime allow you to mark a class as abstract even if none of its members are abstract. You can use an abstract class when you need to encapsulate a basic set of functionality that derived classes can inherit or override when appropriate.

An instance of a .NET Framework class is an object. You get access to an object's functionality by calling its methods and accessing its properties, events, and fields. Each language compiler chooses its own syntax for creating instances of classes. A class can implement any number of interfaces, but it can inherit from exactly one base class. The runtime allows you to pass an instance of a class as a parameter. All classes are required to have at least one constructor, which initialized new instances of the class. Each language compiler that supports the runtime chooses its own syntax for indicating to the compiler that the class or class member has specific characteristics. You just use the syntax required by the language compiler and, when your code is compiled to Microsoft intermediate language (MSIL), the compiler ensures that the characteristics of the class and its members are stored (as metadata) along with the implementation of the class.

The following Table 3–2 provides a description of some of the characteristics that the runtime allows a class to have. Additional characteristics that are available through Attribute classes are not included in this list. Your compiler might not make all of these characteristics available.

INTERFACES

Interfaces define a set of functionality that classes can implement; however, interfaces contain no implementation, except for static methods and static fields. An interface specifies a contract that a class implementing the interface must follow. Interfaces can contain static or virtual methods, static fields, properties, and events. All interface members must be public. Interfaces cannot define constructors. The runtime allows an interface to require that any class that implements it must also implement one or more other interfaces.

To simplify the definition of interfaces, some languages do not require interface characteristics to be applied explicitly because those characteristics already apply implicitly. For example, all interfaces are implicitly abstract, and every member of the interface is implicitly abstract.

Table 3–2

Class characteristic	Meaning
sealed	You cannot derive another class from this one.
implements	The class fulfills the contract specified by one or more interfaces.
abstract	You cannot create an instance of the class. If you want to use it, you must derive another class from it.
inherits	Indicates that instances of the class can be used anywhere the base class is specified. A derived class that inherits from a base class can use the implementation of any virtual methods provided by the base class, or the derived class can override them with its own implementation.
exported or not exported	Indicates whether a class is visible outside the assembly.

Note	The runtime allows you to define members of your class, such as properties, methods, fields, and events. Again, some language compilers might choose not to support all of these member types. The runtime allows class members to have the following characteristics (but language compilers are not required to support all of these characteristics).
abstract	This virtual method has no implementation. If you inherit from the class that it is a member of, you must implement this member if you want to instantiate the derived class.
private, family, assembly, family and assembly, or public	Defines the accessibility of the member:
	private: accessible only from within the same class as the member or assembly, family or within a nested class.
	family: accessible from within the same class as the member and from subtypes that inherit from it.
	assembly: accessible only from within the assembly that contains the member's implementation. .NET applications are partitioned into one or more assemblies, which establish the visibility scope for types at execution time.
	family or assembly: accessible only from classes that qualify for either family or assembly access.
	family and assembly: accessible only from classes that quality for both family and assembly access.
	public: accessible from any class.
final	You cannot override this virtual method in a derived class.

Table 3–2	*Continued*
Member characteristic	**Meaning**
overrides	The virtual method's implementation replaces the implementation supplied by a member of the class from which it derives.
static	The member belongs to the class it is defined on, not to a particular instance of the class; the member exists even if the class is not instantiated, and it is shared among all instances of the class.
overloads	The method has the same name as another member defined in the same type, but it differs in some way from the other method(s) with the same name; for example, its parameter types, the order of parameter types, or the calling convention might be different.
virtual	The method can be implemented by a subclass, and can be invoked either statically or dynamically. If dynamic invocation is used, the type of the instance that is used to make the call at runtime determines which implementation of the method to call, instead of the type known at compile time.
synchronized	The runtime ensures that only one thread of execution at a time can access the implementation. This characteristic can be applied to static methods, as well as instance and virtual methods.

VALUE TYPES

Most programming languages provide built-in data types, like integers and floating point numbers that are copied when they are passed as arguments. This differs from the way objects are treated: they are always passed by reference. The runtime generalized the idea of built-in data types to allow for user-defined data types that are passed by value. These types are called value types. Value types are stored as efficiently as primitive types, yet you can call methods on the value type including the virtual methods defined on the **System.Object** class as well as any methods defined on the value type itself. The .NET Framework defines built-in value types such as **System.Int32** and **System.Boolean**, which correspond to primitive data types used by language compilers; they are identical to your language compiler's primitive types. Value types can be instantiated, passed as parameters, stored as local variables, or stored in a field of another value type or object. Value types do not have the overhead associated with storing an instance of a class, and they do not require a constructor to be called when an instance is created. The contents of a value type are guaranteed to be initially zero (null for object fields).

You can define your own value types by using special syntax that your language compiler supplies. Such value types are derived from **System.ValueType**. If you want to define a type representing a value that is small, such as a complex number (using two floating point numbers), you might choose to define it as a value type because you can pass the value type efficiently by value. If the type you are defining would be more efficiently passed by reference, you should define it as a class instead. For each value type, the runtime supplies a corresponding *boxed* type, which is a class having the same state and behavior as the value type. Some language compilers require you to use special syntax when the *boxed* type is required; others automatically use the *boxed* type when it is needed. When you define a value type, you are defining both the *unboxed* type and the *boxed* type that is associated with the value type.

Value types can have fields, properties, and events. They can also have static and nonstatic methods. When they are *boxed*, they inherit the virtual methods from **System.ValueType**, and they can implement zero or more interfaces. Constructors are not required on value types. Value types are sealed, meaning that no other type can be derived from them. However, you can define virtual methods directly on the value type, and these can be called on either the *boxed* or *unboxed* form of the value type. Even though you cannot derive another type from a value type, you might define virtual methods on a value type when you are using a language in which it is more convenient to work with virtual methods than nonvirtual or static methods.

ENUMERATIONS

An enumeration (enum) is a special form of value type, which inherits from **System.Enum** and supplies an alternate name for an underlying primitive type. An enum type has a name, an underlying type, and a set of fields. The underlying type must be one of the built-in signed or unsigned integer types (such as Int16, Int32, or Int64). The fields are static literal fields, each of which represent a constant. Each field is assigned a specific value of the underlying type by the language compiler. Multiple fields can be assigned the same value. When this occurs, the compiler marks exactly one of the enum values as a "primary" enum value for the value, for the purpose of reflection and string conversion.

You can assign a value of the underlying type to an enum and vice versa (no cast is required by the runtime). You can create an instance of an enum, and you can call the methods of **System.Enum**, as well as any methods defined on the enum's underlying type. However, some language compilers might not allow you to pass an enum as a parameter when an instance of the underlying type is required (or vice versa). The following additional restrictions apply to enumerations:

- They cannot define their own methods.
- They cannot implement interfaces.
- They cannot define properties or events.

Delegates

The runtime supports objects called delegates that serve the same purpose as function pointers in C++. As we mentioned above, there are some 143 predefined delegates associated with the namespaces. Because they are type-save, secure, managed objects, you get all the advantages of pointers without any of their disadvantages. For example, delegates will always point to a valid object and cannot corrupt memory of other objects. Besides their use as the equivalent of function pointers, delegates are also used for event handling and callbacks in the .NET Framework. Each instance of a delegate forwards calls to a method on a particular object. The object and method are chosen when the delegate instance is constructed. Therefore, the definition of a delegate is simply the signature of the method to which it forwards its calls. The implementations of the methods on a delegate are provided by the runtime, not by user code. Developers cannot specify additional members on a delegate.

Two delegate classes are provided by the .NET Framework: Delegate and MulticastDelegate. All delegates have an invocation list, or linked list of delegates, that are executed when the invoke method is called. A delegate that derives from the **System.Delegate** class contains an invocation list with one method, while a delegate that derives from the **System.Multicase Delegate** contains an invocation list with multiple methods. The MulticastDelegate class contains two static methods to add and remove method references from an invocation list: Combine and Remove.

When you declare a delegate, you tell the compiler the type of each parameter and of its return value. These types correspond to the method that the delegate will ultimately call. For example, the following code defines a delegate that takes no parameters and returns no value:

```
public delegate void MyDelegate();
```

You would next declare an instance of the delegate. The delegate constructor takes the name of the method it will call. The following code declares an instance of MyDelegate and makes it call Method1 of Myclass.

```
MyDelegate TheDelegate = new MyDelegate(MyClass.Method1);
```

You can now call MyDelegate, and it will, in turn, call MyClass.Method1, like this:

TheDelegate();

Delegates are particularly suited for event handling. An event is sent by an object or event source in response to an action either performed by a user or some sort of program logic. The event receiver must then act in response to the raised event and perform an action. It is the event delegate's job to act as an intermediary between these two objects. With this in mind, the event delegate is declared with a reference to the method it will call. Once the delegate is invoked, it takes two parameters: the source that raised the event and the data that the target method will need to take as a parameter. The following code shows the declaration for an event delegate called EventHandler:

```
public delegate void EventHandler(object sender, EventArgs e);
```

You next register the event delegate as an event with the following code:

```
public event EventHandler Event;
```

Finally, you pass an EventArgs object to the OnEvent method. The event delegate then takes this pointer and the event object. The following code shows the OnEvent method that will be called when the previously register event is raised:

```
protected virtual void OnEvent(EventArgs e)
{
// Invokes the delegates.
Event(this, e);
}
```

Once invoked, the delegate will take any data passed to it and call the methods that it references.

Common Language Runtime

The .NET Framework provides a runtime environment called the Common Language Runtime (CLR), which manages the execution of code and provides services that make the development process easier. Compilers and tools expose the runtime's functionality and enable you to write code that benefits from this managed execution environment. Code that you develop with a language compiler that targets the runtime is called managed code. It benefits from features such as cross-language integration, cross-language exception handling, enhanced security, versioning and deployment support, a simplified model for component interaction, and debugging and profiling services.

To enable the runtime to provide services to managed code, language compilers are required to emit *metadata*, which means that they provide information that describes the types, members, and references in your code. Metadata is stored along with the code; every loadable common language runtime image contains metadata. The runtime uses metadata to locate and load classes, lay out instances in memory, resolve method invocations, generate native code, enforce security, and set up runtime context boundaries. The runtime automatically handles object layout and manages references to objects, releasing them when they are no longer being used. Objects whose lifetimes are managed in this way by the runtime are called *managed data*. Automatic memory management eliminates memory leaks as well as some other common programming errors. If your code is managed, you can use managed data; however, you can instead use unmanaged data if you wish, or you can use both managed and unmanaged data in your .NET application. Because language compilers supply their own types, such as primitive types, you might not always know (or need to know) whether your data is being managed.

The Common Language Runtime makes it easy to design components and applications whose objects interact across languages. Objects written in different languages can communicate with each other, and their behaviors can be tightly integrated. For example, you can define a class, then, using a different language, derive a class from your original class or call a method on it. You can also pass an instance of a class to a method on a class written in a different language. This cross-language integration is possible because language compilers and tools that target the runtime use a common type system defined by the runtime, and they follow the runtime's rules for defining new types, as well as creating, using, persisting, and binding to types. As part of their metadata, all managed components carry information about the components and resources they were built against. The runtime uses this information to ensure that your component or application has the specified versions of everything it needs; as a result, your code is less likely to break due to some dependency not being met. Registration information and state data are no longer stored in the registry, which can be difficult to establish and maintain; instead, information about the types you define (and their dependencies) is stored with the code as metadata, making the tasks of component replication and removal much less complicated.

Language compilers and tools expose the runtime's functionality in ways that are intended to be useful and intuitive to their developers. This means that some features of the runtime might be more noticeable in one environment than in another. Therefore, how you experience the runtime depends on which language compilers or tools you use. For example, if you are a Visual Basic developer, you might notice that with the Common Language Runtime, the Visual Basic language has more object-oriented features than before. The following benefits of the runtime would be particularly interesting to the developer.

* Performance improvements
* The ability to easily use components developed in other languages
* Extensible types provide by a class library
* A broad set of language features

If you use Visual C++, you can write managed code using managed extensions to C++, which provide the benefits of a managed execution environment while giving you access to powerful capabilities and expressive data types that you are familiar with. You would find the following runtime features especially compelling:

* Cross-language integration, especially cross-language inheritance
* Automatic memory management, which manages object lifetime so that reference counting is unnecessary
* Self-describing objects, which make using IDL (Interface Definition Language) unnecessary
* The ability to compile once and run on any CPU and operating system that support the runtime

Managed Execution

The first step in the managed execution process is designing the source code. If you want your application to have the benefits provided by the CLS, you must use one (or more) language compilers that target the runtime, such as Visual C++, C#, Visual Basic, or one of many third-party compilers such as Perl or COBOL. Because the runtime is a multilanguage execution environment, it supports a wide variety of data types and language features. The language compiler you are using determines what subset of the runtime's functionality is available, and you design your code, using the features available in your compiler. The syntax you use in your code is determined by the compiler, not by the runtime. If your component is required to be completely usable by components written in other languages, you must use only language features that are included in the CLS in your component's exported types.

Once your code is written, you compile it, and the compiler translates it to Microsoft intermediate language (MSIL) and generates the required metadata. When you are ready to execute your code, the MSIL gets compiled into native code by a Just In Time (JIT) compiler. If security policy requires the code to be type-safe, the IL is checked for type-safety as part of the JIT compilation process; if the type-safety check fails, an exception is thrown when the code is executed. During execution, the runtime provides services that include automatic memory management, debugging support, enhanced security, and interoperability and unmanaged code, such as COM components. The following sections provide more detailed information about managed execution.

MICROSOFT INTERMEDIATE LANGUAGE (MSIL)

If you compile your source code to managed code, the compiler translates your source code into Microsoft intermediate language (MSIL), which is a CPU-independent set of instructions that can be efficiently converted to native code. MSIL includes a wide spectrum of instructions, such as instructions for loading, storing, initializing, and calling methods on objects, as well as instructions for arithmetic and logical operations, control flow, direct memory access, and exception handling. Before code can be executed, MSIL must be converted to CPU-specific code by a Just In Time (JIT) compiler. Because the runtime supplies one or more JIT compilers for each computer architecture it supports, the same set of MSIL can be JIT-compiled and executed on any supported architecture.

When a compiler produces MSIL, it also produces metadata, which describes the types in your code, including the definition of each type, the signatures of each type's members, the members that your code references, and other data that the runtime uses at execution time. The MSIL and metadata are contained in a portable executable (PE) file that is based on and extends the published Microsoft Portable Executable (PE) and Common Object File format (COFF) used historically for executable content. This file format, which accommodates MSIL or native code as well as metadata, enables the operating system to recognize Common Language Runtime images. The presence of metadata in the file, along with the MSIL, enables your code to describe itself, which means that there is no need for type libraries or IDL. The runtime locates and extracts the metadata from the file as necessary during execution.

JIT COMPILATION

Before MSIL can be executed, it must be converted by a .NET Framework Just In Time (JIT) compiler to native code, which is CPU-specific code that runs on the same computer architecture that the JIT compiler is running on. Because the runtime supplies a JIT compiler for each CPU architecture that the runtime operates on, developers can write a set of MSIL that can be JIT-compiled and executed on computers with different architectures. There is an MSIL Instruction Set specification with the .NET Framework SDK located in the Tools Developers Guide directory. If the managed code calls platform-specific native APIs or a class library that is platform-specific, your code is limited to running on a specific operating system.

The idea behind JIT compilation recognizes the fact that some code may never get called during execution; therefore, rather than using time and memory to convert all of the MSIL in a PE file to native code, it makes sense to convert the MSIL as it is needed during execution and store the resulting native code so that it is accessible for subsequent calls. The loader creates and attaches a stub to each of the type's methods when the type is loaded; on the initial call to the method, the stub passes control to the JIT compiler, which converts the MSIL for that method into native code and modifies the stub to direct execution to the location of the native code. Subsequent calls of the JIT-compiled method proceed directly to the native code that was previously generated, reducing the time it takes to JIT compile and execute the code.

As part of compiling MSIL to native code, the code must pass a verification process (unless an administrator has established a security policy that allows the code to bypass verification). Verification examines MSIL and metadata to see whether the code can be determined to be type-safe, which means that it is known to access only memory locations it is authorized to access. Type safety is necessary to ensure that objects are safely isolated from each other and, therefore, safe from inadvertent or malicious corruption. It also provides assurance that security restrictions on code can be reliably enforced. For code that is verifiably type-safe, the runtime can rely on the following statements being true:

- A reference to a type is strictly compatible with the type being referenced
- Only appropriately defined operations are invoked on an object
- Identities are what they claim to be

During the verification process, MSIL code is examined in an attempt to confirm that the code can access memory locations and call methods only through properly defined types. For example, code cannot allow an object's fields to be accessed in a manner that allows memory location to be overrun. Additionally, verification inspects code to see whether the MSIL has been correctly generated, since incorrect MSIL could lead to a violation of the type safety rules. The verification process passes a well-defined set of type-safe code, and it passes only code that is type-safe. However, some type-safe code might not pass verification due to limitations of the verification process, and some languages by design do not produce verifiably type-safe code.

Assemblies

An assembly is the functional unit of sharing and reuse in the Common Language Runtime. It provides the CLR with the information it needs to be aware of type implementations. To the runtime, a type does not exist outside the context of any assembly. Assemblies are a fundamental part of the runtime. In physical terms, an assembly is a collection of physical files that are owned by the assembly. These assemblies, called static assemblies, can include .NET Framework types (interfaces and classes), as well as resources for the assembly (bitmaps, JPEG files, resource files, etc.). In addition, the CLR provides APIs that script engines use to create dynamic assemblies when executing scripts. These assemblies are run directly and are never saved to disk, though you can save them to disk if you choose. An assembly forms the boundary for security, deployment, and type resolution. The assembly is also the smallest unit that can be versioned. The runtime can only execute code located in assemblies. All code, whether it be a programming or scripting language, is run from assemblies.

There are several ways assemblies can be created. The same development tools, such as Visual Studio.NET, that you have used in the past to create DLLs or EXEs are now redesigned so you can use them to create assemblies. You can also use additional tools provided in the .NET Framework SDK to create assemblies with modules you created from other development environments. In addition, the CLR provides APIs such as Reflection.Emit that can be used to create dynamic assemblies.

ASSEMBLY CONCEPTS

An assembly forms a logical unit of functionality, a "logical" dll. An assembly forms the fundamental unit of deployment, version control, reuse, activation scooping, and security permissions. Contained in an assembly is the assembly manifest, which contains all the metadata needed to specify the version requirements, security identity, and all information needed to define the scope of the assembly and resolve references to resources and classes. It is a unit of class deployment, much like a dll. An application is built from assemblies, and these assemblies can be packaged for deployment in several ways.

VERSIONING AND DLL CONFLICTS

Currently there are two versioning problems that occur with Win32 applications. First, current applications cannot express versioning rules between pieces of an application having these rules honored and enforced by the operating system. The current approach relies on "common-sense" coding practices that state that interface definitions are static once published and that a single piece of code must maintain backward compatibility with previous versions. Furthermore, code is typically designed so that only a single version of it can be present and executing on a machine at any given time. The second versioning problem is the fact that there is no way to maintain consistency between the sets of components that were built together and the set that will be present at runtime. These two versioning problems combine to create DLL conflicts, where installing one application can inadvertently break an existing application because a certain software component or DLL was installed that was not fully backward compatible with a previous version. Once this situation occurs, there is no support in the system for diagnosing and fixing the problem.

AN END TO DLL CONFLICTS

Windows 2000 introduced some progress toward fixing DLL conflicts. First, Windows 2000 enables you to create client applications where the dependent DLLs are located in the same directory as the application's EXE. Windows 2000 first checks for the component in the directory where the EXE is located before checking the fully qualified path or doing the normal path search. This allows components to be independent of components installed and used by other applications. The second feature in Windows 2000 designed to partially fix DLL conflicts is System File Protection. The operating system locks the files in the System32 directory that are shipped with the OS so they cannot be inadvertently replaced when applications are installed.

The CLR continues this evolution toward a complete solution to DLL conflicts. To solve the remaining problems that lead to DLL conflicts, the runtime:

- Allows developers to specify version rules between different software components
- Provides the infrastructure to enforce versioning rules
- Provides the infrastructure to allow multiple versions of a software component to be run simultaneously (called side-by-side execution)

ASSEMBLIES AND DEPLOYING

An assembly is not a packaging format in and of itself. An assembly to be deployed is usually made up of PE files and resource files, and these files can be deployed in a number of ways. How you choose to create assemblies will dictate much of your deployment story. You can deploy assemblies using the Windows Installer, Internet Explorer, or by copying the assembly. Assemblies can be deployed in as .cab files or as .msi files. You can also simply download or xcopy an assembly to deploy.

The Minimum You Need to Know About Assemblies

As a developer, you can think of an assembly as a "logical" dll. Here is a list of things you should remember about an assembly:

It contains code that the runtime will execute. MSIL code in a PE file will not be executed if it does not have an assembly manifest associated with it. Note, too, that each assembly can have only one entry point (i.e., DLLMain, WinMain, or Main).

It forms a security boundary—an assembly is the unit at which permissions are requested and granted.

It forms a type boundary—Every type has as part of its identity the assembly in which it resides. Therefore, a type MyType loaded in the scope of one assembly is not the same as type MyType loaded in the scope of another assembly.

It forms a reference scope boundary—The assembly's manifest contains the rules for resolving types and resources. It specifies what types and resources are exposed outside the assembly. The manifest also enumerates other assemblies on which it is dependent.

It forms a version boundary—The assembly is the smallest version unit in the CLR; all types and resources in the same assembly are versioned as a unit. The assembly's manifest describes the version dependencies you specify for any dependent assemblies.

It forms a deployment unit—An application when launched only requires those assemblies it initially calls. All assemblies of an application do not have to be present at runtime; other assemblies, such as localization resources, can be retrieved on demand. This allows downloaded applications to be kept simple and thin.

It is the unit at which side-by-side execution is supported.

Some of the information in an assembly manifest can be overridden by an application or machine-wide configuration file.

ASSEMBLY MANIFEST

An assembly's manifest contains information on all items considered part of an assembly; this information is known as the assembly's metadata. The manifest indicates what items are exposed outside of the assembly and what items are accessible only within the current assembly's scope. The assembly's manifest also contains a collection of references to other assemblies. These references are resolved by the runtime based on information stored in the manifest. The assembly's manifest contains all information needed to use an assembly. All assemblies have a manifest, and all applications that use the runtime must be made up of an assembly or assemblies. All files that make up the assembly must be listed in a manifest. Figure 3–4 shows the types of assemblies.

As you can see in Figure 3–4, the manifest can be stored in several ways. For an assembly with one associated file, the manifest is incorporated into the PE file to store a single-file assembly. A multifile assembly can be created with either the manifest as a stand-alone file or incorporated into one of the PE files in the assembly.

From an external view (i.e., that of the assembly consumer), an assembly is a named and version-constrained collection of exported types and resources. From the internal view (i.e., that of the assembly developer), an assembly is a collection of one or more files that implement types and resources. Each assembly's manifest enumerates the file that makes up the assembly and governs how references to the assembly's types and resources

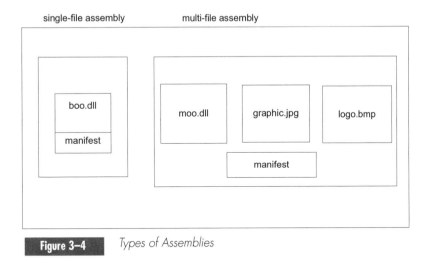

single-file assembly   multi-file assembly

boo.dll

manifest

moo.dll   graphic.jpg   logo.bmp

manifest

Figure 3–4   *Types of Assemblies*

are mapped to the files that contain their declarations and implementations. The manifest also enumerates other assemblies on which it depends. The existence of a manifest provides a level of indirection between consumers of the assembly and the implementation details of the assembly and renders assemblies self-describing. The manifest contains the following information:

- Assembly name—contains a textual string name of the assembly.
- Version information—consists of a major and minor version number, and a revision and build number. These numbers are used by the runtime when enforcing version policy.
- Shared name information—contains the public key from the publisher and a hash of the file containing the manifest signed with the publisher's private key.
- Culture, processor and OS supported—contains information on the cultures, processors, and operating systems the assembly supports. For BETA 1 release, this processor and OS information is ignored by the runtime.
- List of all files in the assembly—consists of a hash of each file contained in the assembly and a relative path to the file from the manifest file. Note that all files that make up the assembly must be in the same directory as the manifest file.
- Type reference information—contains information used by the runtime to map a type reference to the file that contains its declaration and implementation.
- Information on referenced assemblies—contains a list of other assemblies that are statically referenced by the assembly. Each reference includes the dependent assembly's name, metadata (version, culture, OS, etc.), and public key if the assembly is shared.

A developer can also set, in code, custom assembly attributes. These attributes are informational only and are not used by the runtime in any way. Custom attributes include:

- Title—Provides a friendly name, which can include spaces. For example, the assembly name of an assembly might be "comdlg," while the assembly title would be "Microsoft Common Dialog Control."
- Description—a short description of the assembly.
- Default Alias—Provides a friendly default alias in cases where the assembly name is not friendly or a GUID.
- Configuration information—consists of a string that can be set to any value for configuration information such as Retail or Debug.
- Product information such as Trademark, Copyright, Product, Company, and Informational Version.

ASSEMBLY CUSTOM ATTRIBUTES

You can view the attributes assigned to an assembly when it was first created, and you can add information to an assembly by using custom attributes. There are two sets of assembly attributes in BETA 1. The first set of assembly attributes includes four fields from the assembly manifest (Title, Description, DefaultAlias, and Configuration) and five custom attributes for company or product information (Trademark, Copyright, Product, Company, InformationalVersion). These attributes are represented by nine classes in the **System.Reflection** namespace. The runtime adds these values to the assembly manifest when the assembly is created. You can query this information using the class **System.Reflection**.

Assembly Attribute Class	Description
AssemblyDescriptionAttribute	Description of the product or modules that make up the assembly.
AssemblyInformationalVersionAttribute	Additional or supporting version information, such as a commercial product version number.
AssemblyProductAttribute	Product information.
AssemblyTitleAttribute	The assembly's title.
AssemblyTrademarkAttribute	Trademark information

The second set of assembly attributes are contained in the **System.Runtime.CompilerServices** namespace. These are custom attributes that you can add, and this information is added to an assembly when the assembly is created. You can put these custom attributes in any module to be included in the assembly. These attributes include:

Assembly Attribute	Description
AssemblyCultureAttribute	Information on what cultures or languages the assembly supports.
AssemblyDelaySignAttribute	Specifies that the assembly should not be fully signed when created, but rather "delay signed," which means space is reserved for the signature, which is later filled by a signing tool like the sn.exe utility.
AssemblyKeyFileAttribute	Specifies the name of the file containing the key pair used to sign the assembly (i.e., give it a shared name).
AssemblyKeyNameAttribute	Specifies the name of the key container. Instead of placing a key pair in a file, you can store it in a key container in the CSP. If you choose this option, this attribute will contain the name of the key container.
AssemblyOperatingSystemAttribute	Information on which operating system the assembly was built to support.
AssemblyProcessorAttribute	Information on which processors the assembly was built to support.
AssemblyVersionAttribute	Specifies the assembly's version information, in the format major.minor build rev.

CREATING ASSEMBLIES

You can create assemblies using development tools designed to work with the .NET Frameworks, such as Visual Studio.NET, or using the al.exe utility provided in the .NET Frameworks SDK. When creating an assembly, there are several decisions you need to make. These options, explained further in the text below, include:

- Naming—An assembly can have either a simple, string name, or a shared (also called "strong") name created using standard public-key cryptography.
- Location—An assembly can be deployed in an application's root director, in a subdirectory of that application, or in the global assembly cache.
- Loader Optimization—An assembly can have a single copy of the assembly's code shared among all the applications running in a given process. This means that the assembly's code is compiled by the JIT compiler only once, and this compiled code is loaded into multiple application domains in a process.

The simplest assembly you can create for an application would have all the files that make up the assembly deployed in the application folder, would have a simple name, would be loaded into a single application domain, and would not be shared with other applications. The assembly would not be able to be referenced by other assemblies outside the application directory, and would undergo no version checking. To uninstall the application made up of the assembly, you would only need to delete the directory that contained it. For many developers, an assembly with these options is all that is needed for deploying an application.

You also can create an assembly designed to be shared by multiple applications. This assembly would have a shared name, be deployed in the global assembly cache, and you could determine what load optimization setting best fit the application. If a host runs the same application in several domains within a process, you would specify the Loader Optimization setting. This assembly would have been built explicitly for sharing.

NAMING AN ASSEMBLY

The naming of an assembly has a significant impact on the assembly's scope and use by multiple applications. An assembly that is intended for use by one application and deployed in the application's directory most likely will need only the name assigned when the assembly is created. Note that there is nothing in the runtime to prevent name collisions. This option for naming an assembly is appropriate for assemblies intended for use by the application it is deployed with, but for code that is intended to be shared by multiple applications, a stronger notion of naming is required.

This stronger notion of naming is addressed by giving the assembly what is known as a shared (also called "strong") name using standard public-key cryptography. A shared name is a simple text name accompanied by a public key and a digit signature that was generated over the assembly file (the file that contains the assembly manifest, which in turn contains the names and hashes of all the files that make up the assembly) using the corresponding private key. Assigning an assembly a shared name allows the assembly to be deployed in the global assembly cache. An assembly with a shared name is often called a shared assembly.

ASSEMBLY LOCATION

You can deploy an assembly in several locations. The location of the assembly will determine if the assembly is able to be shared with other assemblies, and can impact if the runtime can locate the assembly when references are made to it. The most common location for an assembly is in the application's directory. This is the preferred location if the assembly is only going to be used with the application it was deployed with. You can also deploy an assembly into the global assembly cache, a machine-wide cache that is installed on each machine that has the CLR installed. In most cases, if you intend to share an assembly with multiple applications, you should deploy it into the global assembly cache.

LOADER OPTIMIZATION

An assembly can also be designated as usable by multiple applications. The assembly can be mapped into all domains in a process. The assembly's code is compiled using the JIT compiler once for use by multiple application domains, and one copy of the assembly is available per process. Each domain gets its own copy of global static data. Designating an assembly as useable by multiple applications can have several advantages. When a type from such an assembly is loaded the first time, it is automatically mapped into all application domains instead of being loaded into each application domain separately. As a result, the assembly consumes fewer resources if multiple application domains refer to it. In addition, such an assembly speeds up the creation of application domains since the runtime does not need to recompile the code or build multiple copies of the data structures used to represent the types. Assemblies designated as useable by multiple applications are not unloaded until the process ends.

While using such an assembly does reduce memory usage, its use results in slightly larger JIT-compiled code. In addition, since statics are scoped by application domain, references to statics must be in-directed when the assembly is loaded instead of being accessed by direct memory reference. As a result, access to statics is slower when the assembly is designated as useable by multiple applications than when it is not. A setting called "Loader Optimization" is used to designate an assembly as useable by multiple applications. This setting can have one of three values:

- Single Domain—the loader optimizes for single application domain application. This is the default setting, and means that the assembly is not optimized for use by multiple applications.
- Multi Domain—the loader optimized for multiple application domain application, where each domain is running the same code.
- Multi Domain Host—loader optimized for multi application domain applications, where each domain is hosting different code.

You can designate an assembly at the process level to be domain neutral in two ways:

- Through the unmanaged hosting API, by calling CorBindToRuntimeEx() with appropriate flags
- By setting a custom attribute (of type **System.LoaderOptimizationAttribute**) on an .exe's Main method

You can also designate an assembly to be domain neutral on a per domain basis by calling AppDomain.SetData(AppDomainFlags.LoaderOptimization, x), where x is an instance of the LoaderOptimization enum. This function, of course, must be called before the domain is used. If not set, the default value is single domain.

Shared Name

A shared (or "strong") name is a simple text name accompanied by a public key and a digital signature. It is generated over the assembly file (the file that contains the assembly manifest, which in turn contains the names and hashes of all the files that make up the assembly) using the corresponding private key. Visual Studio.NET and other development tools can create shared names for an assembly. Assemblies with the same shared name are expected to be identical. A developer can ensure that a name is globally unique by assigning an assembly a shared name. In particular, shared names satisfy the following requirements:

- Shared names guarantee name uniqueness by relying on unique key-pairs.
- Shared names prevent others from "taking over your namespace." Because only you have your private key, no one can generate the same name that you can. An assembly generated with on private key has a different name than an assembly generated with another private key.
- Shared names also protect the version lineage of an assembly. This means that a shared name can ensure a developer that no one can produce a subsequent version of his or her assembly. Users can be sure that a version of the assembly they are loading comes from the same publisher that created the version the application was built with.
- Shared names provide some notion of integrity. If the .NET Frameworks security checks pass, you are guaranteed that the contents of the assembly have not been changed since it was built. Note, however, that shared names in and of themselves do not provide a level of trust. Trust is accomplished through full digital signatures complete with certificates.

Shared assemblies installed in the assembly cache must have shared names.

How to Assign and Reference a Shared Name

In general, the process of giving an assembly a shared (or "strong") name, and later referencing by that name, works as follows:

- Assembly A is created with a shared name, using either a development environment that supports creating shared names or by first using the al.exe utility to create an assembly and then using the sn.exe utility to assign it a shared name. Both tools are in the CLR SDK. The development environment or tool signs the hash of the file containing the assembly's manifest with the developer's private key. This digital signature is stored in the PE file, containing the assembly manifest in Assembly A.

- Assembly B, a consumer of Assembly A, would include a "token" that represents Assembly A's public key in the reference section of Assembly B's manifest. A "token" of the public key is stored rather than the key itself to save space—the token is a portion of the full public key.
- The runtime verifies the shared name signature when the assembly is placed in the global assembly cache. When binding by shared name at runtime, the runtime compares the key stored in Assembly B's manifest with the key used to generate the shared name for Assembly A. If the .NET Frameworks security checks pass and the bind succeeds, Assembly B has a guarantee that the bits it is getting haven't been tampered with and that they do, in fact, come from the developers of Assembly A.

The above scenario does not address trust issues. Assemblies can also carry full Authenticode signatures in addition to a shared name. These Authenticode signatures include a certificate that establishes trust. It is important to note that shared names do not require code to be signed in this way. In fact, the keys used to generate the shared name signature do not have to be the same keys used to generate an Authenticode signature.

Assemblies and Security Considerations

The runtime examines the set of permissions in an assembly when granting access privileges. When an assembly is built, the developer can specify a minimum set of permissions that the assembly requires to run. Additional permissions can be granted by security policy set on the machine on which the assembly will run. For example, if the developer writes code that accesses the disk, the assembly should request "File I/O Permission." The set of required permissions to run the assembly is stored in the assembly manifest. At load time, the assembly's permission request is used as input to security policy. Security policy is established by the administrator and is used to determine the set of permissions that is granted to all managed code when executed. Security policy can be established for the publisher of the assembly if it is signed with an AuthentiCode signature, as well as the Web site and zone (in Internet Explorer terms) the assembly was downloaded from, or the assembly's shared name. For example, an administrator can establish security policy that states that all code downloaded form the Internet and signed by a given software company can display a user interface on a machine but cannot access a disk drive.

You can give a shared (or "strong") name and an AuthentiCode digital signature to a single-file assembly, or you can use either alone. AuthentiCode can sign only one file at a time, so, in the case of a multifile assembly, you sign the file that contains the assembly manifest. A shared name is stored in the assembly manifest, but an AuthentiCode signature is stored in a specially reserved slot in the PE file (not as part of the manifest). AuthentiCode signing of an assembly can be used (with or without a shared name) when you already have a trust hierarchy that already relies on AuthentiCode signatures, or when your policy uses the key portion and does not check a chain of trust.

To allow policy to be based on either AuthentiCode signatures or shared names, the runtime must be able to guarantee that the contents of the assembly have not been changed since it was built. That is, it must be able to guarantee the integrity of each assembly it runs. It does this through hash verification: The assembly manifest contains a list of all files that make up the assembly, including a hash of each file, as it existed when the manifest was built. As each file is loaded at load time, its contents are hashed and compared with the hash value stored in the manifest. If the two hashes don't match, the assembly fails to load. In addition to the hash checks described here, the runtime also validates the assembly's signature—either the shared name or the AuthentiCode signature.

Assemblies and Versioning

All versioning of assemblies that use the CLR is done at the assembly level. The specific version of an assembly and the versions of dependent assemblies are recorded in the assembly's manifest. Version policy, that is, which version should be used, is specified by configuration files. These files—the assembly manifest, the optional application configuration file, and the machine's administrator configuration file—provide the means for expressing version and version policy, and the runtime then enforces the policy at runtime. Note: Versioning is done only on assemblies with shared names (also known as strong names).

Each assembly has two distinct ways of expressing version information. The first "number" is called a compatibility version, and is used by the runtime for version comparisons. This version number is part of the assembly's identity and is a key part in the type resolution process at runtime. It is called a compatibility number because this number is used by the runtime when enforcing version policy to determine a particular version's compatibility with previous versions. The second version "number" is called an informational version. The informational version is a string and is used to represent additional version information that is included for documentation purposes only. This textual version information corresponds to the product's marketing literature, packaging, or product name and is not used by the runtime. For example, an information version could be "Common Language Runtime Beta1" or ".Net Control SP2."

How the Common Language Runtime Works with Assemblies

The Common Language Runtime can only execute code in assemblies. The runtime works with two types of assemblies: static assemblies and dynamic assemblies. A static assembly is the kind of assembly you will most often work with: the unit produced when working with most developer environments. A static assembly consists of code modules and resources that are loaded from disk or downloaded for use by the runtime.

In contrast, a dynamic assembly is one built "on-the-fly" by the runtime from scripts on a Web page or with **Reflection.Emit**. These dynamic assemblies can be transient—never persisted to disk—or they can be persisted and saved to disk. Persisted dynamic assemblies can be emitted with **Reflection.Emit** and saved for later use.

HOW THE RUNTIME LOCATES ASSEMBLIES

The Common Language Runtime goes through a number of steps when attempting to locate an assembly and resolve an assembly reference. The term "probing" is often used when talking about how the runtime locates assemblies as it refers to the set of heuristics used to locate the assembly base on its name and culture. Each step is explained in the following descriptions.

STEP 1: INITIATING THE BIND

The process of locating an assembly begins when the runtime is asked to resolve a reference to another assembly. This reference can be to either a static or dynamic assembly. Static references are recorded in the assembly manifest's metadata at build time by the compiler. Dynamic references are constructed "on-the-fly" as a result of calling various APIs such as **System.Reflection.Assembly.Load**. In either case, the reference contains the name, version, culture, and originator of the desired assembly. The runtime then uses this information to locate the assembly, following the steps described below. There is no difference in the resolution process based on whether the reference was static or dynamic.

STEP 2: VERSION POLICY IN THE APPLICATION CONFIGURATION

The next step in binding to an assembly is to retrieve the application configuration file, if one exists. For client executables, the configuration file resides in the same directory as the executable and has the same name as the exe, substituting a .cfg extension for the .exe file extension of the executable. For example, the configuration file for c:\program files\myapp\myapp.exe would be c:\program files\myapp\myapp.cfg. In a browser-based scenario, the configuration file must explicitly be pointed to in the html file.

The <BindingPolicy> tag in the application configuration file can be used to redirect the reference to a particular version, or all versions, of an assembly to a different version. These version policies only apply when the reference is to an assembly with a shared name. References to private assemblies cannot have such policies applied; in fact, version checking is not done at all for binds to private assemblies. The following entry from an application configuration file redirects references to all versions of an assembly call calcr to version 2.1.0.0:

```
<BindingPolicy>
    <BindingRedire Name="Calcr"
            Originator="32ab4ba45e0a69a1"
            Version="*.*" VersionNew="2.1.0.0"
            UseLatestBuildRevision="yes"/>
</BindingPolicy>
```

If a version redirect for the requested assembly is encountered, the runtime proceeds as if the original bind had requested the version specified in the redirect. In the example above, the bind will continue as if the original bind request was for version 2.1.0.0 of calcr.

The default behavior of the runtime is to match versions based on major and minor numbers, and take the latest build and revision numbers. The policy of taking the latest build and revision is often referred to as Automatic QFE Policy (QFE is an abbreviation of Quick Fix Engineering). This QFE policy allows software vendors to release critical bug fixes without requiring dependent applications to be rebuilt or reconfigured. It is worth noting that this policy is implicit in that there is nothing that the runtime does to enforce that a QFE is, in fact, backward compatible with the version it is replacing. Also note that the runtime never implicitly takes the latest major and minor numbers because they are, by definition, incompatible with what is being requested. The automatic QFE policy can be overridden in one of two ways using the application configuration file. First, QFE policy can be disabled for references to particular assemblies using the "UseLatestBuildRevision" attribute of BindingPolicy. For example, the following entry turns off QFE policies for all references to an assembly named Parser:

```
<BindingPolicy>
    <BindingRedir Name="Parser"
            Originator="32ab4ba45e0a69a1"
            Version="*" VersionNew="12.3.0.0"
            UseLatestBuildRevision="no"/>
```

Second, the application configuration file can be used to specify that all references to assemblies made within the application should bind to the exact versions that were present at build time, as recorded in the manifest. This is called Safe Mode. When running an application in Safe Mode,

automatic QFE policy is never applied. Safe Mode is turned on using the
<BindingMode> tag.

```
<BindingMode>
        <AppBindingMode Mode="safe'/>
</BindingMode>
```

STEP 3: LOCATING THE ASSEMBLY THROUGH CODEBASES OR PROBING

After the desired version has been determined by combining the information
in the reference with that in the application configuration file, the runtime
attempts to find the assembly. The runtime does this either by a process
called probing or a codebase specified in the configuration file or through
the current binding context.

LOCATING THE ASSEMBLY THROUGH CODEBASES

The application configuration file can be used to point directly to the file
containing a particular assembly's manifest. This prevents the runtime from
probing for it. For example, the following entry indicates to the runtime that
version 1.0.0.1 of calcr can be found at http://internaltools/utils/caclr.dll:

```
<Assemblies>
    <CodeBaseHint Name="Calcr"
            Originator="8e47bfla5ed0ec84"
            Version="1.0.0.1"
            CodeBase="http://internaltools/utils/caclr.dll"/>
</Assemblies>
```

When the file at the given codebase is loaded, the runtime checks to be
sure that the name, version, culture, and originator match what is in the reference. By default, the revision and build numbers can be higher than what
is requested. Regardless of whether the given assembly matches the bind criteria, Step 3 is done at this point. If no match is found, the bind fails and no
further steps are taken. If the runtime finds a match, it continues to Step 4. In
some scenarios, codebase information can also be available in the current
binding context. This most often applies in a browser-based scenario. Given
an assembly that references another assembly, the first assembly's codebase
is considered a "hint" as to where to find the referenced assembly. For example, if Asm1 references Asm2 and Asm1 were downloaded from
http://mystuff/utils this will be considered a hint as to where to find
Asm2.dll. If Asm2 is not found at that location, the runtime will continue by
probing for the assembly as described below.

LOCATING THE ASSEMBLY THROUGH PROBING

In the absence of a codebase describing the location of the assembly, the
runtime probes for the assembly under the AppBase. Note that the version of
the assembly probed for may differ from the original reference if rules in the

application configuration file redirected the original bind to a different version. By default, the assemblies that are actually deployed in the application directory need not match the bind reference exactly. It is possible for an application author to deploy new assemblies in the application directory that will still satisfy the bind, provided the newer assemblies only contain updates in the revision and/or build number of the assembly. The runtime always probes for the name of the assembly concatenated with three extensions (listed in order of priority): .MCL, .DLL, and .EXE.

The runtime always begins probing in the AppBase directory. That is, the first probing URLs generated will always be the concatenation of the AppBase, the assembly name, and extension. For example, if the AppBase is c:\program files\myapp and the assembly name is MYCODE, then the first probing URLs generated will be:

> c:\program files\myapp\mycode.mcl
> c:\program files\myapp\mycode.dll
> c:\program files\mycode.exe.

If the assembly is not found in the AppBase, probing continues in the directories on the assembly search path. The search path is specified using the <AppDomain> tag in the application configuration file:

> <AppDomain PrivatePath="utils"/>

The directories given on the search path are relative to the AppBase and must be subdirectories of the AppBase. You cannot use this path to bind to assemblies outside the AppBase. Assemblies outside the AppBase must have shared names and must either be installed in the global assembly cache or pointed to using a codebase as described above. In addition to the subdirectories given in the configuration file, the runtime always prep ends a directory corresponding to the name of the assembly being probed for. For example, given the path specified above, if the runtime were probing for "caclr" it would modify the search path to be:

> Calcr;utils.

The runtime also considers the culture of the assembly when generating probing URLs. Specifically, the runtime looks in the culture-specific subdirectories under each directory on the search path. Probing is best understood by looking at all the URLs generated for a specific example:

> NAME=MyName
> APPBASE=http://www.code.microsoft.com
> SEARCH PATH=bin (The AssemblyResolver changes this to: MyName;bin)
> LOCALE=de

EXPLICIT CODEBASES:

Binding context CODEBASE=http://www.all.code.microsoft.com/codebase.exe
App.cfg CODEBASE=[none]

PROBING URLS:

1. http://www.all.code.microsoft.com/codebase.exe
1. http://www.code.microsoft.com/MyName.MCL
2. http://www.code.microsoft.com/MyName.DLL
3. http://www.code.microsoft.com/MyName.EXE
1. http://www.code.microsoft.com/MyName.MCL
2. http://www.code.microsoft.com/MyName/de/MyName.MCL
3. http://www.code.microsoft.com/bin/MyName.MCL
4. http://www.code.microsoft.com/bin/de/MyName.MCL
1. http://www.code.microsoft.com/MyName/MyName.DLL
2. http://www.code.microsoft.com/MyName/de/MyNAME.DLL
3. http://www.code.microsoft.com/bin/MyName.DLL
4. http://www.code.microsoft.com/bin/de/MyName.DLL
1. http://www.code.microsoft.com/MyName/MyName.EXE
2. http://www.code.microsoft.com/MyName/de/MyName.EXE
3. http://www.code.microsoft.com/bin/MyName.EXE
4. http://www.code.microsoft.com/bin/de/MyName.EXE

If the reference did not contain an originator (i.e., was to a private assembly), the binding process stops at this point. If a match is found, that assembly is loaded. If no match was found, an error is raised. This error ends up as a TypeLoadException in managed code. If the reference was to an assembly with a shared name, the binding process continues by looking in the global assembly cache.

STEP 4: THE GLOBAL ASSEMBLY CACHE AND AUTO-QFE POLICY

The global assembly cache caches assemblies that are meant to be used by several applications on a machine. All assemblies in the global store must have shared names. If an assembly was found via probing or through a codebase, and QFE policy has not been turned off, the runtime looks in the global assembly cache to see if any QFEs exist for that assembly. If there is a version of the assembly in the cache that has a higher build and/or revision number, this assembly is loaded instead of the one found by probing. If no assembly was found via probing or through a codebase, the runtime looks in the global cache for an assembly that matches the criteria given in the

AssemblyRef. If automatic QFE policy has not been turned off, the runtime takes the match that has the higher build/revision number. This policy of always looking for latest revision/build number in the global assembly cache allows an administrator to put certain shared assemblies in a location that will affect all assembly bindings on the system. The common scenario for this would be to apply a security fix to a well-known shared assembly.

STEP 5: ADMINISTRATOR POLICY

The final step in the binding process is to apply any version policy specified by the administrator. Administration policy is specified in a file called admin.cfg, located in the Windows directory. The syntax for specifying administration version policy is the same as that used in the application configuration file. The following example redirects all references to "calcr" made by any application on the machine to version 5.0.11.0:

```
<BindingPolicy>
    <BindingRedire Name="Calcr"
                   Originator="32ab4ba45e0a69a1"
                   Version="*" VersionNew="5.0.11.0"
                   UseLatesBuildRevision="yes"/>
</BindingPolicy>
```

Administrator policy is the strongest form of policy. The version determined by the administrator policy file is final, and cannot be overridden. It is required that if a policy redirect occurs as a result of administrator policy, the target assembly version must preexist in the global assembly cache (i.e., it cannot be installed at the time of the redirect). That is to say that the runtime will not reissue a probe for the post-administrator-policy assembly, but rather it is assumed that such a version redirect is a result of an explicit administrator action, which involved preinstalling the desired target assembly in the global assembly cache.

PARTIALLY SPECIFIED REFERENCES

A complete AssemblyRef includes the textual name of the assembly, the version, the culture, and the originator (if the assembly has a shared name). Only the assembly text name is strictly required for location. If a full assembly reference is not given, the runtime attempts to locate the assembly based on the first match to the name.

Partial references are often convenient to use in source code, but they do introduce some variability into the binding process. For example, if you issue a bind to an assembly with a shared name but don't include the originator in your reference, you have no assurance that the assembly you get back came from the publisher you expect. Also, references that do not include the Originator are not subject to version policy, so the application and administrator configuration files are never checked. To be absolutely sure you're getting what you want, include all the parameters when referencing an assembly.

How the Runtime Determines Type Identity

Assemblies are the construct used by the runtime to locate and load types. The assembly manifest contains the information that the runtime uses to resolve all type references made within the scope of the assembly. A type name in the runtime has two logical parts: the assembly name and the name of the type within the assembly. Two types with the same name but in different assemblies are defined as two distinct types. Assemblies provide consistency between the scope of names seen by the developer and the scope of names seen by the runtime system. Developers author types in the context of an assembly. The contents of the assembly a developer is building establishes the scope of names that will be available at runtime.

NAMESPACES

To the runtime, a namespace is just a collection of type names. Particular languages have constructs (and corresponding syntax) that help developers form logical groups of classes, but these constructs are not used by the runtime when binding types. For example, you can build a single assembly that exposes types that look like they come from two different hierarchical namespaces, such as **System.Collections** and **System.WinForms**. You can also build two assemblies that both export types whose names contain "MyDLL.MyClass." If you wanted to create a tool to present types in an assembly as belonging to a hierarchical namespace, the tool would have to enumerate the types in an assembly or group of assemblies and parse the type names to derive a hierarchical relationship.

How the Runtime Uses Assembly Version Information

Each assembly has a specific compatibility version number as part of its identity. As such, two assemblies that differ by compatibility version are considered by the runtime to be completely different assemblies. This compatibility version number is physically represented as a four-part number with the following format:

<major version>.<minor version>.<build number>.<revision>

For example, version 1.5.1254.0. each portion of this number has a specific meaning to the runtime as it determines which version of an assembly to load. It is important that you understand the significance of each number.

The runtime views the four numbers as three logical parts:

- The major and minor version numbers form the incompatible part of the version number. Any change in these two numbers indicates to the runtime that this version is incompatible with other assemblies with different major and minor version numbers. In other words, changes in the major and minor version numbers indicate a significant new release of an assembly.
- The build number forms a compatible part of the version number. A change in the build number indicates to the runtime that a change has been made to the assembly that may still be compatible and carries less risk than an incompatible change. Backwards compatibility is not assumed, though. For example, a service pack or daily build would change this number.
- The revision number forms the QFE (Quick Fix Engineering) part of the version number. A change in the revision number indicates to the runtime that this is an emergency fix and the runtime will assume this is a compatible assembly unless instructed to not use it by a configuration file override.

For example, an assembly with compatibility version number 5.4.0.0 is considered incompatible with an assembly whose compatibility number is 4.1.11.00. An assembly with a version number of 3.5.1342.0 may be compatible with an assembly with version number 3.5.1340.0. Finally, an assembly with a revision number of 5.4.0.23 is considered a QFE for an assembly with a version number of 5.4.0.0. The compatibility version number is stored in the assembly's manifest along with other identity information, including the assembly name and originator, as well as information on relationships and identities of other assemblies connected with the application. Because the version number is integral to the assembly, two assemblies with different version numbers are treated as different assemblies by the runtime.

When an assembly is built, the development tool records dependency information for each assembly that is referenced. This information is kept in the assembly manifest as AssemblyRefs. The runtime uses these version numbers, in conjunction with configuration information set by an administrator, to load the proper version of a referenced assembly. The runtime distinguishes between private and shared assemblies for the purpose of versioning. No version checking is done when resolving references to private assemblies. Since a private assembly is deployed along with the application and is placed in the same directory or subdirectory as the application, the application author has control over the contents and distribution of the assembly.

An Assembly's Informational Version

As discussed above, the informational version is a string used to attach additional version information to an assembly for documentation purposes only;

this information is not used at runtime. In the BETA 1 release, the information is displayed by admin tools and the property pages visible in the shell. The informational version is represented using the custom attribute **System.Reflection.AssemblyInformationalVersionAttribute.** The definition of that attribute is:

```
[AttributeUsage (AttributeTargets.Assembly, AllowMultiple=false)]
public class AssemblyInformationalVersionAttribute: Attribute
{
    private String m_informationalVersion;

    public            AssemblyInformationVersionAttribute(String
informationalVersion)
    {
            m_informationalVersion = informationalVersion;
    }
    public String InformationVersion
    {
            get {return m_informationalVersion;}
    }
}
```

Specifying Version Policies in Configuration Files

The rules that specify the acceptable versions of an assembly are called version policies. Version policies are expressed using the <BindingPolicy> tag in the configuration files. Configuration files can be used to override the manifest information. For example, the manifest of any assembly records the version number of each dependency at the time the assembly was compiled. In some cases, it may be acceptable to run with different versions of the dependent assemblies than those present at build time. For example, even if version 5.0.0.0 of a dependent assembly was present at build time, a more recent version, such as version 5.0.1.0, may be acceptable at runtime. Configuration files can also be used to change version policy if a version of a dependency causes an application to stop working. In this case, configuration information can be used to "roll back" to a specific version of a dependency that was present at build time. The version policies supported in configuration files include:

DEFAULT VERSION POLICY

The default version policy takes the version of the dependent assembly that is recorded in the manifest and matches the major and minor numbers exactly, then takes the latest build and revision numbers. In other words, of the four numbers that make up the version number, the first two must match exactly and the highest of the build and revision numbers are used. For example, if the runtime is given a reference to version 5.0.11.0, and version 5.0.11.12 is present in the global assembly cache, version 5.0.11.12 will be used. There are a few points to consider about the default version policy. First, the "use latest" behavior described above only applies to the build and revision portions of the version number. The policy of taking the latest build and revision is often referred to as Automatic QFE Policy. This QFE policy allows software vendors to release critical bug fixes without requiring dependent applications to be rebuilt or reconfigured. It is worth noting that this policy is implicit in that there is nothing that the runtime does to enforce that a QFE is in fact backward compatible with the version it is replacing. The runtime never implicitly takes the latest major and minor numbers because they are, by definition, incompatible with what is being requested. Second, the runtime only looks in the global assembly cache for QFEs. This is important. If a search path is specified in a configuration file, the runtime does not look at all assemblies on the path, searching for the one with the highest build and revision number. The performance cost of doing this would be prohibitive. Note that as stated above, the runtime will take an assembly with a higher build or revision number if it locates it through probing.

BIND TO A SPECIFIC VERSION

The Bind to a specific version policy allows the developer to specify a particular assembly version using the BindingPolicy tag in a configuration file. This policy allows you to bind to a different version of an assembly than the version recorded in the manifest. The policy can be used to map either references to a specific version of a dependency or references to all versions of a dependency. For example, the following configuration file entry maps references to all versions of an assembly called calcr to version 6.0.0.0:

```
<BindingPolicy>
    <BindingRedir Name="Calcr"
            Originator="32ab4ba45e0a69a1"
            Version="*" VersionNew="6.0.0.0"
            UseLatestBuildRevision="yes"/>
</BindingPolicy>
```

Note   To obtain the Originator value, run the utility SN.exe, at the command prompt, with the –T option on an assembly or with the –t on a keyfile. For example, c:\>sn –T strasm.dll

DON'T ACCEPT IMPLICIT QFES

The two previously described policies employ automatic QFE policy, that is, they will use the latest build and revision number available. There are times when this is not desirable, such as when a QFE is applied and it works for some applications but breaks others. In this scenario, the administrator or developer could disable the automatic QFE policy that has broken because of the update. This policy also uses the BindingPolicy tag in a configuration file. The attribute UseLatestBuildRevision is set to "no" to disable automatic QFE policy for references to a particular assembly. For example, this excerpt from a configuration file binds all references to an assembly called calcr to exactly version 6.1.1212.14; no QFEs to that version will be picked up:

```
<BindingPolicy>
   <BindingRedir Name="Calcr"
               Originator="32ab4ba45e0a69a1"
               Version="*" VersionNew="6.1.1212.14"
               UseLatestBuildRevision="no"/>
</BindingPolicy>
```

SAFE MODE

The Safe Mode policy is used to ensure that the versions of the assemblies built and tested together are the same versions that are run together after the application is deployed. The Safe Mode policy can also be used to revert to a known state in the presence of failures caused by running with incompatible or buggy versions of dependent assemblies.

Safe Mode always applies to an entire application, not to individual assembly references. The runtime ignores any other version policies and binds to exactly the versions of the dependent assemblies specified in the manifest. All four parts of the version number are checked; no QFEs are applied. The Safe Mode policy uses the BindingMode tag in the configuration files. The following example enables the Safe Mode policy:

```
<BindingMode>
   <AppBindingMode Mode="safe"/>
</BindingMode>
```

Application Domains

The Common Language Runtime provides a secure, lightweight, and versatile unit of processing called an *application domain*. Application domains benefit from .NET Framework security features and are the unit of enforcing security policy. Application domains also provide fault tolerance at a much smaller resource cost than with a traditional process. In fact, multiple application domains can run in a single Win32 process. Operating systems and runtime environments typically provide some form of isolation between applications running on the system. This isolation is necessary to ensure that code running in one application cannot adversely affect other unrelated applications. Typically, isolation means:

- Faults in one application cannot affect other applications by bringing down the entire process.
- Applications can be independently stopped and debugged.
- Code running in one application cannot directly access code or resources from another application; doing so could introduce a security hole.
- The behavior of running code is scoped by the application it runs in.

In modern operating systems, this isolation has historically been achieved using process boundaries. A process runs exactly on application and that process scopes the resources that are available for that process to use. For example, memory addresses in Win32 are process relative—a pointer in one process is meaningless in the context of another process. The CLR relies on the fact that code is type safe and verifiable to provide fault isolation between domains. By relying on the type safe nature of the code, application domains provide fault isolation at a much lower cost than the process isolation used in Win32. Because isolation is based on static type verification, there is no need for hardware ring transitions or process switches. In many respects, application domains are the CLR equivalent of a Win32 process.

The runtime creates an application domain for each runtime application; each application domain can have an associated configuration file. Application domains isolate separate applications, which run within a process. The combination of an application domain and configuration information create isolation for the application. The way in which application domains are created affects the permissions that assemblies have when running in the domain. For basic Web-application scenarios, where the Web page does not provide a LINK tag to a configuration file, the runtime creates an application domain on a per-site basis. Domain-neutral assemblies are only shared between application domains and assemblies with identical permission sets. A domain-neutral assembly called by two application domains with dissimilar permission sets is loaded into the domain neutral area twice. With the exception of mscorlib, of which there is only one copy of the code, all static and local data are cloned.

An application can have multiple application domains running on its behalf. An application domain is the unit of code loading and unloading. Note that you can have multiple application domains in one process. Each type is loaded into the same application domain as its caller, or a caller can request that a type be loaded into a new application domain. There are no direct calls between objects in different application domains; instead, a proxy is used. Application domains can be debugged independently.

UNLOADING AND THREADS

Application domains represent the unit of code unloading in the CLR. The runtime does not unload code at a more granular level than an application domain, such as by class or by assembly. Each application domain is a process that can be unloaded independently of the other application domains using the **Unload** method on **System.AppDomain**. A new application domain runs on the same thread as the code that created it. There is not a one-to-one correspondence between threads and application domains. Web server scenarios can require hundreds of application domains per process, whereby the ideal number of threads is some small multiple of the number processes on the machine.

At any given time, every thread is executing one application domain. The CLR keeps track of which threads are running in which application domains. This information, coupled with the fact that direct references are not allowed between domains, allows the runtime to provide clean shutdown of application domains. When a shutdown request is made, the runtime unwinds the thread until it gets to the application domain boundary. At this point, it can "detach" all proxies to objects in other application domains.

Metadata and Self-Describing Components

In the past, a compiled component (.exe or .dll) was only able to communicate with another compiled component through a binary interface. Furthermore, since different languages sometime had conflicting protocols for defining and storing data, interlanguage communication was made difficult. One way that the .NET Framework solves these problems is by allowing compilers to emit additional declarative information into all .NET Framework files and assemblies. This information, called *metadata*, serves as a roadmap for compiled files to seamlessly interact. Metadata, however, does not work alone to solve these and other problems. It is aided by additional components of the Common Language Runtime like the common type system.

What Is Metadata?

Metadata is binary information describing your code that is either stored in a .NET Framework portable executable (PE) file or in memory. When your code is compiled into a PE file, metadata is inserted into one portion of the file while your code is converted to Microsoft intermediate language (MSIL) and inserted into another. Every type and member defined and referenced in a file or assembly is described within metadata. When code is executed, the

CLR loads metadata information into in-memory data structures that it references when it requires information about your code's classes, members, inheritance, etc. Runtime reflection services are used to retrieve information from in-memory data structures.

Many key .NET Framework benefits stem from the runtime's use of metadata. Metadata provides a common frame of reference that enables communication between the runtime, compilers, debuggers, and code that has been compiled into MSIL. It enables the runtime to locate and load your code, generate native code at runtime, and provide memory management services. The runtime is able to track which portions of memory your code is allowed to access and prevent it from accessing memory that it shouldn't. Metadata also helps the runtime and garbage collection keep track of memory that will be released back to the operating system when it is no longer needed. The information stored in metadata also enables the CLR to enforce security by tracking the access-privileges that your code requests and is granted. The following list is a more precise explanation of the information stored in metadata:

DESCRIPTION OF PE OR ASSEMBLY

- Identity: name, version, culture, public key
- What types are exported
- Other assemblies on which it depends
- Security permissions needed to run

DESCRIPTION OF TYPES

- Name, visibility, base class, interfaces implemented
- Members (methods, fields, properties, events, nested types)

ATTRIBUTES

- Additional descriptive elements that modify types and members

The Benefits of Metadata

Metadata provides so much information about compiled code that you can actually inherit a class from a PE file written in a different language. You can create an instance of any accessible class in PE files written in any managed language without having to worry about explicit marshalling or using custom interoperability code. The CLR allows you to access compiled code in a manner that was previously only possible with noncompiled files.

.NET Framework files and assemblies are self-describing. Everything one component needs in order to interact with another component is provided within that component's metadata. This architecture eliminates the need for IDL files, type libraries, or any external method of component reference. .NET Framework files and assemblies do not even require registration with the operating system. In this manner, the descriptions used by the runtime will always reflect the actual code inside your compiled file and application reliability will be increased.

Since the compiler is responsible for creating metadata, you do not directly control much of what is emitted. However, the CLR allows you to declare specific kinds of metadata, called attributes, in your compiled file. Attributes can be found throughout the .NET Framework and are used to control in more detail how your program behaves at runtime. Additionally, you can emit your own custom metadata into .NET Framework files through the use of user-defined custom attributes.

Visual C++ 7.0

Introduction

In this chapter and associated appendices we will primarily be covering the Microsoft Visual C++ 7.0 and its use in the .NET Framework environment to do applications with Windows 2000. The .NET Framework Base Classes (base classes) for all intents and purposes completely wrap the Win32 APIs that we covered in Chapter 1. Therefore, we will be doing our applications by working with the base classes. Of course, as we discussed in Chapter 3, the Common Language Runtime (CLR), which sets underneath the base classes, is the primary interface to the Win32 APIs and is controlled by the base class methods we work with. The developer will not normally have any contact directly with the CLR. There are a few APIs for the CLR but they are not normally used and we will not cover those. We will be creating Assemblies or, as they are sometimes called, Components for our different examples. We will look at how the Application Domain is used to house our Assemblies. A good analogy to the Application Domain is the Win32 process we discussed in Chapter 1. The Application Domain was discussed in some detail in Chapter 3. In Chapter 5 we will cover the C# Compiler and its use in the .NET Framework environment to do applications with Windows 2000. In the case of both these compilers, we are not going to discuss the language as such, but how to use the language to implement applications using the new .NET Framework and the Windows 2000 Operating System. In Microsoft Visual C++.NET many new features are provided besides the two compilers. The following list shows the new features provided.

- C# Programming Language
- Managed Code and Targeting COM+

- Attribute Programming
- C++ Compiler, Linker, and C++ Language
- Debugger
- Development Environment
- Libraries
  1. Active Template Library (ATL)
  2. ATL Server
  3. C Run-Time Library
  4. Microsoft Foundation Classes (MFC)
  5. OLE DB Templates
  6. Shared Classes
  7. Standard C++ Library
  8. Old iostream library

We covered most of these features in Chapter 3; however, let's touch upon some of these new features again.

C# Programming Language

C# (pronounced C Sharp) is a new programming language introduced in Visual Studio.NET. An evolution of C and C++, C# is simple, modern, type safe, and object oriented. C# was designed for building a wide range of enterprise applications that run on the .NET Platform. Code that you write with C# is compiled as managed code, which means it benefits from the services of the Common Language Runtime. These services include language interoperability, garbage collection, enhanced security, and improved versioning support. C# is fully supported within Visual Studio.NET by project templates, designers, property pages, code assistants, an object model, and other features of the development environment. The library for C# programming is the .NET Framework.

Managed Code and Targeting the .NET Framework

A primary focus of Visual C++.NET is to provide a powerful and simple way to design applications that target the .NET Framework Common Language Runtime (CLR). The CLR offers a run-time environment that manages the execution of code. When you develop code using Visual C++.NET, you can compile your application or component to managed code, which is code that the CLR supports with services that make component programming easier. Because managed code is self-describing, it has easy access to benefits such as cross-language integration, automatic memory management, cross-language exception handling, enhanced security, and a simplified model for component interaction.

Programming in Native Code

In addition to the new support for managed code, Visual C++.NET includes significant enhancements for those developing in native C++. This includes improved libraries, faster and smaller executables, and added support for Windows and Web development.

Attributed Programming

Attributes are designed to provide an efficient and quick method to simplify COM programming in Visual C++. Attributes, like C++ keywords, are used in your source files and interpreted by the compiler. Attributes can modify the behavior of your existing code and even insert additional framework code to accomplish basic tasks, such as ActiveX control implementation, class factory creation, or formatting a database command. Attributes can be applied to nearly any C++ object, such as classes, data members, and member functions, or you can insert attributes into your source code as stand-alone statements. Attributes extend C++ in directions not currently possible without breaking the classic structure of the language. Attributes allow providers (separate DLLs) to extend language functionality dynamically. As we mentioned, the primary goal of attributes is to simplify the authoring of COM components, in addition to increasing the productivity level of the component develop. We could write a whole chapter on just the use and description of Attribute Programming. In Appendix H, titled "Attributes", we have put together several samples of using attributes with Visual C++ 7.0.

ATL Server

ATL Server is a set of classes and IDE features that allows you to create server applications, particularly Web-based ISAPI applications, in native C++ code. Like the other ATL classes, the ATL Server classes are designed to provide high-performance code for the most commonly implemented parts of an application. The ATL Server ISAPI classes provide a thin C++ layer on top of the ISAPI EXTENSION_CONTROL_BLOCK, a model for separating static and dynamic content with the use of server response files (SRF), and a number of higher level abstractions for cookies, uploaded files, and request and response objects.

ATL Server offers several server classes that can be configured and used together or independently of each other, including the following:

- Thread pool
- Cache classes
- Performance monitoring helpers
- Cryptography services
- SMTP mail client functionality

New Integrated Debugger

Visual Studio.NET provides a single integrated debugger for all Visual Studio languages. A new, unified interface combines features of the old Visual C++ and Visual Basic debuggers, as well as many new features. The new Visual Studio debugger offers many new features for cross-language debugging, .NET Common Language Runtime debugging, the ability to attach to and debug processes already running, and the ability to debug multiple programs. In Appendix I, titled "Debugging Visual C++", we have put together information on debugging techniques for Visual C++ 7.0.

Event Handling in Visual C++

Event handling in Visual C++ now uses the Unified Event Model, which allows you to use the same programming model for event handling in all types of classes in Visual C++:

- Native C++ classes (C++ classes that do not implement COM objects)
- COM classes (C++ classes that implement COM objects, typically using ATL classes or the coclass attribute)
- Managed classes (C++ classes declared with the __gc keyword or by declaration in a managed context)

In Appendix J, titled "Event Handling in Visual C++," we have put together an explanation and several samples of using events with Visual C++ 7.0.

Visual C++ Editions

The Microsoft Visual C++ 7.0 Compiler is available in three editions: Standard, Professional, and Enterprise.

- The Standard Edition—Learn the C++ language while using the professional Visual C++ tool set. The Standard Edition contains all the features of the Professional Edition except code optimizations and static linking to the MFC Library.
- The Professional Edition—Develop applications, services, and controls for Win32 platforms, including Windows 95/98, Windows NT, and Windows 2000. You can target the operating system's graphical user interface or console APIs.
- The Enterprise Edition—Develop and debug client-server applications for Internet or intranet use. The Enterprise Edition includes tools for working with SQL databases and debugging SQL stored

procedures in addition to all the features of the Professional Edition. The Visual SourceSafe source-code control system simplifies developing in a team environment.

What's Included in the Visual C++ Standard Edition

The Microsoft Visual C++ 7.0 Standard Edition (formerly called the Learning Edition) includes a rich variety of professional tools to help you learn C, C++, C#, and many other professional technologies such as MFC, OLE, ATL, ATL Server, Managed Extensions for C++, ODBC, DAO, ActiveX, and .NET. The Standard Edition is packaged with a book and C++ tutorial on CD-ROM that helps you learn how to use Visual C++.

The Standard Edition contains the features found in the Professional Edition but does not include the following features:

- Static linkage to MFC. Static linking allows you to include the MFC library in your program's compilation, resolving MFC references at link time and not at run time. If you write programs that use the MFC library with the Standard Edition, the resulting executable will require that the MFC library code be available as a shared library (DLL). Calls to the MFC library that you place in your code are resolved at run time and not at link time.
- Code optimization. Code optimization, implemented with the compiler's /O compiler options, makes your final executable files (EXE) and dynamic-link library (DLL) files smaller or faster.
- RemoteData control and other data-bound controls. The RemoteData control and DBGrid, DBCombo, and DBList controls are for use with data-access clients and are only found in the Professional and Enterprise Editions.
- Custom Application Wizard. The Custom Application Wizard project type allows you to create an application wizard that you will subsequently use to create projects with customized started files.
- InstallShield. InstallShield is a program package with the Professional and Enterprise Editions that lets you package your application in a setup program for easy installation.
- Cluster Resource Wizard. The Cluster Resource Type Wizard generates two projects for implementing a Microsoft Cluster Server resource type. Writing a custom resource type allows an application to be more closely managed and monitored by MSCS. The two generated projects are a resource DLL project, which produces a DLL that is loaded by an MSCS resource monitor on a cluster node to manage and monitor the application, and a Cluster Administrator extension DLL project, which produces a COM in-proc server DLL for providing a user interface for managing resources of this new type.

What's Included in the Visual C++ Professional Edition

The Professional Edition of Microsoft Visual C++ 7.0 provides features that let you develop and distribute commercial-quality software products. The Professional Edition includes the following features:

PROGRAMMING FEATURES

- C# Programming Language
- Microsoft Foundation Classes
- Active Template Library
- ATL Server
- Component Object Model (COM)
- Compiler COM Support
- OLE DB Provider and Consumer Templates
- C/C++ Run-Time Libraries
- Standard C++ Library
- Support for Common Controls in Internet Explorer
- Active Document Containment

INTERNET

- Internet Server API (ISAPI) Extensions
- ChttpConnection (and other CHttp* MFC classes)
- CinternetConnection (and other CInternet* classes)

ACTIVEX CONTROLS

- Composite Control Fundamentals
- Developing MFC ActiveX Controls
- Developing ATL ActiveX Controls
- Adding an ActiveX Control to a Project

PROJECT FEATURES

- Wizard Support for Creating Applications
- Integrated Development Environment and more IDE topics
- Debugging Your Application
- Component and Object Gallery
- InstallShield

OPTIMIZATIONS

- Inline Optimizing of Your Code
- Compiler Optimization Options
- Linker Optimizations (/OPT)
- C++ Exception Handling

DATABASE SUPPORT

- ActiveX Controls for Databinding
- ADO
- Read-only versions of Microsoft Visual Database Tools (Enterprise Edition has full-feature Visual Database Tools)

What's Included in the Visual C++ Enterprise Edition

The Enterprise Edition of Microsoft Visual C++ provides many tools and components for building and validating enterprise-level distributed COM applications. Visual C++ Enterprise Edition is best suited for developers building distributed database applications in a team environment. For these developers, SQL debugging and MTS are integrated into the development environment making development of distributed-transaction-oriented applications faster and easier. (SQL Server and MTS come with the Enterprise Edition of Visual C++.) The Enterprise Edition also includes Microsoft Visual SourceSafe, a tool that allows a team of developers to share and mutually update a common repository of source code. The Visual C++ Enterprise Edition includes all the features in the Professional Edition, plus the following features:

- Microsoft Transaction Server
- Visual Database Tools
- SQL Editor
- SQL Debugger
- MFC Database Classes
- ADO Databinding
- Application Wizard and Data Sources
- Remote Automation Components
- MFC Data Binding
- Visual SourceSafe
- Remote Automation

Programming with Managed Extensions for C++

Starting with Visual C++ 7.0, the standard C++ language has been extended to provide support for managed programming. Managed Extensions for C++ are mainly comprised of a set of keywords and attributes. See Appendix K, "Managed Extensions for C++ Reference." To use Managed Extensions for C++, your C++ application must include the following code:

```
#using <mscorlib.dll>
using namespace System;          // Needed to access the .NET Framework classes
```

In addition, you must use the /CLR (Common Language Runtime Compilation) compiler option when compiling the application. See Appendix L, "/CLR (Common Language Runtime Compilation)." There are quite a few considerations to be looked at before using the /CLR, as detailed in Appendix L.

When to Use Managed Extensions for C++

Managed Extensions for C++ are a set of language extensions to C++ that help Visual C++ developers write .NET Framework applications. Managed Extensions allow you to intermix traditional unmanaged and managed C++ code within the same application. New applications written with Managed Extensions can take advantage of unmanaged code features and new managed code features. Existing components can easily be wrapped as .NET Framework components using Managed Extensions, preserving the investment in existing code while integrating with the .NET Framework.

Managed Extensions are the best choice for the following development scenarios:

- Rapid migration of unmanaged C++ applications to the .NET Framework. If you have an existing unmanaged C++ application, Managed Extensions provide a smooth transition to the .NET Framework. Because you can mix unmanaged and managed code in the same application—even in the same file—you can move code over time, component by component, to the .NET Framework. Or you can continue to write components in unmanaged C++, taking advantage of the full power and flexibility of the language, and only use Managed Extensions to write thin, high-performance wrappers that make your C++ code callable from .NET Framework components.

- Accessing a C++ component from a .NET Framework-compatible language. Managed Extensions support calling a C++ class from any .NET Framework-compatible language. This is made possible by writing a simple wrapper class using Managed Extensions that exposes your C++ class and methods as a managed class. The wrapper is a fully managed class and can be called from any .NET Framework-compatible language. The wrapper class acts as a mapping layer between the managed class and the unmanaged C++ class — it simply passes method calls directly into the unmanaged class. Managed Extensions support calls to any unmanaged DLL or library, as well as unmanaged classes.

- Accessing .NET Framework classes from unmanaged code. With Managed Extensions you can directly create, and call, .NET Framework class from your C++ code. In addition, you can write C++ code that treats the .NET Framework component like any other managed C++ class. You can also use the unmanaged COM support (in the .NET Framework) to call .NET Framework classes. Depending on your project, you can use unmanaged COM support or Managed Extensions to access .NET Framework components. This decision will depend on your project. In some cases, leveraging the existing COM support will be the best option. In other cases, it may be possible to increase performance and developer productivity by using Managed Extensions.

- Managed and unmanaged code in one executable file. The Visual C++ compiler translates data, pointers, exceptions, and instruction flow between managed and unmanaged contexts automatically and transparently. This process allows managed code to interoperate seamlessly with unmanaged C++ code. The developer is given fine-grained control over what data and code should be managed. This feature is supported by the ability to choose whether each class and function is managed or unmanaged. This flexibility is needed as some types of code or data perform better in an unmanaged environment. However, managed code typically offers enhanced developer productivity due to features such as garbage collection and managed class libraries.

Introduction to Managed Extension for C++

Because Managed Extensions for C++ use a garbage-collected heap and target the .NET Framework platform, several areas related to code and general programming procedures are new to C++ developers. The following sections provide a general overview of these areas. Each topic contains information on various subjects related to Managed Extensions and provides some sample code to illustrate the points of the topic.

MANAGED TYPES

Managed types are a powerful and versatile feature of Managed Extensions for C++. In addition to the standard features of a C++ type, the .NET Framework and the Visual C++ compiler provide new features for managed types:

- Extensible metadata. A key concept for implementing modern component software, Managed Extensions provide built-in support for metadata and enable declaring new types and categories of metadata.
- Garbage collection. Managed Extensions allow the developer to specify that certain types be allocated exclusively on the garbage-collected Common Language Runtime heap, thereby removing the burden of lifetime management for the developer. Specifically, this means that you no longer must deal with complex bugs associated with reference counting or circular-reference leaks.

- Simplified language interoperability. Any managed type written in Managed Extensions is immediately usable from Visual Basic or any other language that targets the Common Language Runtime. This ability removes the need for error-prone MIDL files or the restriction of using only BSTRs for your string objects.
- Versionable. A new version of managed objects that includes new methods and data members can be deployed, while maintaining binary compatibility with existing client software.
- Binary headers. Any file type that is able to contain metadata (.exe, .obj, or .dll) can be directly included in a Managed Extension source file. The precompiled form also increases compilation speed. Note: An ordinary C++ type is referred to as an unmanaged type. Unmanaged types are always allocated from the standard C++ runtime heap.

There are three kinds of managed types:

1.	Garbage-Collected Classes	Allocated on the Common Language Runtime heap and the most general-purpose type of managed type.
2.	Value Classes	Represent a small, short-lived data item (allocated on the stack) for which full garbage collection would be too costly.
3.	Managed Interface Classes	Offer direct support for COM-style interface programming in C++.

The following features apply to all managed types:

- A managed type can inherit from any number of managed interfaces, or a garbage-collected class, or any number of managed interfaces and a garbage-collected class.
- A managed type can declare a static class constructor.
- A managed type can contain properties.
- A managed type can have a visibility specified.
- A managed type can implement any number of constructors and a destructor.
- A managed type can have pointers to unmanaged classes as data members.

The following restrictions apply to all managed types:

- A managed type cannot inherit from unmanaged types, and unmanaged types cannot inherit from managed types.
- A managed type does not support friends.
- A managed type cannot contain an instance of or a reference to an unmanaged type with non-static member functions.
- A managed type should not be used with the size of operator.

GARBAGE-COLLECTED CLASSES

Because garbage-collected classes are allocated from the Common Language Runtime heap, the following usage restrictions exist:

- A garbage-collected class has exactly one base class. There is no multiple inheritance of garbage-collected classes. If no base class is specified, it is assumed to be the .NET Framework root class System.Object.
- All instances of a garbage-collected class are created on the .NET Framework garbage-collected heap using the built-in operator new. This means that only pointers to a garbage-collected class type are allowed. Object or parameter declarations or a function return of a garbage-collected class type is not allowed.
- The __gc keyword cannot be used to qualify an unmanaged class type in an object declaration.
- A garbage-collected class cannot have a copy constructor.
- A garbage-collected class cannot override operator& or operator new.

Note   Usage of the __asm keyword or setjmp function within a function forces the compilation of the function to unmanaged native code. This can cause various errors or warnings if the function contains any managed code, takes garbage-collected types as parameters, or returns a garbage-collected type.

DESTROYING A GARBAGE-COLLECTED CLASS

As in standard C++, a garbage-collected class may have a destructor, which can be called explicitly.

Note   During garbage-collection, the destructor is invoked before the associated memory is released.

A garbage-collected class may be explicitly destructed, either by calling the destructor directly or by using the delete operator. This allows an object to release its resources at a well-defined point. The destructor will not be called again when the garbage collector runs; only the memory will be reclaimed.

The following example demonstrates the explicit invoking of a garbage-collected object destructor:

```
#using <mscorlib.dll>

void main()
{
        ManagedObject* mObj1 = new ManagedObject();
        mObj1->AllocateResources(); // Allocate resources from the managed heap.
        delete mObj1;                      // Frees those resources now.
        / Alternatively, the objects destructor may be called directly
        mObj1 = new ManagedObject();
        mObj1->~ManagedObject();
}
```

If a garbage-collected class derives from a garbage-collected class authored in another language, the finalization method (if any) of the base class is treated as the destructor and is called automatically at the end of the destructor for the derived class.

Note   A garbage-collected class may implement a finalization method. This method is called before unloading the object and is automatically called only once for each class.

If you are not certain that an object is destroyed, you can assign the value 0 to the pointer that references it. If that is the last pointer to the object, the garbage collector will automatically reclaim it.

VALUE CLASSES

A value class differs from a garbage-collected class in that instances can be allocated on the run-time stack and as static or heap-allocated variables under certain conditions. A value class is declared by applying the __value keyword to a class or struct declaration. Value classes are designed to hold small data items with short lifetimes, so as not to have the overhead of garbage collection for every allocation. They can also be members of a garbage-collection class. In addition to those features common to all managed classes, the following features are also supported for value classes:

- A value class cannot implement a copy constructor. You cannot declare a pointer to a value class.
- A value class can derive from one or more managed interfaces.
- A value class can override any method of the System.ValueType class.
- A value class can be allocated from the run-time stack or from the Common Language Runtime heap as a member of a managed class.

- A value class that does not contain any managed pointers can be allocated anywhere an unmanaged class can be allocated.

In addition to those restrictions common to all managed classes, the following restrictions are also in effect for value classes:

- A value class can only inherit from one or more managed interfaces. It cannot inherit from a garbage-collected or another value class.
- A value class cannot declare any virtual methods not previously defined by System.ValueType.
- A value class cannot have the __abstract keyword applied to it.
- By definition, a value class is sealed and therefore a value class cannot be used as a base class.
- A value class cannot be allocated directly from the Common Language Runtime heap. However, instances of the value class may exist in the Common Language Runtime heap by embedding in garbage-collected classes or boxing.

Value classes cannot use an initialized list if the value class contains managed objects.

Note	Usage of the __asm keyword or setjmp function within a function forces the compilation of the function to unmanaged native code. This can cause various errors or warnings if the function contains any managed code, takes garbage-collected types as parameters, or returns a garbage-collected type.

VALUE CLASSES AND BOXING

When the __box keyword is applied to a class or struct object, it is referred to as boxing the class or struct. This instance can then be treated as a managed object. For every definition of a value class, there exists a unique boxed value class type corresponding to the original value class. All boxed value class types inherit from the garbage-collected class System.ValueType. Enumerated types that are boxed (sometimes referred to as managed enums) inherit from the garbage-collected class System.Enum. You cannot define boxed types directly; the compiler generates them on demand as needed. Referring to the boxed value class by its boxed type is more precise than using the generic type System.Object and allows the user to avoid expensive dynamic cast operations when accessing the underlying value type.

Because a boxed value class implicitly inherits from System.ValueType and System.Object, a value class may directly call any function it specifically implements without being boxed first. This includes any overrides of virtual member functions defined in System.ValueType. The following example overrides the ToString member of System.ValueType and then invokes it directly from an instance of the value class v:

```
#using <mscorlib.dll>
using namespace System;        // Needed to access the .NET Framework
classes

__value struct v
{
    // Override ValueType::ToString
    String *ToString()
    {
    return i.ToString();
    }
    int i;
};

void main()
{
    V v = {10};
    Console::WriteLine(v.ToString());        // Boxing not required
}
```

A value class member can be accessed from the boxed version using the same syntax as accessing an unboxed value member. The following example demonstrates this by accessing the data member (i) of a boxed value class (V):

```
#using <mscorlib.dll>
#include "assert.h"

__value struct V
{
    int i;
};

void main ()
{
    V v = {10};
    __box V* pbV = __box(v);
    assert(pbV->i == 10);
}
```

To call a virtual function System.ValueType that has not been overridden in the value type, boxing is required. The following example uses the same value class (without the explicit override of ToString), ToString by boxing the value class first:

```
#using <mscorlib.dll>
using namespace System;        // Needed to access the .NET Framework
Classes

__value struct V
{
    int i;
};

void main()
{
    V v = {10};
    v.i = 10;
    Console::WriteLine(v.ToString());        // Error: boxing required
    Console::WriteLine(__box(v)->ToString());     // OK: prints V
}
```

MANAGED INTERFACES

A managed interface embodies the COM notion of an interface (with the added benefits of being managed) and is declared by applying the __gc keyword to an existing interface declaration:

```
__gc __interface IMyInterface
{
    void method_one();
};
```

The previous code sample declares a managed interface (IMyInterface) that is essentially a managed C++ abstract base class. Like an abstract base class, the methods of a managed interface are implicitly pure virtual methods. The following rules apply to managed interfaces:

- A managed interface cannot contain data members or static members.
- A managed interface can contain only the public access specifier, which is the default.
- A managed interface cannot provide implementations for any declared methods of the managed interface.
- A managed interface can only inherit from other managed interfaces.
- A managed interface cannot have the __sealed keyword applied to it.

IMPLEMENTATION OF AMBIGUOUS BASE INTERFACE METHODS

Managed Extensions for C++ allow two or more base interfaces of a class to declare identical methods. These ambiguous interface methods are implemented by providing a fully qualified name in the definition. The following example demonstrates this by declaring and defining the Calculate method for both sample interfaces IAccount and IStatement:

```
__gc __interface IAccount
{
    void Calculate();
};


__gc __interface IStatement
{
    void Calculate();
};


__gc struct CMyStatement: IAccount, IStatement
{
    void IAccount::Calculate() {};          // OK
    void IStatement::Calculate() {};            // OK
};
```

DEFAULT IMPLEMENTATION OF A METHOD

Managed Extensions for C++ automatically provide a default implementation for methods that are not defined by the child class. Default implementation can also be used to implement ambiguous base interface methods. For example, the following code sample declares a class (CMyBase) and a managed interface (IMyInterface). Another class (CMyChild) is derived from CMyBase and IMyInterface but does not provide an implementation for the derived method Calculate:

```
#using <mscorlib.dll>

__gc __interface IMyInterface
{
    void Calculate();
};
__gc struct CMyBase
{
    void Calculate() {};
};
__gc struct CMyChild : CMyBase, IMyInterface
```

```
{
    // By default, CMyChild uses CMyBase::Calculate to implement
    // IMyInterface::Calculate
};
void main()
{
    IMyInterface* pI = new CmyChild;    // OK: CMyChild is not
abstract
    pI->Calculate();                    // OK: calls CMyChild::Calculate (via default
                                        // implementation)

}
```

MANAGED ARRAYS

Using Managed Extension for C++, a managed array can be declared by using the __gc keyword or by containing a managed object type. Because managed arrays are allocated from the managed heap, these arrays have additional criteria and features for declaration and usage when compared to standard (unmanaged) arrays:

- The definition of a managed array variable may not specify a size. The array size is given in the call to the managed operator new.
- All managed arrays must be dynamically allocated using the managed operator new.
- The indices of a managed array are zero based.
- Because managed arrays automatically inherit from System.Array, any method from System.Array can be applied directly to the array variable.
- When accessing static members of an object in a managed array, no bounds checking is performed. This means that accessing past the end of the array will not cause an error.

The following example declares and instantiates a simple managed array of integers:

```
#using <mscorlib.dll>

void main()
{
    int MyIntArray __gc[] = new int __gc[100];
}
```

To construct a managed String object from an array of type wchar_t characters, there is no need to zero-terminate the array if it is managed. However, if the wchar_t array is unmanaged, it must be zero-terminated. The following code example demonstrates this:

```
#using <mscorlib.dll>
using namespace System;    // Needed to access the .NET Framework classes

void main()
{
    String* s = new String(L"ab");
    wchar_t s1__gc[] = new wchar_t __gc[2];      // array of two wchar_t's
s1[0] = L'a';
s1[1] = L'b';
// no zero termination

wchar_t s2[3];
s2[0] = L'a';
s2[1] = L'b';
s2[2] = 0;                              // must be zero-terminated

String* str1 = new String(s1);

if(s->Equals(str1))
    Console::WriteLine(S"managed passed");

if(s->Equals(s2))
    Console::WriteLine(S"unmanaged passed");
}
```

AUTOMATIC ARRAY INITIALIZATION

When allocating a managed array, the values of the array are automatically initialized to a standard value. This value is determined by the type of the managed array. The following table lists the possible value types and their respective default initialization values.

Value type of array	Default initialization value
C++ primitive data type (int, char, and others)	Zero initialized.
Managed class	Zero initialized.
Value type V (a value array)	The default constructor for the value type is applied to each array element.

MULTIDIMENSIONAL ARRAYS

Managed Extensions also support managed arrays with multiple dimensions. The number of dimensions is equal to the number of commas in the declaration plus one. The following example declares a two-dimensional managed array of type Int32:

```
Int32 MyArray[ , ] = new Int32[10, 20];           // Two dimensions
for(int row = 0; row < MyArray->GetLength(0); ++row)
{
__—for(int col = 0; col < MyArray->GetLength(1); ++col)
_____— —MyArray[row, col] = row+col;
}
```

Note   The standard C++ comma operator cannot be used inside managed array indices unless it is nested within parentheses.

ARRAY COVARIANCE

For managed arrays, Managed Extensions support the concept of covariance. Array covariance means that, given two types (A and B), an array value of type A can be treated as a reference to an array value of type B, provided there is an implicit reference conversion from B to A. With Managed Extensions, this implicit conversion is available if one class is a direct or indirect base class of the other.

Note   Array covariance is not supported for arrays of value class types.

For instance, the following code sample demonstrates this relationship by declaring several classes (Base, Derived, Derived2, and Derived3) and then initializing them in various ways:

```
#using <mscorlib.dll>

__gc struct Base { int i; };
struct Derived : Base {};
struct Derived2 : Base {};
struct Derived3 : Derived {};
__gc struct Other { short s };

void main()
{
    Derived* d[] = new Derived* [100];
    base* b[] = d;          // OK by array covariance
    b[0] = new Other;       // Error (compile time)
    b[1] = new Derived2;    // Error (run-time exception)
    b[0] = new Base;        // Error (run-time exception), must be "at least" a
                            Derived.
```

```
        b[1] = new Derived;     //OK
        b[0] = new Derived3;    // OK
}
```

As part of the support for array covariance, assignments to elements of reference type arrays include a run-time check that ensures that the value being assigned to the array element is actually of a permitted type. If the type is not permitted, an exception System.ArrayTypeMismatchException is thrown.

DELEGATES IN MANAGED EXTENSIONS FOR C++

Delegates provide the underlying mechanism for events in the .NET Framework Component Model. Delegates are implemented as abstract classes within the .NET Framework. There are two types of delegates: single cast and multicast. The single-case delegates (implemented by System.Delegate) enables binding a function pointer to only one method. The multicast delegate (implemented by System.MultiCastDelegate) may bind a function pointer to a single method or many methods. Delegates differ from C++ function pointers in that they may only point to members of managed classes and may bind to an object to support calling method of that type of instance.

Note　　For simplicity, the term "delegate" will refer to both the single-case and multicast versions. If only one of these classes is intended, it will be explicitly stated.

Under Managed Extensions for C++ delegates are supported by the __delegate keyword. The __delegate keyword defines a single-cast delegate type with a specific method signature. A variant of the __delegate keyword, __delegate(multicast), declares a multicast delegate type with a specific method signature.

SINGLE-CAST DELEGATES

The single-cast delegate only binds the delegate to one method. The following example declares a single-cast delegate GetDayOfWeek.

__delegate int GetDayOfWeek();

Single-case delegate objects are implemented by the Ddelegate base class.

MULTICAST DELEGATES

Another version of a delegate is the multicast delegate. This delegate is able to bind to multiple methods. Multicast delegates are declared by using a variant of the __delegate keyword, __delegate(multicast). The following example declares a multicast delegate DayOfWeekChanged.

__delegate(multicast) void DayOfWeekChanged();

Multicase delegate objects are implemented by the MultiCastDelegate base class.

Note   Multicast delegates are not permitted to return a value or out parameters. This limitation is due to the properties of return values and out parameters being supplied by one callee and a multicast delegate having many callees.

Although the syntax for the __delegate keyword is similar to the syntax of the standard C++ typedef keyword, the compiler actually generates a definition of a managed class. The managed class has the following characteristics:

- It inherits from either System.Delegate(single-cast delegates) or SystemMulticastDelegate(multicast delegates).
- The constructor takes two arguments: a managed referenced or NULL and a fully qualified method of the specified type.
- It has a method called Invoke, whose signature matches the declared signature of the delegate. This method makes the actual call to the bound method to all delegates (clients).

The following example declares a single-cast delegate and illustrates that the delegate is actually implemented by the Delegate base class:

__delegate int GetDayOfWeek();

```
__gc class MyCalendar
{
public:
    int MyGetDayOfWeek()
    {
// Function implementation
    }
};

void UsesDelegate()
{
MyCalendar* pCal = new MyCalendar;
    GetDayOfWeek* pGetDayOfWeek = new GetDayOfWeek(pCal,
                            &MyCalendar::MyGetDayOfWeek);
    int DayOfWeek = pGetDayOfWeek->Invoke();
}
```

Managed Extensions support a special case for a delegate that uses a single argument constructor where the syntax can be automatically constructed to include both the object reference and method. The previous statement, creating a GetDayOfWeek delegate, could be written as:

GetDayOfWeek* pGetDayOfWeek = new GetDayOfWeek
(pcal>MyGetDayOfWeek);

PROPERTIES OF MANAGED OBJECTS

In Managed Extensions for C++, you can implement a property for a managed class using the __property keyword. To client code, a property has the appearance of an ordinary data member and can be written to or read from using the same syntax as a data member. However, instead of declaring an actual data member, you declare a pair of methods that implement the property. The compiler then generates a pseudo-data member, corresponding to the property methods. This pseudo-data member can be referenced in your source code as if it were an actual data member of the containing class.

Note   You cannot take the address of a pseudo-data member.

The naming convention for a managed property has the following properties:
  • The identifier of the Get method must begin with "get_".
  • The identifier of the Set method must begin with "set_".

The following example declares a size property for the CMyClass class and then manipulates the property using the declared accessor functions:

```
#using <mscorlib.dll>

__gc class MyClass
{
public:
__property int get_Size() {...};
__property void set_Size(int I) {...};
// Pseudo-data member Size generated by compiler
};

void main()
{
    CMyClass* pC = new CMyClass;
    pC->Size = 10;                      // calls set_Size
    int i = pC>Size;                    // calls get_Size
}
```

The following usage notes apply to the __property keyword:

- The name of the Get and Set methods are the same except for the prefix.
- The virtual keyword can be applied to either the Get or Set method.
- The accessibility of the Get and Set methods may differ.
- It is not necessary for a property to have both a Get and Set method.
- A property can be made pure virtual by appending "=0" to the end of the Get and Set method declarations (like an ordinary method).
- The definition of a Get and Set method can appear outside the class body (like an ordinary method).

Some restrictions apply for managed properties:

- A property name cannot match the name of the managed class containing it.
- In a managed class, any member whose identifiedr follows the managed property-naming convention (as described above) must define either a Get or a Set property method.
- If the static keyword is applied to either the Get or Set method, it must also be applied to the other method.
- The last argument of the Set method must match the return type of the Get method.

PROPERTY TYPES IN MANAGED EXTENSIONS

Managed Extensions for C++ support two types of managed properties: scalar and indexed.

SCALAR PROPERTIES

A property is scalar if the Get and Set methods have the following characteristics:

- The Get method has no parameters and has a return type T.
- The Set method has a single parameter of type T, and a void return type.

INDEXED PROPERTIES

A property is indexed if its Get and Set methods have the following characteristics:

- The Get method has a parameter list (p1, ..., pn) and has return type T.
- The Set method has a parameter list (p1, ..., pn) and a void return type.

Given the previous information, a pseudo-data member array is generated with the following form (assuming a property name of Dimension):

```
/*  T Dimension[p1, ..., pn];  */
```

This property provides array-like access to the pseudo-member. However, because it is implemented using method calls, any parameter type can be used to index the pseudo-data member array. The following example demonstrates this access. First, two classes are declared (Employee and Manager). Second, an instance of the Manager class (Ed) and two instances of the Employee (Bob and Gus) are created. The Report property (implemented by class Manager) is then accessed for both Bob and Gus:

```
#using <mscorlib.dll>

__gc class Employee
{
public:
String* name;

......
}__gc class Manager
{
public:
__property Employee* get_Report(String*) { ... }
__property void set_Report(String*, Employee*) { ... }
// Pseudo-array member
/* Employee* Report[ String* ];  */
};

void main()
{
Manager* Ed = new Manager;
Employee* Bob = new Employee(S"Bob");
Employee* Gus = Employee(S"Gus");

// Track Ed's reports
Ed->Report[ Bob->name ] = Bob; // indexed by String* type
Ed->Report[ Gus->name ] = Gus; // indexed by String* type
}
```

Adding Support for Managed Extensions for C++ to an Existing Application

One of the strongest reasons for using Managed Extensions for C++ is the ease in converting existing C++ applications to Managed Extensions applications. The procedure is simple and straightforward and consists of two steps:

* Modifying the Existing Project Settings
* Employing New Managed Extensions Functionality in Existing Applications

MODIFYING THE EXISTING PROJECT SETTINGS

The first step is to modify the compiler options by adding the /CLR option and recompile the target application. The /CLR option enables support for Managed Extensions and forces a link to the proper library. To modify the project settings, do the following steps:

1. Load the target project into Visual Studio.
2. From the Solution Explorer, right-click the project node and click Property Pages.
3. Click the C/C++ folder in the left pane.
4. Click General folder under C/C++.
5. Set the Enable Common Language Runtime property to Assembly Support (/CLR).
6. Click OK and rebuild the project.

Once the project has been rebuilt, support for Managed Extensions is now available.

EMPLOYING NEW MANAGED EXTENSIONS FUNCTIONALITY IN EXISTING APPLICATIONS

Once the target application has been built with Managed Extensions support, all .NET Framework features, from managed objects to .NET Framework base classes (such as String), can be easily added. For the purposes of this section, it is sufficient to demonstrate this step using the .NET Framework base classes String and Console. The following code declares two instances of the String class and a managed array of int type.

```
String MyLiteral = L"Current array values";
String MyLiteral2 = L"Current array values (after initialization)";
__gc int a1[] = new __gc int[20];
```

Note	Because the a1 array is a managed array, the managed operator new is used to declare and initialize the memory to 0.

After the variables have been declared, an instance of the System.Console class is created and the current values (all equal to 0) in the array is printed using the Write method of the System.Console class and the Length method of the System.Array class:

```
Console::Write(MyLiteral);
Console::Write('\n');
for(i=0; i < a1->Length; ++i)              // Use the Length member
{
Console::Write(a1[i]);
Console::Write(L' ');
}
```

Finally, the array is reinitialized and the values are again printed:

```
for(i=0; i < 20; ++i)
a1[i] = i;

for(i=0; i < a1->Length; ++i)              // Use the Length member
{
Console::Write(a1[i]);
Console::Write(L' ');
}
```

Examining the example code reveals some of the benefits of using Managed Extensions in a C++ application:

- Single-dimensional arrays are dynamic until they are created.
- The array is automatically destroyed and all resources freed by the managed heap.
- The array values are automatically initialized to 0.
- .NET Framework base classes are easily accessible and managed classes themselves.

Handling Exceptions Using Managed Extensions for C++

You can use both structured exception handling (SHE) and C++ exception handling in Managed Extensions for C++. Managed Extensions extend native exception handling by supporting the handling of managed exceptions. A managed exception is any exception thrown by a managed type. The System.Exception class provides many useful methods for processing managed exceptions and is recommended as a base class for user-defined exception classes.

Note	Catching exception types derived from an interface is not supported by Managed Extensions.

BASIC CONCEPTS IN USING MANAGED EXCEPTIONS

In this section, the basic concepts for exception handling in managed applications are discussed.

THROWING EXCEPTION USING MANAGED EXTENSIONS

The C++ throw expression is extended to throw a pointer to any managed object. The following example creates a custom exception type and then throws an instance of that type:

```
__gc struct MyStruct : public System::Exception { int i; };

void GlobalFunction()
{
MyStruct* pMyStruct = new MyStruct;
Throw pMyStruct;
}
```

Value classes must be boxed before they can be thrown:

```
__value struct MyValueStruct { int i };

void Global Function ()
{
MyValueStruct v = {11};
Throw __box(v);
}
```

TRY/CATCH BLOCKS USING MANAGED EXTENSIONS

The same try/catch block structure can be used for catching both managed and unmanaged exceptions. The following example demonstrates a simple try/catch block with managed and unmanaged structures:

```
// file: ehtest.cpp
// compile with cl /CLR /GX ehtest.cpp
#using <mscorlib.dll>

// Needed to access the .NET Framework classes; otherwise you need to
// use the System:: prefix for .NET Framework classes.
Using namespace System;

__gc struct MyStruct : public System::Exception {
 int i;
 };
struct CMyClass {
 double d;
 };
void GlobalFunction()
{
MyStruct* pMyStruct = new MyStruct;
pMyStruct->i = 11;
throw pMyStruct;
}
void Global Function2()
{
CMyClass c = {2.0};
throw c;
}
void main()
{
for(int i = 1; i >=0; —i)
{
    try
{
if( i == 1 )
GlobalFunction2();
if( i == 0 )
GlobalFunction();
}
catch( CMyClass& catchC )
{
Console::WriteLine(L"Inside 'catch(CMyClass& catchC) ' ");
Console::WriteLine(catchC.d);
}
catch(MyStruct* catchException)
{
Console::WriteLine(L"Inside 'catch(MyStruct* catchException) ' ");
```

```
Console::WriteLine(catchException->i);
                }
         }
}
```

Program Output
     Inside 'catch(CMyClass& catchC)'
     2
     Inside 'catch(MyStruct* catchException)'
     11

ORDER OF UNWINDING FOR C++ OBJECTS

As usual, unwinding occurs for any C++ objects with destructors that may be on the run-time stack between the throwing function and the handling function. Because garbage-collected classes are allocated on the heap, unwinding does not apply to them.

CATCHING UNMANAGED C++ TYPES

When an unmanaged C++ object type is thrown, it is wrapped with an exception of type System.Runtime.InteropServices.SEHException. When searching for the appropriate catch clause, there are two possibilities. If an unmanaged C++ type is encountered, the exception is unwrapped and compared to the type encountered. This comparison allows an unmanaged C++ type to be caught in the normal way. However, if a catch clause of type SEHException or any of its base classes is examined first, the clause will intercept the exception. Therefore, you should place all catch clauses that catch unmanaged C++ types first before any catch clauses of managed types.

MANAGED EXTENSIONS AND THE __FINALLY KEYWORD

In addition to try and catch clauses, Managed Extensions support a __finally clause. The semantics are identical to the __finally block in structured exception handling (SHE). A __finally block can follow a try or catch block. The purpose of the __finally block is to clean up any resources left after the exception occurred. Note that the __finally block is always executed, even if no exception was thrown. The catch block is only executed if a managed exception is thrown within the associated try block. The following example demonstrates a simple __finally block:

```
#using <mscorlib.dll>
using namespace System;          // Needed to access the .NET Framework classes

__gc class MyException : public System::Exception
{
```

```
.......
};
void ThrowMyException()
{
throw new MyException;
}
void main()
{
try
{
ThrowMyException();
}
catch(MyException *e)
{
Console::WriteLine("in catch");
Console::WriteLine(e->GetType());
}
__finally
{
Console::WriteLine("in finally")
}
}
```

Program Output
    in catch
    MyException
    in finally

C++ EXCEPTION EXAMPLES

The real power of C++ exception handling lies not only in its ability to deal with exceptions of varying types, but also in its ability to automatically call destructor functions during stack unwinding for all local objects constructed before the exception was thrown. The context, which exists between the throw site and the catch handler, is referred to as the "exception stack frame." This frame may contain objects with destructor semantics. If an exception is thrown during execution of the guarded section or in any routine the guarded section calls (directly or indirectly), an exception object is created from the object created by the throw operand. (This implies that a copy constructor may be involved.) At this point, the compiler looks for a catch clause in a higher execution context that can handle an exception of the type thrown, or a catch handler that can handle any type of exception. The catch handlers are examined in order of their appearance following the try block. If no appropriate handler is found, the next dynamically enclosing try block is examined. This process continues until the outermost enclosing try block is examined.

    If a matching handler is still not found, or if an exception occurs while unwinding but before the handler gets control, the predefined run-time function terminate is called. If an exception occurs after throwing the exception but before the unwind begins, the terminate function is called. You can install a custom termination function to handle such situations. The following example demonstrates C++ exception handling using classes with destructor semantics. It declares two C++ classes; one (class CTest) for defining the exception object itself, and the second (class CDtorDemo) for demonstrating the destruction of a separate frame object during stack unwinding:

```
#include <iostream>

using namespace std;
void MyFunc(void);

class CTest
{
public:
CTest() {};
~CTest() {};
const char *ShowReason() {
return "Exception in CTest class.";
}
};

class CdtorDemo
{
public:
CDtorDemo();
~CDtorDemo();
};

CDtorDemo::CDtorDemo()
{
cout << "Constructing CDtorDemo." << end1;
}

CDtorDemo::~CDtorDemo()
{
cout << "Destructing CDtorDemo. " << end1;
}
```

```
void MyFunc()
{
CDtorDemo D;
cout << "In MyFunc(). Throwing CTest exception." << end1;
throw CTest();
}
int main()
{
cout << "In main." << end1
try
{
cout << "In try block, calling MyFunc()." << end1;
MyFunc();
}
catch (CTest E)
{
cout << "In catch handler." << end1;
cout << "Caught CTest exception type: ";
cout << E.ShowReason() << end1;
}
catch (char *str)
{
cout << "Caught some other exception: " << str << end1;
}
cout << "Back in main. Execution resumes here." << end1;
return 0;
}
```

If a matching catch handler is found, and it catches by value, its formal parameter is initialized by copying the exception object. If it catches by reference, the parameter is initialized to refer to the exception object. After the formal parameter is initialized, the process of "unwinding the stack" begins. This involves the destruction of all automatic objects that were constructed (but not yet destructed), between the beginning of the try block associated with the catch handler and the exception's throw site. Destruction occurs in reverse order of construction. The catch handler is executed and the program resumes execution following the last handler (that is, the first statement or construct that is not a catch handler). This is the output from the preceding example:

```
In main.
In try block, calling MyFunc().
Constructing CDtorDemo.
In MyFunc(). Throwing CTest exception.
```

Destructing CDtorDemo.
In catch handler.
Caught CTest exception type: Exception in CTest class.
Back in main. Execution resumes here.

Note the declaration of the exception parameter in both catch handlers:

```
catch(CTest E)
{// ...
}
catch(char *str)
{// ...
}
```

You do not need to declare this parameter; in many cases it may be sufficient to notify the handler that a particular type of exception has occurred. However, if you do not declare an exception object in the exception declaration, you will not have access to the object in the catch handler clause. For example:

```
catch(CTest)
{
// No access to a CTest exception object in this handler.
}
```

A throw expression with no operand re-throws the exception currently being handled. Such an expression should appear only in a catch handler or in a function called from within a catch handler. The re-thrown exception object is the original exception object (note a copy). For example:

```
try
{
throw CsomeOtherException();
}
catch(...)                              // Handle all exceptions
{
// Respond (perhaps only partially) to exceptions
// ...

throw;                         // Pass exception to some other handler
}
```

C#

Introduction

C# is a simple, modern, object-oriented, and type-safe programming language derived from C and C++. C# (pronounced "C sharp") is firmly planted in the C and C++ family tree of languages, and will immediately be familiar to C and C++ programmers. The purpose of C# is to combine the high productivity of Visual Basic and the raw power of C++. C# is provided as part of Microsoft Visual Studio 7.0. In addition to C#, Visual Studio supports Visual Basic, Visual C++, and the scripting languages VBScript and JScript. All of these languages provide access to the Microsoft .NET platform, which as we covered in Chapter 3, includes a common execution engine and a rich class library. The Microsoft .NET platform defines a "Common Language Subset" (CLS), a sort of lingua franca that ensures seamless interoperability between CLS-compliant languages and class libraries. For C# developers, this means that even though C# is a new language, it has complete access to the same rich class libraries that are used by seasoned tools such as Visual Basic and Visual C++. C# itself does not include a class library.

The thing to keep in mind is this compiler, as well as the Visual C++ compiler with Managed Extensions, sits on top of the .NET Framework, which sits on top of the Windows 2000 operating system. The C# use of the .Net Framework Base Class (base classes) libraries is to set up and control the Windows 2000 operating system (via the Win32 APIs). The base class libraries are classes that almost completely encapsulate the Win32 APIs. The most difficult thing will not be to learn the C# syntax but to understand the member functions and member data of the base classes. Appendix G shows the .NET Framework Namespaces that are involved in wrapping the Win32 APIs. This is why Chapters 1 and 2 were devoted to understanding the primary elements of developing applications (via Win32 APIs), to operate in the Windows 2000 environment. Appendices D and E show all the Win32 APIs. Again, a book such as my *Win32 System Services The Heart of Windows 98 and Windows 2000* will give you a more in-depth understanding of the Windows 2000 operating system engine and the associated Win32 APIs. It is not absolutely necessary to go down to, or completely understand, the Win32 API level to do C# and Visual C++ .NET Framework application development. However, it is helpful in gaining an insight into how this overall application programming META structure fits together and works. Also, in the .NET Framework Base Classes they have added to or enhanced the utility type base classes beyond that found in the Win32 APIs. It is interesting to note that the .NET Framework programming interface elements are classes, not just APIs, as with the Win32 APIs. Thus, we have a much richer set of semantics available to us for application development. It is my opinion, with .NET Framework base classes, that we are finally beginning to capitalize on the potential of using objects in developing complex application. After all, that's how we humans communicate and control things—by using the object metaphor. Thus, it is possible to form a powerful synergy between the programmer, the compiler, and the base classes. We are starting to let the software do what it is good at, more and more, and let the human (programmer) do what we are good at.

Comparison Between C++ and C#

A lot of you developers reading this will have a background in C++. Therefore, I will start this part off a little differently by having Table 5–1 show important comparisons between C++ and C# features. As a C++ programmer, this table will give you the most important differences between the two languages at a glance. Also, in Appendix M we show the C# compiler options, both alphabetically and by category. We also show some sample uses of these from the command line. In Appendix N we show the C# keywords, the built-in keyword C# types, and the C# Operators. This table and the appendices should start to give you a flavor of the C# controls for programming.

General Structure of a C# Program

The above gives us a general feel for the differences between C++ and C#. Let's look at the general structure of a C# program. C# programs can consist of one or more files. Each file can contain one or more namespaces. A namespace can contain types, such as classes, structs, interfaces, enumerations,

Table 5-1	
Feature	**Types**
Inheritance: A class can inherit implementation from one base class only. Also, a class or an interface can implement multiple interfaces.	class interface
Arrays: The syntax of declaring C# arrays is different from that of C++ arrays. The tokens "[]" appear following the array type in C#.	Arrays
The bool type: There is no conversion between the bool type and other types (specifically int).	bool
The struct type: In C#, classes and structs are semantically different. A struct is a value type, while a class is a reference type.	struct class
The switch statement: Unlike the C++ switch statement, C# does not support fall through from one case label to another.	switch
The delegate type: Delegates are roughly similar to function pointers in C++, but they are type-safe and secure.	delegate
Calling the overridden base class members from derived classes.	base
Using the new modifier to explicitly hide an inherited member.	new
Declaring override methods requires the override keyword.	override
Preprocessor directives are used for conditional compilation. No header files are used in C#.	Preprocessor Directives (See Appendix N)
Exception handling: Using the finally statement.	try-finally try-catch-finally
C# operators: C# supports additional operators such as is and typeof. It also introduced different functionality of some logical operators.	& Operator etc. (See Appendix N)
Use of the extern keyword.	extern
Use of the static keyword.	static
The Main method is declared differently from the main function in C++.	Main
Method parameters: C# supports ref and out parameters, which are used instead of pointers in passing parameters by reference.	ref out
Pointers are allowed in C# but only in unsafe mode.	Unsafe
Overloading operators is performed differently in C#	C# Operators
Strings: C# strings are different from C++ strings.	String

and delegates, in addition to other namespaces. The following is the skeleton
C# program that contains all of these elements.

```
// A skeleton of a C# program
using System;
namespace MyNamespace1
{
    class MyClass1
    {
    }
    struct MyStruct
    {
    }
    interface IMyInterface
    {
    }
    delegate int MyDelegate();
    enum MyEnum
    {
    }
    namespace MyNamespace2
    {
    }
    class MyClass2
    {
        public static void Main(string[] args)
        {
        }
    }
}
```

Notice how the namespace keyword is used to declare a scope. This namespace scope lets you organize code and gives you a way to create globally
unique types.

```
namespace name[.name1] ...] {
type declarations
}
```

where:
name, name1

A namespace name can be any legal identifier. A namespace name can
contain periods.
type declarations

Within a namespace, you can declare one or more of the following types:

- another namespace
- class
- interface
- struct
- enum
- delegate

Even if you do not explicitly declare one, a default namespace is created. This unnamed namespace, sometimes called the global namespace, is present in every file. Any identifier in the global namespace is available for use in a named namespace. Namespaces implicitly have public access and this is not modifiable. It is possible to define a namespace in two or more declarations. For example, the following sample defines both classes as part of namespace MyCompany.

```
namespace MyCompany.Proj1
{
    class MyClass
    {
    }
}
namespace MyCompany.Proj1
{
    class MyClass1
    {
    }
}
```

Example:

```
using System;
namespace SomeNameSpace
{
    public class MyClass
    {
        public static void Main()
        {
            Nested.NestedNameSpaceClass.SayHello();
        }
    }
    namespace Nested                    // a nested namespace
    {
        public class NestedNameSpaceClass
```

```
        {
                public static void SayHello()
                {
                        Console.WriteLine("Hello");
                }
        }
    }
}
```

Output
    Hello

As shown above, C# is an elegant, simple, type-safe, object-oriented language. C# gives you the capability to build durable system-level components by virtue of the following features:

- Full COM/Platform support for existing code integration
- Robustness through garbage collection and type safety
- Security provided through intrinsic code trust mechanisms
- Full support of extensible metadata concepts

It can also interoperate with other languages, across platforms, with legacy data, by virtue of the following features:

- Full interoperability support through COM+ 1.0 and .NET services with tight library-based access
- XML support for Web-based component interaction
- Versionability to provide ease of administration and deployment

See Appendix O for a libraries tutorial and how to create C# DLLs. Appendix M covers the C# Compiler Options that are used in Appendix O.

C# Version of Hello World

The following console program is the C# version of the traditional "Hello World!" program, which displays the string Hello World!.

```
// A "Hello, world" program in C#
using System;
class Hello
{
    static void Main()
    {
        Console.WriteLine("Hello, world");
    }
}
```

The source code for a C# program is typically stored in one or more text files with a file extension of .cs, as in hello.cs. Using the command-line compiler provided with Visual Studio, such a program can be compiled with the command line directive

csc hello.cs

which produces an executable program named hello.exe. The output of the program is:

Hello, world

Close examination of this program is illuminating:

- The using System; directive references a namespace called **System** that is provided by the Microsoft .NET class library. This namespace contains the Console class referred to in the Main method. Namespaces provide a hierarchical means of organizing the elements of a class library. A "using" directive enables unqualified use of the types that are members of the namespace. The "Hello, world" program uses Console.WriteLine as a shorthand for System.Console.WriteLine.
- The Main method is a member of the class Hello. It has the static modifier, and so it is a method on the class Hello rather than on instances of this class.
- The main entry point for a program—the method that is called to begin execution—is always a static method named Main.
- The "Hello, world" output is produced through the use of a class library. The language does not provide a class library. Instead, it uses a common class library that is also used by languages such as Visual Basic and Visual C++.

For C and C++ developers, it is interesting to note a few things that do not appear in the "Hello, world" program.

- The program does not use a global method for Main. Methods and variables are not supported at the global level; such elements are always contained within type declarations (e.g., class and struct declarations).
- The program does not use either "::" or "->" operators. The "::" is not an operator at all, and the "->" operator is used in only a small fraction of programs. The separator "." is used in compound names such as Console.WriteLine.
- The program does not contain forward declarations. Forward declarations are never needed, as declaration order is not significant.
- The program does not use #include to import program text. Dependencies among programs are handled symbolically rather

than textually. This system eliminates barriers between programs written in different languages. For example, the Console class could be written in another language.

You can compile the "Hello, world" program by creating a C# client EXE project in the Visual Studio IDE, or by using the command line. To compile the program from the command line:

- Create the source file using the text editor and save it using a name such as Hello.cs. C# source code files use the extension .cs.
- To invoke the compiler, enter the command:
      csc Hello.cs
  If your program does not contain any compilation errors, a Hello.exe file will be created.
- To run the program, enter the command:
  Hello

Appendix M contains information on the C# Compiler Options.

Developing a Simple Windows Forms Control

To round out our understanding of the program structure of a C# program, let's walk through the key steps that are required to create a custom Windows Forms control. If you have created controls before, the steps may seem familiar. However, even if are an experienced control developer, it is recommended that you browse through the steps described here. Chapter 4 covered the properties, events, and attributes that are being used in the development. Before we get into the development let's look at Class versus Component versus Control to eliminate some of the confusion that sometimes arises.

Class versus Component versus Control

A managed class can be versioned through assemblies. Additionally, if it exposes only Common Language Specification (CLS) compliant members, it can be used seamlessly from other CLS-compliant languages. A managed class thus satisfies the major requirements for software reuse. Why then is another entity called component defined, and what is its role?

A Component is a class with emphasis on cleanup and containment. A component can be hosted in a container, and has the ability to query and get services from its container. A component ensures that resources are released explicitly through its Dispose method, without waiting for automatic memory management. During teardown of a container, it is guaranteed that all resources allocate to the container, and its components will be released. Containment is logical and does not have to be visual. A middle tier container that sites database components is an example of logical containment.

Note   The Windows Forms and Web Forms designers in Visual Studio.NET require that a class must be a component to be displayed in the designer. This requirement is based on considerations such as those described above.

The definitions of a component and a control are as follows:

Component: To be a component, a class must implement the **System.ComponentModel.Icomponent** interface, and provide a constructor that requires no parameters. A class can also be a component if it derives from a class that implements **System.ComponentModel.Icomponent** such as **System.ComponentModelComponent**. A component can be contained and sited by a container. When sited in a container, a component interacts with the container through its container provided site.

Control: A control is a component with user interface (UI) capabilities. The only controls in .NET Framework are classes that derive from **System.WinForms.Control** or **System.Web.UI.Control**, and their subclasses. **System.WinForms.Control** itself provides basic UI capabilities, while **System.Web.UI.Control** provides the infrastructure on which it is easy to add UI.

```
//MyWinControl is a control since RichControl drives from
System.Winforms.Control
using System.WinForms;
public class MyWinControl : RichControl {...}
```

```
//MyWebControl is a control since WebControl derives from
System.Web.UI.Control
using System.Web.UI;
public class MyWebControl : WebControl {...}
```

If you are developing components and control for Windows Forms or Web Forms, you will not have to implement containers or sites. The Windows Forms and Web Forms designers are containers for Windows Forms and Web Forms controls. Containers are used for providing services. At design time, controls are sited in the designer and obtain services from the designer. For completeness, the definitions of a container and a site are given below.

Container: To be a container, a class must implement the System.ComponentModel.Icontainer interface and provide a constructor that requires no parameters. A class can also be a container if it derives from a class that implements System.ComponentModel.Icontainer. A container logically contains one or more components that are called the container's child components.

Site: Sites are provided by a container to manage and communicate with its child components. Typically, a container and a site are implemented as a unit. To be a site, a class must implement the **System.Component Model.Isite** interface.

A Windows Forms control sited in Microsoft Internet Explorer 5.5 is another example of a component sited in a container. The browser provides services, such as ambient properties, to the control through its site.

The control that we will develop in this section merely allows the alignment of text to be changed. To create a simple custom control:

1. Define a class that derives from **System.WinForms.RichControl**
   public class FirstControl : RichControl {...}

2. Define properties. (You are required to define a property, but a custom control that does anything meaningful will generally need to define additional properties.) The code fragment below defines a property TextAlignment that will be used to format the **Text** property inherited from **RichControl**.

```
private ContentAlignment alignment = Content1Alignment.Left;
public ContentAlignment TextAlignment {
  get {
      return alignment;
  }
  set {
      alignment = value;
      // Invalidate invokes the OnPaint method described in step 3 below.
      Invalidate();
  }
}
```

3. Override the protected **OnPaint** method inherited from **RichControl** to provide paint logic to your control. Unless you override **OnPaint** your control will not be able to draw. In the code fragment given below, the **OnPaint** method displays the **Text** properly inherited from **RichControl** with a default alignment. The code example at the end of this section shows how **OnPaint** can change the alignment to that specified by TextAlignment defined in step 2 above.

```
public class FirstControl : RichControl {
    public FirstControl() {...}
```

```
protected override void OnPaint(PaintEventArgs e) {
    base.OnPaint(e);
    e.Graphics.DrawString(Text, font, new SolidBrush (ForeColor),
                                ClientRectangle);
    }
}
```

4. Provide attributes for your control. Attributes allow your control and its properties and events to be displayed appropriately at design-time. The code fragment shown below applies attributes to the TextAlignment property. In a designer such as Visual Studio.NET, the **Category** attribute (applied below) will cause the property to be displayed under a logical category. The **Description** attribute will cause a descriptive string to be displayed at the bottom of the property window when the TextAlignment property is selected.

```
[
Category("Alignment"),
Description("Specifies the alignment of text.")
]
public ContentAlignment TextAlignment {…}
```

5. (optional) Provide resources for your control. You can provide resources, such as a bitmap for your control, by packaging them with your control. This can be accomplished by using a compiler option (/res for C#). At run time, the resource can be retrieved using methods of the **System.Resources.ResourceManager** class.

The code for FirstControl is shown below. The control is created in the namespace CustomWinControls. A namespace provides a logical grouping of related types. You can create your control in a new or existing namespace. In C#, the using declaration allows types to be accessed from a namespace without using the fully qualified name of the type. For example, with the using declaration below, you can access the class **RichControl** from **System.Winforms** simply by typing **RichControl** instead of **System.WinForms.RichControl.**

If you compile FirstControl and create an assembly (which will be a .dll file in this case), you will be able to add it to the toolbox of a Windows Forms designer such as Visual Studio.NET.

```
namespace CustomWinControls {
    using System;
    using System.ComponentModel;
    using System.WinForms;
    using System.Drawing;
    public class FirstControl : RichControl {
```

```
        private ContentAlignment alignment = ContentAlignment.Left;
    [
        Categroory("Alignment"),
        Description("Specifies the alignment of text.")
    ]
        public ContentAlignment TextAlignment {
            get {
                return alignment;
            }
            set {
            alignment = value;
            // InValidate invokes the OnPaint method
            InValidate();
            }
        }
// OnPaint aligns text as specified by the TextAlignment property, by passing
            a parameter
// to the DrawString method of the Graphics object.
    protected override void OnPaint(PaintEventArgs e) {
        base.OnPaint(e);
        // TextFormat style = (TextFormat) 0;
        StringFormat style = new StringFormat();
        style.Alignment = StringAlignment.Near;
        switch (alignment) {
                case ContentAlignment.Left:
                  style.Alignment = StringAlignment.Near;
                break;
                case ContentAlignment.Right:
                  style.Alignment = StringAlignment.Far;
                break;
            case ContentAlignment.Center:
                style.Alignment = StringAlignment.Center;
                break;
            }
    // Call the DrawString method of the System.Drawing class to write text.
    // Text and ClientRectangle are properties inherited from
    // RichControl and Control respectively.

        e.Graphics.DrawString(Text, font, new SolidBrush (ForeColor),
                    ClientRectangle, style);
        }
    }
}
```

APIs

The following APIs (functions) are used with **processes**.

Function	Description
CommandLineToArgvW	Parses a Unicode command-line string.
CreateProcess	Creates a new process and its primary thread.
CreateProcessAsUser	Creates a new process and its primary thread. The new process runs in the security context of the specified user.
CreateProcessWithLongonW	Creates a new process and its primary thread. The new process then runs the specified executable file in the security context of the specified credentials (user, domain, and password).
ExitProcess	Ends a process and all its threads.
FreeEnvironmentStrings	Frees a block of environment strings.
GetCommandLine	Retrieves the command-line string for the current process.
GetCurrentProcess	Retrieves a pseudo handle for the current process.
GetCurrentProcessId	Retrieves the process identified as the calling process.
GetEnvironmentStrings	Retrieves the environment block for the current process.
GetEnvironmentVariable	Retrieves the value of the specified variable from the environment block of the calling process.
GetExitCodeProcess	Retrieves the termination status of the specified process.
GetGuiResources	Retrieves the count of handles to graphical user interface (GUI) objects in use by the specified process.
GetPriorityClass	Retrieves the priority class for the specified process.
GetProcessAffinityMask	Retrieves a process affinity mask for the specified process and the system affinity mask for the system.
GetProcessIoCounters	Retrieves accounting information for all I/O operations performed by the specified process.

GetProcessPriorityBoost	Retrieves the priority boost control state of the specified process.
GetProcessShutdownParameters	Retrieves shutdown parameters for the currently calling process.
GetProcessTimes	Retrieves timing information for the specified process.
GetProcessVersion	Retrieves the major and minor version numbers of the system on which the specified process expects to run.
GetProcessWorkingSetSize	Retrieves the minimum and maximum working set sizes of the specified process.
GetStartupInfor	Retrieves the contents of the STARTUPINFO structure that was specified when the calling process was created.
OpenProcess	Opens an existing process object.
SetEnvironmentVariable	Sets the value of an environment variable for the current process.
SetPriorityClass	Sets the priority class for the specified process.
SetProcessAffinityMask	Sets a processor affinity mask for the threads of a specified process.
SetProcessPriorityBoost	Disables the ability of the system to temporarily boost the priority of the threads of the specified process.
SetProcessShutdownParameters	Sets shutdown parameters for the currently calling process.
SetProcessWorkingSetSize	Sets the minimum and maximum working set sizes for the specified process.
TerminateProcess	Terminates the specified process and all of its threads.

The following APIs (functions) are used with **threads**.

Function	Description
AttachThreadInput	Attaches the input processing mechanism of one thread to that of another thread.
CreatRemoteThread	Creates a thread that runs in the virtual address space of another process.
CreateThread	Creates a thread to execute within the virtual address space of the calling process.
ExitThread	Ends a thread.
GetCurrentThread	Retrieves a pseudo handle for the current thread.
GetCurrentThreadId	Retrieves the thread identifier of the calling thread.
GetExitCodeThread	Retrieves the termination status of the specified thread.
GetThreadPriority	Retrieves the priority value for the specified thread.
GetThreadPriorityBoost	Retrieves the priority boost control state of the specified thread.
GetThreadTimes	Retrieves timing information for the specified thread.
OpenThread	Opens an existing thread object.
ResumeThread	Decrements a thread's suspend count.
SetThreadAffinityMask	Sets a processor affinity mask for the specified thread.

SetThreadIdealProcessor	Specifies a preferred processor for a thread.
SetThreadPriority	Sets the priority value for the specified thread.
SetThreadPriorityBoost	Disables the ability of the system to temporarily boost the priority of a thread.
Sleep	Suspends the execution of the current thread for a specified interval.
SleepEx	Suspends the current thread until the specified condition is met.
SuspendThread	Suspends the specified thread.
SwitchToThread	Causes the calling thread to yield execution to another thread that is ready to run on the current processor.
TerminateThread	Terminates a thread.
ThreadProc	An application-defined function that serves as the starting address for a thread.
TlsAlloc	Allocates a thread local storage (TLS) index.
TlsFree	Releases a TLS index.
TlsGetValue	Retrieves the value in the calling thread's TLS slot for a specified TLS index.
TlsSetValue	Stores a value in the calling thread's TLS slot for a specified TLS index.
WaitForInputIdle	Waits until the specified process is waiting for user input with no input pending, or until the time-out interval has elapsed.

The following APIs (functions) are used with **job objects**.

Function	Description
AssignProcessToJobObject	Associates a process with an existing job object.
CreateJobObject	Creates or opens a job object.
OpenJobObject	Opens an existing job object.
QueryInformationJobObject	Retrieves limit and job state information from the job object.
SetInformationJobObject	Sets limits for a job object.
TerminateJobObject	Terminates all process currently associated with the job.
UserHandleGrantAccess	Grants or denies access to a handle to a User object to a job that has a user-interface restriction.

The following APIs (functions) are used in **thread pooling**.

Function	Description
BindIoCompletionCallback	Binds the specified file handle to the thread pool's I/O completion port.
QueueUserWorkItem	Queues a work item to a worker thread in the thread pool.

Base Priority

The priority level of a thread is determined by both the priority class of the process and its priority level. The priority class and priority level are combined to form the base priority of each thread.

Level	Process Priority Class	Thread Priority Level
1	IDLE_PRIORITY_CLASS	THREAD_PRIORITY_IDLE
1	BELOW_NORMAL_PRIORITY_CLASS	THREAD_PRIORITY_IDLE
1	NORMAL_PRIORITY_CLASS	THREAD_PRIORITY_IDLE
1	ABOVE_NORMAL_PRIORITY_CLASS	THREAD_PRIORITY_IDLE
1	HIGH_PRIORITY_CLASS	THREAD_PRIORITY_IDLE
2	IDLE_PRIORITY_CLASS	THREAD_PRIORITY_LOWEST
3	IDLE_PRIORITY_CLASS	THREAD_PRIORITY_BELOW_NORMAL
4	IDLE_PRIORITY_CLASS	THREAD_PRIORITY_NORMAL
4	BELOW_NORMAL_PRIORITY_CLASS	THREAD_PRIORITY_LOWEST
5	IDLE_PRIORITY_CLASS	THREAD_PRIORITY_ABOVE_NORMAL
5	BELOW_NORMAL_PRIORITY_CLASS	THREAD_PRIORITY_BELOW_NORMAL
5	Background NORMAL_PRIORITY_CLASS	THREAD_PRIORITY_LOWEST
6	IDLE_PRIORITY_CLASS	THREAD_PRIORITY_HIGHEST
6	BELOW_NORMAL_PRIORITY_CLASS	THREAD_PRIORITY_NORMAL
6	Background NORMAL_PRIORITY_CLASS	THREAD_PRIORITY_BELOW_NORMAL
7	BELOW_NORMAL_PRIORITY_CLASS	THREAD_PRIORITY_ABOVE_NORMAL

7	Background NORMAL_PRIORITY_CLASS	THREAD_PRIORITY_NORMAL
7	Foreground NORMAL_PRIORITY_CLASS	THREAD_PRIORITY_LOWEST
8	BELOW_NORMAL_PRIORITY_CLASS	THREAD_PRIORITY_HIGHEST
8	NORMAL_PRIORITY_CLASS	THREAD_PRIORITY_ABOVE_NORMAL
8	Foreground NORMAL_PRIORITY_CLASS	THREAD_PRIORITY_BELOW_NORMAL
8	ABOVE_NORMAL_PRIORITY_CLASS	THREAD_PRIORITY_LOWEST
9	NORMAL_PRIORITY_CLASS	THREAD_PRIORITY_HIGHEST
9	Foreground NORMAL_PRIORITY_CLASS	THREAD_PRIORITY_NORMAL
9	ABOVE_NORMAL_PRIORITY_CLASS	THREAD_PRIORITY_BELOW_NORMAL
10	Foreground NORMAL_PRIORITY_CLASS	THREAD_PRIORITY_ABOVE_NORMAL
10	ABOVE_NORMAL_PRIORITY_CLASS	THREAD_PRIORITY_NORMAL
11	Foreground NORMAL_PRIORITY_CLASS	THREAD_PRIORITY_HIGHEST
11	ABOVE_NORMAL_PRIORITY_CLASS	THREAD_PRIORITY_ABOVE_NORMAL
11	HIGH_PRIORITY_CLASS	THREAD_PRIORITY_LOWEST
12	ABOVE_NORMAL_PRIORITY_CLASS	THREAD_PRIORITY_HIGHEST
12	HIGH_PRIORITY_CLASS	THREAD_PRIORITY_BELOW_NORMAL
13	HIGH_PRIORITY_CLASS	THREAD_PRIORITY_NORMAL
14	HIGH_PRIORITY_CLASS	THREAD_PRIORITY_ABOVE_NORMAL
15	HIGH_PRIORITY_CLASS	THREAD_PRIORITY_HIGHEST
15	HIGH_PRIORITY_CLASS	THREAD_PRIORITY_TIME_CRITICAL
15	IDLE_PRIORITY_CLASS	THREAD_PRIORITY_TIME_CRITICAL
15	BELOW_NORMAL_PRIORITY_CLASS	THREAD_PRIORITY_TIME_CRITICAL
15	NORMAL_PRIORITY_CLASS	THREAD_PRIORITY_TIME_CRITICAL
15	ABOVE_NORMAL_PRIORITY_CLASS	THREAD_PRIORITY_TIME_CRITICAL
16	REALTIME_PRIORITY_CLASS	THREAD_PRIORITY_IDLE
17	REALTIME_PRIORITY_CLASS	-7
18	REALTIME_PRIORITY_CLASS	-6
19	REALTIME_PRIORITY_CLASS	-5
20	REALTIME_PRIORITY_CLASS	-4
21	REALTIME_PRIORITY_CLASS	-3
22	REALTIME_PRIORITY_CLASS	THREAD_PRIORITY_LOWEST

23	REALTIME_PRIORITY_CLASS	THREAD_PRIORITY_BELOW_NORMAL
24	REALTIME_PRIORITY_CLASS	THREAD_PRIORITY_NORMAL
25	REALTIME_PRIORITY_CLASS	THREAD_PRIORITY_ABOVE_NORMAL
26	REALTIME_PRIORITY_CLASS	THREAD_PRIORITY_HIGHEST
27	REALTIME_PRIORITY_CLASS	3
28	REALTIME_PRIORITY_CLASS	4
29	REALTIME_PRIORITY_CLASS	5
30	REALTIME_PRIORITY_CLASS	6
31	REALTIME_PRIORITY_CLASS	THREAD_PRIORITY_TIME_CRITICAL

Note: The values -7, -6, -5, -4, -3, 3, 4, 5, and 6 are supported only on Windows 2000

Object Categories

Go to MSDN Library and search for "Interprocess Communication." At about item 81, this category of Object Categories comes up. You can then click on the Overview item and extract the information you need on an object.

User Object	Overview
Accelerator table	Keyboard Accelerators
Caret	Carets
Cursor	Cursors
DDE conversation	Dynamic Data Exchange Management Library
Desktop	Window Stations and Desktops
Hook	Hooks
Icon	Icons
Menu	Menus
Window	Windows
Window position	Windows
Window station	Window Stations and Desktops

GDI Object	Overview
Bitmap	Bitmaps
Brush	Brushes
DC	Device Contexts
Enhanced metafile	Metafiles
Enhanced-metafile DC	Metafiles

Font	Fonts and Text
Memory DC	Device Contexts
Metafile	Metafiles
Metafile DC	Metafiles
Palette	Colors
Pen and extended pen	Pens
Region	Regions

Kernel Object	**Overview**
Access token	Access Control
Change notification	File I/O
Communications device	Communications
Console input	Consoles and Character-Mode Support
Console screen buffer	Consoles and Character-Mode Support
Event	Synchronization
Event log	Event Logging
File	File I/O
File mapping	File Mapping
Find file	File I/O
Heap	Memory Management
Job	Job Objects
Mailslot	Mailslots
Module	Dynamic-Link Libraries
Mutex	Synchronization
Pipe	Pipes
Process	Processes and Threads
Semaphore	Synchronization
Socket	Windows Socket 2
Thread	Processes and Threads
Timer	Synchronization
Update resource	Resources

Functions in Alphabetical Order (1939 APIs)

A Functions
AbnormalTermination
AbortDoc
AbortPath
AbortPrinter
AbortProc
AbortSystemShutdown
AccessCheck
AccessCheckAndAuditAlarm
AccessCheckByType
AccessCheckByTypeAndAuditAlarm
AccessCheckByTypeResultList
AccessCheckByTypeResultListAnd-
AuditAlarmByHandle
ActivateKeyboardLayout
AddAccessAllowAce
AddAccessAllowAceEx
AddAccessAllowedObjectAce
AddAccessDeniedAce
AddAccessDeniedAceEx
AddAccessDeniedObjectAce
AddAce
AddAtom
AddAuditAccessAce
AddAuditAccessAceEx
AddAuditAccessObjectAce
AddFontMemResourceEx

AddFontResource
AddFontResourceEx
AddForm
AddJob
AddMonitor
AddPort
AddPrinter
AddPrinterConnection
AddPrinterDriver
AddPrinterDriverEx
AddPrintProcessor
AddPrintProvidor
AddUsersToEncryptedFile
AdjustTokenGroups
AdjustTokenPrivileges
AdjustWindowRect
AdjustWindowRectEx
AdvancedDocumentProperties
AllocateAndInitializeSid
AllocateLocallyUniqueId
AllocateUserPhysicalPages
AllocConsole
AllowSetForegroundWindow
AlphaBlend
AngleArc
AnimatePalette
AnimateWindow

AnsiLower
AnsiLowerBuff
AnsiNext
AnsiPrev
AnsiToOem
AnsiToOemBuff
AnsiUpper
AnsiUpperBuff
AnyPopup
AppendMenu
Arc
ArcTo
AreAllAccessesGranted
AreAnyAccessesGranted
AreFileApisANSI
ArrangeIconicWindows
AssignProcessToJobObject
AttachThreadInput

B Functions
BackupEventLog
BackupRead
BackupSeek
BackupWrite
Beep
BeginDeferWindowPos
BeginPaint
BeginPath
BeginUpdateResource
BindIoCompletionCallback
BitBlt
BlockInput
BroadcastSystemMessage
BuildCommDCB
BuildCommDCBAndTimeouts
BuildExplicitAccessWithName
BuildImpersonateExplicitAccessWithName
BuildImpersonateTrustee
BuildSecurityDescriptor
BuildTrusteeWithName
BuildTrusteeWithObjectsAndName
BuildTrusteeWithObjectsAndSid
BuildTrusteeWithSid

C Functions
CallMsgFilter
CallNamedPipe
CallNextHookEx
CallWindowProc
CallWndProc
CallWndRetProc
CancelDC
CancelIo
CancelWaitableTimer
CascadeWindows
CBTProc
CCHookProc
CFHookProc
ChangeClipboardChain
ChangeDisplaySettings
ChangeDisplaySettingsEx
ChangeServiceConfig
ChangeServiceConfig2
ChangeTimerQueueTimer
CharLower
CharLowerBuff
CharNext
CharNextExA
CharPrev
CharPrevExA
CharToOem
CharToOemBuff
CharUpper
CharUpperBuff
CheckDlgButton
CheckMenuItem
CheckMenuRadioItem
CheckRadioButton
CheckTokenMembership
ChildWindowFromPoint
ChildWindowFromPointEx
ChooseColor
ChooseFont
Chord
ClearCommBreak
ClearCommError
ClearEventLog

ClientToScreen
ClipCursor
CloseClipboard
CloseDesktop
CloseEnhMetaFile
CloseEventLog
CloseFigure
CloseHandle
CloseMetaFile
ClosePrinter
·CloseServiceHandle
CloseWindow
CloseWindowStation
CombineRgn
CombineTransform
CommandLineToArgvW
CommConfigDialog
CommDlgExtendedError
CompareFileTime
CompareString
ConfigurePort
ConnectNamedPipe
ConnectToPrinterDlg
ContinueDebugEvent
ControlService
ConvertDefaultLocale
ConvertSecurityDescriptorToStringSecurity-
Descriptor
ConvertSidToStringSid
ConvertStringSecurityDescriptorToSecurity-
Descriptor
ConvertStringSidToSid
ConvertThreadToFiber
ConvertToAutoInheritPrivateObjectSecurity
CopyAcceleratorTable
CopyCursor
CopyEnhMetaFile
CopyFile
CopyFileEx
CopyIcon
CopyImage
CopyLZFile
CopyMemory
CopyMetaFile

CopyProgressRoutine
CopyRect
CopySid
CountClipboardFormats
CreateAcceleratorTable
CreateBitmap
CreateBitmapIndirect
CreateBrushIndirect
CreateCaret
CreateCompatibleBitmap
CreateCompatibleDC
CreateConsoleScreenBuffer
CreateCursor
CreateDC
CreateDesktop
CreateDialog
CreateDialogIndirect
CreateDialogIndirectParam
CreateDialogParam
CreateDIBitmap
CreateDIBPatternBrush
CreateDIBPatternBrushPt
CreateDIBSection
CreateDirectory
CreateDirectoryEx
CreateDiscardableBitmap
CreateEllipticRgn
CreateEllipticRgnIndirect
CreateEnhMetaFile
CreateEnvironmentBlock
CreateEvent
CreateFiber
CreateFile
CreateFileMapping
CreateFont
CreateFontIndirect
CreateFontIndirectEx
CreateHalftonePalette
CreateHardLink
CreateHatchBrush
CreateIC
CreateIcon
CreateIconFromResource
CreateIconFromResourceEx

CreateIconIndirect
CreateIoCompletionPort
CreateJobObject
CreateMailslot
CreateMDIWindow
CreateMenu
CreateMetaFile
CreateMutex
CreateNamedPipe
CreatePalette
CreatePatternBrush
CreatePen
CreatePenIndirect
CreatePipe
CreatePolygonRgn
CreatePolyPolygonRgn
CreatePopupMenu
CreatePrivateObjectSecurity
CreatePrivateObjectSecurityEx
CreateProcess
CreateProcessAsUser
CreateProcessWithLogonW
CreateRectRgn
CreateRectRgnIndirect
CreateRemoteThread
CreateRestrictedToken
CreateRoundRectRgn
CreateScalableFontResource
CreateSemaphore
CreateService
CreateSolidBrush
CreateTapePartition
CreateThread
CreateTimerQueue
CreateTimerQueueTimer
CreateToolhelp32Snapshot
CreateWaitableTimer
CreateWindow
CreateWindowEx
CreateWindowStation

D Functions

DdeAbandonTransaction

DdeAccessData
DdeAddData
DdeCallback
DdeClientTransaction
DdeCmpStringHandles
DdeConnect
DdeConnectList
DdeCreateDataHandle
DdeCreateStringHandle
DdeDisconnect
DdeDisconnectList
DdeEnableCallback
DdeFreeDataHandle
DdeFreeStringHandle
DdeGetData
DdeGetLastError
DdeImpersonateClient
DdeInitialize
DdeKeepStringHandle
DdeNameService
DdePostAdvise
DdeQueryConvInfo
DdeQueryNextServer
DdeQueryString
DdeReconnect
DdeSetQualityOfService
DdeSetUserHandle
DdeUnaccessData
DdeUninitialize
DebugActiveProcess
DebugBreak
DebugProc
DecryptFile
DefDlgProc
DeferWindowPos
DefFrameProc
DefHookProc
DefineDosDevice
DefineHandleTable
DefMDIChildProc
DefWindowProc
DeleteAce
DeleteAtom
DeleteCriticalSection

DeleteDC
DeleteEnhMetaFile
DeleteFiber
DeleteFile
DeleteForm
DeleteMenu
DeleteMetaFile
DeleteMonitor
DeleteObject
DeletePort
DeletePrinter
DeletePrinterConnection
DeletePrinterData
DeletePrinterDataEx
DeletePrinterDriver
DeletePrinterDriverEx
DeletePrinterKey
DeletePrintProcessor
DeletePrintProvidor
DeleteProfile
DeleteService
DeleteTimerQueue
DeleteTimerQueueEx
DeleteTimerQueueTimer
DeleteVolumeMountPoint
DeregisterEventSource
DestroyAcceleratorTable
DestroyCaret
DestroyCursor
DestroyEnvironmentBlock
DestroyIcon
DestroyMenu
DestroyPrivateObjectSecurity
DestroyWindow
DeviceCapabilities
DeviceIoControl
DialogBox
DialogBoxIndirect
DialogBoxIndirectParam
DialogBoxParam
DialogProc
DisableThreadLibraryCalls
DisconnectNamedPipe
DispatchMessage

DlgDirList
DlgDirListComboBox
DlgDirSelectComboBoxEx
DlgDirSelectEx
DllMain
DnsHostnameToComputerName
DocumentProperties
DosDateTimeToFileTime
DPtoLP
DragDetect
DrawAnimatedRects
DrawCaption
DrawEdge
DrawEscape
DrawFocusRect
DrawFrameControl
DrawIcon
DrawIconEx
DrawMenuBar
DrawState
DrawStateProc
DrawText
DrawTextEx
DuplicateHandle
DuplicateIcon
DuplicateToken
DuplicateTokenEx

E Functions
EditWordBreakProc
Ellipse
EmptyClipboard
EnableMenuItem
EnableScrollBar
EnableWindow
EncryptFile
EncryptionDisable
EndDeferWindowPos
EndDialog
EndDoc
EndDocPrinter
EndMenu
EndPage

EndPagePrinter
EndPaint
EndPath
EndUpdateResource
EnhMetaFileProc
EnterCriticalSection
EnumCalendarInfo
EnumCalendarInfoEx
EnumCalendarInfoProc
EnumCalendarInfroProcEx
EnumChildProc
EnumChildWindows
EnumClipboardFormats
EnumCodePagesProc
EnumDateFormats
EnumDateFormatsEx
EnumDateFormatsProc
EnumDateFormatsProcEx
EnumDependentServices
EnumDesktopProc
EnumDesktops
EnumDesktopWindows
EnumDisplayDevices
EnumDisplayMonitors
EnumDisplaySettings
EnumDisplaySettingsEx
EnumEnhMetaFile
EnumFontFamExProc
EnumFontFamilies
EnumFontFamiliesEx
EnumFontFamProc
EnumFonts
EnumFontsProc
EnumForms
EnumInputContext
EnumJobs
EnumLanguageGroupLocales
EnumLanguageGroupLocalesProc
EnumLanguageGroupsProc
EnumLocalesProc
EnumMetaFile
EnumMetaFileProc
EnumMonitors
EnumObjects

EnumObjectsProc
EnumPorts
EnumPrinterData
EnumPrinterDataEx
EnumPrinterDrivers
EnumPrinterKey
EnumPrinters
EnumPrintProcessorDatatypes
EnumPrintProcessors
EnumProps
EnumPropsEx
EnumRegisterWordProc
EnumResLangProc
EnumResNameProc
EnumResourceLanguages
EnumResourceNames
EnumResourceTypes
EnumResTypeProc
EnumServicesStatus
EnumServicesStatusEx
EnumSystemCodePages
EnumSystemLanguageGroups
EnumSystemLocales
EnumTaskWindows
EnumThreadWindows
EnumThreadWndProc
EnumTimeFormats
EnumTimeFormatsProc
EnumUILanguages
EnumUILanguagesProc
EnumWindows
EnumWindowsProc
EnumWindowStationProc
EnumWindowStations
EqualPrefixSid
EqualRect
EqualRgn
EqualSid
EraseTape
Escape
EscapeCommFunction
ExcludeClipRect
ExcludeUpdateRgn
ExitProcess

ExitThread
ExitWindows
ExitWindowsEx
ExpandEnvironmentStrings
ExpandEnvironmentStringsForUser
ExtCreatePen
ExtCreateRegion
ExtEscape
ExtFloodFill
ExtractAssociatedIcon
ExtractIcon
ExtractIconEx
ExtSelectClipRgn
ExtTextOut

F Functions
FatalAppExit
FatalExit
FiberProc
FileEncryptionStatus
FileIOCompletionRoutine
FileTimeToDosDateTime
FileTimeToLocalFileTime
FileTimeToSystemTime
FillConsoleOutputAttribute
FillConsoleOutputCharacter
FillMemory
FillPath
FillRect
FillRgn
FindAtom
FindClose
FindCloseChangeNotification
FindClosePrinterChangeNotification
FindFirstChangeNotification
FindFirstFile
FindFirstFileEx
FindFirstFreeAce
FindFirstPrinterChangeNotification
FindFirstVolume
FindFirstVolumeMountPoint
FindNextChangeNotification
FindNextFile
FindNextPrinterChangeNotification

FindNextVolume
FindNextVolumeMountPoint
FindResource
FindResourceEx
FindText
FindVolumeClose
FindVolumeMountPointClose
FindWindow
FindWindowEx
FixBrushOrgEx
FlashWindow
FlashWindowEx
FlattenPath
FloodFill
FlushConsoleInputBuffer
FlushFileBuffers
FlushInstructionCache
FlushPrinter
FlushViewOfFile
FoldString
ForegroundIdleProc
FormatMessage
FrameRect
FrameRgn
FreeConsole
FreeDDElParam
FreeEncryptionCertificateHashList
FreeEnvironmentStrings
FreeLibrary
FreeLibraryAndExitThread
FreeModule
FreePrinterNotifyInfo
FreeProcInstance
FreeResource
FreeSid
FreeUserPhysicalPages
FRHookProc

G Functions
GdiComment
GdiFlush
GdiGetBatchLimit
GdiSetBatchLimit
GenerateConsoleCtrlEvent

GetAce
GetAclInformation
GetACP
GetActiveWindow
GetAllUsersProfileDirectory
GetAltTabInfo
GetAncestor
GetArcDirection
GetAspectRatioFilterEx
GetAsyncKeyState
GetAtomName
GetAuditedPermissionsFromAcl
GetBinaryType
GetBitmapBits
GetBitmapDimensionEx
GetBkColor
GetBkMode
GetBoundsRect
GetBrushOrgEx
GetCalendarInfo
GetCapture
GetCaretBlinkTime
GetCaretPos
GetCharABCWidths
GetCharABCWidthsFloat
GetCharABCWidthsI
GetCharacterPlacement
GetCharWidth
GetCharWidth32
GetCharWidthFloat
GetCharWidthI
GetClassInfo
GetClassInfoEx
GetClassLong
GetClassLongPtr
GetClassName
GetClassWord
GetClientRect
GetClipboardData
GetClipboardFormatName
GetClipboardOwner
GetClipboardSequenceNumber
GetClipboardViewer
GetClipBox

GetClipCursor
GetClipRgn
GetColorAdjustment
GetComboBoxInfo
GetCommandLine
GetCommConfig
GetCommMask
GetCommModemStatus
GetCommProperties
GetCommState
GetCommTimeouts
GetCompressedFileSize
GetComputerName
GetComputerNameEx
GetComputerObjectname
GetConsoleCP
GetConsoleCursorInfo
GetconsoleMode
GetConsoleOutputCP
GetConsoleScreenBufferInfo
GetConsoleTitle
GetCPInfo
GetCPInfoEx
GetCurrencyFormat
GetCurrentDirectory
GetCurrentHwProfile
GetCurrentObject
GetCurrentPositionEx
GetCurrentProcess
GetCurrentProcessId
GetCurrentThread
GetCurrentThreadId
GetCurrentTime
GetCursor
GetCursorInfo
GetCursorPos
GetDateFormat
GetDC
GetDCBrushColor
GetDCEx
GetDCOrgEx
GetDCPenColor
GetDefaultCommConfig
GetDefaultPrinter

GetDefaultUserProfileDirectory
GetDesktopWindow
GetDeviceCaps
GetDevicePowerState
GetDialogBaseUnits
GetDIBColorTable
GetDIBits
GetDiskFreeSpace
GetDiskFreeSpaceEx
GetDlgCtrlID
GetDlgItem
GetDlgItemInt
GetDlgItemText
GetDoubleClickTime
GetDriveType
GetEffectiveRightsFromAcl
GetEnhMetaFile
GetEnhMetaFileBits
GetEnhMetaFileDescription
GetEnhMetaFileHeader
GetEnhMetaFilePaletteEntries
GetEnvironmentStrings
GetEnvironmentVariable
GetEventLogInformation
GetExceptionCode
GetExceptionInformation
GetExitCodeProcess
GetExitCodeThread
GetExpandName
GetExplicitEntriesFromAcl
GetFileAttributes
GetFileAttributesEx
GetFileInformationByHandle
GetFileSecurity
GetFileSize
GetFileSizeEx
GetFileTime
GetFileTitle
GetFileType
GetFileVersionInfo
GetFileVersionInfoSize
GetFocus
GetFontData
GetFontLanguageInfo

GetFontUnicodeRanges
GetForegroundWindow
GetForm
GetFreeSpace
GetFullPathName
GetGlyphIndices
GetGlyphOutline
GetGraphicsMode
GetGuiResource
GetGUIThreadInfo
GetHandleInformation
GetIconInfo
GetInputState
GetJob
GetKBCodePage
GetKernelObjectSecurity
GetKerningPairs
GetKeyboardLayout
GetKeyboardLayoutList
GetKeyboardLayoutName
GetKeyboardState
GetKeyboardType
GetKeyNameText
GetKeyState
GetLargestConsoleWindowSize
GetLastActivePopup
GetLastError
GetLastInputInfo
GetLayout
GetLengthSid
GetListBoxInfo
GetLocaleInfo
GetLocalTime
GetLogicalDrives
GetLogicalDriveStrings
GetLongPathName
GetMailslotInfo
GetMapMode
GetMenu
GetMenuBarInfo
GetMenuCheckMarkDimensions
GetMenuDefaultItem
GetMenuInfo
GetMenuItemCount

GetMenuItemID
GetMenuItemInfo
GetMenuItemRect
GetMenuState
GetMenuString
GetMessage
GetMessageExtraInfo
GetMessagePos
GetMessageTime
GetMetaFile
GetMetaFileBitsEx
GetMetaRgn
GetMiterLimit
GetModuleFileName
GetModuleHandle
GetMonitorInfo
GetMouseMovePointsEx
GetMsgProc
GetMultipleTrustee
GetMultipleTrusteeOperation
GetNamedPipeHandleState
GetNamedPipeInfo
GetNamedSecurityInfo
GetNearestColor
GetNearestPaletteIndex
GetNextDlgGroupItem
GetNextDlgTabItem
GetNextWindow
GetNumberFormat
GetNumberOfConsoleInputEvents
GetNumberOfConsoleMouseButtons
GetNumberOfEventLogRecords
GetObject
GetObjectType
GetOEMCP
GetOldestEventLogRecord
GetOpenClipboardWindow
GetOpenFileName
GetOutlineTextMetrics
GetOverlappedResult
GetPaletteEntries
GetParent
GetPath
GetPixel

GetPolyFillMode
GetPrinter
GetPrinterData
GetPrinterDataEx
GetPrinterDriver
GetPrinterDriverDirectory
GetPrintProcessorDirectory
GetPriorityClass
GetPriorityClipboardFormat
GetPrivateObjectSecurity
GetPrivateProfileInt
GetPrivateProfileSection
GetPrivateProfileSectionNames
GetPrivateProfileString
GetPrivateProfileStruct
GetProcAddress
GetProcessAffinityMask
GetProcessDefaultLayout
GetProcessHeap
GetProcessHeaps
GetProcessIoCounters
GetProcessPriorityBoost
GetProcessShutdownParameters
GetProcessTimes
GetProcessVersion
GetProcessWindowStation
GetProcessworkingSetSize
GetProfileInt
GetProfilesDirectory
GetProfileSection
GetProfileString
GetProfileType
GetProp
GetQueuedCompletionStatus
GetQueueStatus
GetRandomRgn
GetRasterizeCaps
GetRegionData
GetRgnBox
GetROP2
GetSaveFileName
GetScrollBarInfo
GetScrollInfo
GetScrollPos

GetScrollRange
GetSecurityDescriptorControl
GetSecurityDescriptorDacl
GetSecurityDescriptorGroup
GetSecurityDescriptorLength
GetSecurityDescriptorOwner
GetSecurityDescriptorRMControl
GetSecurityDescriptorSacl
GetSecurityInfo
GetServiceDisplayName
GetServiceKeyName
GetShortPathName
GetSidIdentifierAuthority
GetSidLengthRequired
GetSidSubAuthority
GetSidSubAuthorityCount
GetStartupInfo
GetStdHandle
GetStockObject
GetStretchBltMode
GetStringTypeA
GetStringTypeEx
GetStringTypeW
GetSubMenu
GetSysColor
GetSysColorBrush
GetSysModalWindow
GetSystemDefaultLangID
GetSystemDefaultCID
GetSystemDefaultUILanguage
GetSystemDirectory
GetSystemInfo
GetSystemMenu
GetSystemMetrics
GetSystemPaletteEntries
GetSystemPaletteUse
GetSystemPowerStatus
GetSystemTime
GetSystemTimeAdjustment
GetSystemTimeAsFileTime
GetSystemWindowsDirectory
GetTabbedTextExtent
GetTapeParameters
GetTapePosition

GetTapeStatus
GetTempFileName
GetTempPath
GetTextAlign
GetTextCharacterExtra
GetTextCharset
GetTextCharsetInfo
GetTextColor
GetTextExtentExPoint
GetTextExtentExPointI
GetTextExtentPoint
GetTextExtentPoint32
GetTextExtentPointI
GetTextFace
GetTextMetrics
GetThreadContext
GetThreadDesktop
GetThreadLocale
GetThreadPriority
GetThreadPriorityBoost
GetThreadSelectorEntry
GetThreadTimes
GetTickCount
GetTimeFormat
GetTimeZoneInformation
GetTitleBarInfo
GetTokenInformation
GetTopWindow
GetTrusteeForm
GetTrusteeName
GetTrusteeType
GetUpdateRect
GetUpdateRgn
GetUserDefaultLangID
GetUserDefaultLCID
GetUserDefaultUILanguage
GetUserName
GetUserNameEx
GetUserObjectInformation
GetUserObjectSecurity
GetUserProfileDirectory
GetVersion
GetVersionEx
GetViewportExtEx

GetViewportOrgEx
GetVolumeInformation
GetVolumeNameForVolumeMountPoint
GetVolumePathName
GetWindow
GetWindowDC
GetWindowExtEx
GetWindowInfo
GetWindowLong
GetWindowLongPtr
GetWindowModuleFileName
GetWindowOrgEx
GetWindowPlacement
GetWindowRect
GetWindowRgn
GetWindowsDirectory
GetWindowTask
GetWindowText
GetWindowTextLength
GetWindowThreadProcessId
GetWindowWord
GetWinMetaFileBits
GetWorldTransform
GetWriteWatch
GlobalAddAtom
GlobalAlloc
GlobalCompact
GlobalDeleteAtom
GlobalDiscard
GlobalFindAtom
GlobalFix
GlobalFlags
GlobalFree
GlobalGetAtomName
GlobalHandle
GlobalLock
GlobalLRUNewest
GlobalLRUOldest
GlobalMemoryStatus
GlobalMemoryStatusEx
GlobalReAlloc
GlobalSize
GlobalUnfix
GlobalUnlock

GlobalUnWire
GlobalWire
GradientFill
GrayString

H Functions
Handler
HandleEx
HandlerRoutine
Heap32First
Heap32ListFirst
Heap32ListNext
Heap32Next
HeapAlloc
HeapCompact
HeapCreate
HeapDestroy
HeapFree
HeapLock
HeapReAlloc
HeapSize
HeapUnlock
HeapValidate
HeapWalk
HideCaret
HiliteMenuItem

I Functions
ImmAssociateContext
ImmAssociateContextEx
ImmConfigureIME
ImmCreateContext
ImmDestroyContext
ImmDisableIME
ImmEnumInputContext
ImmEnumRegisterWord
ImmEscape
ImmGetCandidateList
ImmGetCandidateListCount
ImmGetCandidateWindow
ImmGetCompositionFont
ImmGetCompositionString
ImmGetCompositionWindow

ImmGetContext
ImmGetConversionList
ImmGetConversionStatus
ImmGetDefaultIMEWnd
ImmGetDescription
ImmGetGuideLine
ImmGetIMEFileName
ImmGetImeMenuItems
ImmGetOpenStatus
ImmGetProperty
ImmGetRegisterWordStyle
ImmGetStatusWindowPos
ImmGetVirtualKey
ImmInstallIME
ImmIsIME
ImmIsUIMessage
ImmNotifyIME
ImmRegisterWord
ImmReleaseContext
ImmSetCandidateWindow
ImmSetCompositionFont
ImmSetCompositionString
ImmSetCompositionWindow
ImmSetConversionStatus
ImmSetOpenStatus
ImmSetStatusWindowPos
ImmSimulateHotKey
ImmUnregisterWord
ImpersonateAnonymousToken
ImpersonateDdeClientWindow
ImpersonateLoggedOnUser
ImpersonateNamedPipeclient
ImpersonateSelf
InflatRect
InitAtomTable
InitializeAcl
InitializeCriticalSection
InitializeCriticalSectionAndSpinCount
InitializeSecurityDescriptor
InitializeSid
InitiateSystemShutdown
InitiateSystemShutdownEx
InSendMessage
InSendMessageEx

InsertMenu
InsertMenuItem
Int32x32To64
Int64ShllMod32
Int64ShraMod32
Int64ShrlMod32
InterlockedCompareExchange
InterlockedCompareExchangePointer
InterlockedDecrement
InterlockedExchange
InterlockedExchangeAdd
InterlockedExchangePointer
InterlockedIncrement
IntersectClipRect
IntersectRect
InvalidateRect
InvalidateRgn
InvertRect
InvertRgn
IsBadCodePtr
IsBadHugeReadPtr
IsBadHugeWritePtr
IsBadReadPtr
IsBadStringPtr
IsBadWritePtr
IsCharAlpha
IsCharAlphaNumeric
IsCharLower
IsCharUpper
IsChild
IsClipboardFormatAvailable
IsDBCSLeadByte
IsDBCSLeadByteEx
IsDebuggerPresent
IsDialogMessage
IsDlgButtonChecked
IsIconic
IsMenu
IsProcessorFeaturePresent
IsRectEmpty
IsSystemResumeAutomatic
IsTextUnicode
IsTokenRestricted
IsValidAcl

IsValidCodePage
IsValidLanguageGroup
IsValidLocale
IsValidSecurityDescriptor
IsValidSid
IsWindow
IsWindowEnabled
IsWindowUnicode
IsWindowVisible
IsZoomed

J Functions
JournalPlayBackProc
JournalRecordProc

K Functions
keybd_event
KeyboardProc
KillTimer

L Functions
LCMapString
LeaveCriticalSection
LimitEmsPages
LineDDA
LineDDAProc
LineTo
LoadAccelerators
LoadBitmap
LoadCursor
LoadCursorFromFile
LoadIcon
LoadImage
LoadKeyboardLayout
LoadLibrary
LoadLibraryEx
LoadMenu
LoadMenuIndirect
LoadModule
LoadResource
LoadString
LoadUserProfile
LocalAlloc
LocalCompact

LocalDiscard
LocalFileTimeToFileTime
LocalFlags
LocalFree
LocalHandle
LocalLock
LocalReAlloc
LocalShrink
LocalSize
LocalUnlock
LockFile
LockFileEx
LockResource
LockSegment
LockServiceDatabase
LockSetForegroundWindow
LockWindowUpdate
LockWorkStation
LogonUser
LookupAccountName
LookupAccountSid
LookupIconIdFromDirectory
LookupIconIdFromDirectoryEx
LookupPrivilegeDisplayName
LookupPrivilegeName
LookupPrivilegeValue
LookupSecurityDescriptorParts
LowLevelKeyboardProc
LowLevelMouseProc
LptoDP
lstrcat
lstrcmp
lstrcmpi
lstrcpy
lstrcpyn
lstrlen
LZClose
LZCopy
LZDone
LZInit
LZOpenFile
LZRead
LZSeek
LZStart

M Functions

MakeAbsoluteSD
MakeProcInstance
MakeSelfRelativeSD
MapDialogRect
MapGenericMask
MapUserPhysicalPages
MapUserPhysicalPagesScatter
MapViewOfFile
MapViewOfFileEx
MapVirtualKey
MapVirtualKeyEx
MapWindowPoints
MaskBlt
MenuItemFromPoint
MessageBeep
MessageBox
MessageBoxEx
MessageBoxIndirect
MessageProc
ModifyMenu
ModifyWorldTransform
Module32First
Module32Next
MonitorEnumProc
MonitorFromPoint
MonitorFromRect
MonitorFromWindow
mouse_event
MouseProc
MoveFile
MoveFileEx
MoveFileWithProgress
MoveMemory
MoveToEx
MoveWindow
MsgWaitForMultipleObjects
MsgWaitForMultipleObjectsEx
MulDiv
MultiByteToWideChar

N Functions

NetAccessAdd
NetAccessCheck
NetAccessDel
NetAccessEnum
NetAccessGetInfo
NetAccessGetUserPerms
NetAccessSetInfo
NetAlertRaise
NetAlertRaiseEx
NetApiBufferAllocate
NetApiBufferFree
NetApiBufferReallocate
NetApiBufferSize
NetAuditClear
NetAuditRead
NetAuditWrite
NetConfigGet
NetConfigGetAll
NetConfigSet
NetConnectionEnum
NetDfsAdd
NetDfsAddFtRoot
NetDfsAddStdRoot
NetDfsAddStdRootForced
NetDfsEnum
NetDfsGetClientInfo
NetDfsGetInfo
NetDfsManagerInitialize
NetDfsRemove
NetDfsRemoveFtRoot
NetDfsRemoveFtRootForced
NetDfsRemoveStdRoot
NetDfsSetClientInfo
NetDfsSetInfo
NetErrorLogClear
NetErrorLogRead
NetErrorLogWrite
NetFileClose
NetFileClose2
NetFileEnum
NetFileGetInfo
NetGetAnyDCName
NetGetDCName
NetGetDisplayInformationIndex
NetGetJoinableOUs
NetGetJoinInformation
NetGroupAdd
NetGroupAddUser

NetGroupDel
NetGroupDelUser
NetGroupEnum
NetGroupGetInfo
NetGroupGetUsers
NetGroupSetInfo
NetGroupSetUsers
NetJoinDomain
NetLocalGroupAdd
NetLocalGroupAddMember
NetLocalGroupAddMembers
NetLocalGroupDel
NetLocalGroupDelMember
NetLocalGroupDelMembers
NetLocalGroupEnum
NetLocalGroupGetInfo
NetLocalGroupGetMembers
NetLocalGroupSetInfo
NetLocalGroupSetMembers
NetMessagBufferSend
NetMessageNameAdd
NetMessageNameDel
NetMessageNameEnum
NetMessageNameGetInfo
NetQueryDisplayInformation
NetRemoteComputerSupports
NetRemoteTOD
NetRenameMachineInDomain
NetReplExportDirAdd
NetReplExportDirDel
NetReplExportDirEnum
NetReplExportDirGetInfo
NetReplExportDirLock
NetReplExportDirSetInfo
NetReplExportDirUnlock
NetReplGetInfo
NetReplImportDirAdd
NetReplImportDirDel
NetReplImportDirEnum
NetReplImportDirGetInfo
NetReplImportDirLock
NetReplImportDirUnlock
NetReplSetInfo
NetScheduleJobAdd

NetScheduleJobDel
NetScheduleJobEnum
NetScheduleJobGetInfo
NetSecurityGetInfo
NetServerComputerNameAdd
NetServerComputerNameDel
NetServerDiskEnum
NetServerEnum
NetServerGetInfo
NetServerSetInfo
NetServerTransportAdd
NetServerTransportAddEx
NetServerTransportDel
NetServerTransportEnum
NetServiceControl
NetServiceEnum
NetServiceGetInfo
NetServiceInstall
NetSessionDel
NetSessionEnum
NetSessionGetInfo
NetShareAdd
NetShareCheck
NetShareDel
NetShareEnum
NetShareGetInfo
NetShareSetInfo
NetStatisticsGet
NetUnjoinDomain
NetUseAdd
NetUseDel
NetUseEnum
NetUseGetInfo
NetUserAdd
NetUserChangePassword
NetUserDel
NetUserEnum
NetUserGetGroups
NetUserGetInfo
NetUserGetLocalGroups
NetUserModalsGet
NetUserModalsSet
NetUserSetGroups
NetUserSetInfo

NetValidateName
NetWkstaGetInfo
NetWkstaSetInfo
NetWkstaTransportAdd
NetWkstaTransportDel
NetWkstaTransportEnum
NetWkstaUserEnum
NetWkstaUserGetInfo
NetWkstaUserSetInfo
NotifyBootConfigStatus
NotifyChangeEventLog

O Functions

ObjectCloseAuditAlarm
ObjectDeleteAuditAlarm
ObjectOpenAuditAlarm
ObjectPrivilegeAuditAlarm
OemKeyScan
OemToAnsi
OemToAnsiBuff
OemToChar
OemToCharBuff
OffsetClipRgn
OffsetRect
OffsetRgn
OffsetViewportOrgEx
OffsetWindowOrgEx
OFNHookProc
OFNHookProcOldStyle
OpenBackupEventLog
OpenClipboard
OpenDesktop
OpenEvent
OpenEventLog
OpenFile
OpenFileMapping
OpenIcon
OpenInputDesktop
OpenJobObject
OpenMutex
OpenPrinter
OpenProcess
OpenProcessToken
OpenSCManager

OpenSemaphore
OpenService
OpenThread
OpenThreadToken
OpenWaitableTimer
OpenWindowStation
OutputDebugString
OutputProc

P Functions

PackDDElParam
PagePaintHook
PageSetupDlg
PageSetupHook
PaintDesktop
PaintRgn
PatBit
PathToRegion
PeekConsoleInput
PeekMessage
PeekNamedPipe
Pie
PlayEnhMetaFile
PlayEnhMetaFileRecord
PlayMetaFile
PlayMetaFileRecord
PlgBit
PolyBezier
PolyBezierTo
PolyDraw
Polygon
Polyline
PolylineTo
PolyPolygon
PolyPolyline
PolyTextOut
PostAppMessage
PostMessage
PostQueuedCompletionStatus
PostQuitMessage
PostThreadMessage
PrepareTape
PrintDlg
PrintDlgEx

PrintMessageBox
PrinterProperties
PrintHookProc
PrivilegeCheck
PrivilegedServiceAuditAlarm
Process32First
Process32Next
PropEnumProc
PropEnumProcEx
PtInRect
PtInRegion
PtVisible
PulseEvent
PurgeComm

Q Functions
QueryDosDevice
QueryInformationJobObject
QueryPerformanceCounter
QueryPerformanceFrequency
QueryRecoveryAgentsOnEncryptedFile
QueryServiceConfig
QueryServiceconfig2
QueryServiceLockStatus
QueryServiceObjectSecurity
QueryServiceStatus
QueryServiceStatusEx
QueryUsersOnEncryptedFile
QueueUserAPC
QueueUserWorkItem

R Functions
RaiseException
ReadConsole
ReadConsoleInput
ReadConsoleOutput
ReadConsoleOutputAttribute
ReadConsoleOutputCharacter
ReadDirectoryChangesW
ReadEventLog
ReadFile
ReadFileEx
ReadFileScatter

ReadPrinter
ReadProcessMemory
RealChildWindowFromPoint
RealGetWindowClass
RealizePalette
Rectangle
RectInRegion
RectVisible
RedrawWindow
RegCloseKey
RegConnectRegistry
RegCreateKey
RegCreateKeyEx
RegDeleteKey
RegDeleteValue
RegDisablePredefinedCache
RegEnumKey
RegEnumKeyEx
RegEnumValue
RegFlushKey
RegGetKeySecurity
RegisterClass
RegisterClassEx
RegisterClipboardFormat
RegisterDeviceNotification
RegisterEventSource
RegisterHotKey
RegisterServiceCtrlHandler
RegisterServiceCtrlHandlerEx
RegisterWaitForSingleObject
RegisterWindowMessage
RegLoadKey
RegNotifyChangeKeyValue
RegOpenCurrentUser
RegOpenKey
RegOpenKeyEx
RegOpenUserClassesRoot
RegOverridePredefKey
RegQueryInfoKey
RegQueryMultipleValues
RegQueryValue
RegQueryValueEx
RegReplaceKey
RegRestoreKey

RegSaveKey
RegSetKeySecurity
RegSetValue
RegSetValueEx
RegUnloadKey
ReleaseCapture
ReleaseDC
ReleaseMutex
ReleaseSemaphore
RemoveDirectory
RemoveFontMemResourceEx
RemoveFontResource
RemoveFontResourceEx
RemoveMenu
RemoveProp
RemoveUsersFromEncryptedFile
ReplaceFile
ReplaceText
ReplyMessage
ReportEvent
RequestWakeupLatency
ResetDC
ResetEvent
ResetPrinter
ResetWriteWatch
ResizePalette
RestoreDC
ResumeThread
ReuseDDElParam
RevertToSelf

S Functions
SaveDC
ScaleViewportExtEx
ScaleWindowExtEx
ScheduleJob
ScreenToClient
ScriptApplyDigitSubstitution
ScriptApplyLogicalWidth
ScriptBreak
ScriptCacheGetHeight
ScriptCPtoX
ScriptFreeCache
ScriptGetCMap

ScriptGetFontProperties
ScriptGetGlyphABCWidth
ScriptGetLogicalWidths
ScriptGetProperties
ScriptIsComplex
ScriptItemize
ScriptJustify
ScriptLayout
ScriptPlace
ScriptRecordDigitSubstitution
ScriptShape
ScriptString_pcOutChars
ScriptString_pLogAttr
ScriptString_pSize
ScriptStringAnalyse
ScriptStringCPtoX
ScriptStringFree
ScriptStringGetLogicalWidths
ScriptStringGetOrder
ScriptStringOut
ScriptStringValidate
ScriptStringXtoCP
ScriptTextOut
ScriptXtoCP
ScrollConsoleScreenBuffer
ScrollDC
ScrollWindow
ScrollwindowEx
SearchPath
SelectClipPath
SelectClipRgn
SelectObject
SelectPalette
SendAsyncProc
SendDlgItemMessage
SendInput
SendMessage
SendMessageCallback
SendMessageTimeout
SendNotifyMessage
ServiceMain
SetAbortProc
SetAclInformation
SetActiveWindow
SetArcDirection

SetBitmapBits
SetBitmapDimensionEx
SetBkColor
SetBkMode
SetBoundsRect
SetBrushOrgEx
SetCalendarInfo
SetCapture
SetCaretBlinkTime
SetCaretPos
SetClassLong
SetClassLongPtr
SetClassWord
SetClipboardData
SetClipboardViewer
SetColorAdjustment
SetCommBreak
SetCommConfig
SetCommMask
SetCommState
SetCommTimeouts
SetComputerName
SetComputerNameEx
SetConsoleActiveScreenBuffer
SetConsoleCP
SetConsoleCtrHandler
SetConsoleCursorInfo
SetConsoleCursorPosition
SetConsoleMode
SetConsoleOutputCP
SetConsoleScreenBufferSize
SetConsoleTextAttribute
SetConsoleTitle
SetConsoleWindowInfo
SetCriticalSectionSpinCount
SetCurrentDirectory
SetCursor
SetCursorPos
SetDCBrushColor
SetDCPenColor
SetDebugErrorLevel
SetDefaultCommConfig
SetDefaultPrinter
SetDIBColorTable
SetDIBits

SetDIBitsToDevice
SetDlgItemInt
SetDlgItemText
SetDoubleClickTime
SetEndOfFile
SetEnhMetaFileBits
SetEntriesInAcl
SetEnvironmentVariable
SetErrorMode
SetEvent
SetFileApisToANSI
SetFileApisToOEM
SetFileAttributes
SetFilePointer
SetFilePointerEx
SetFileSecurity
SetFileTime
SetFocus
SetForegroundWindow
SetForm
SetGraphicsMode
SetHandleCount
SetHandleInformation
SetInformationJobObject
SetJob
SetKernelObjectSecurity
SetKeyboardState
SetLastError
SetLastErrorEx
SetLayeredWindowAttributes
SetLayout
SetLocalInfo
SetLocalTime
SetMailslotInfo
SetMapMode
SetMapperFlags
SetMenu
SetMenuDefaultItem
SetMenuInfo
SetMenuItemBitmaps
SetMenuItemInfo
SetMessageExtraInfo
SetMessageQueue
SetMetaFileBitsEx
SetMetaRgn

SetMiterLimit
SetNamedPipeHandleState
SetNamedSecurityInfo
SetPaletteEntries
SetParent
SetPixel
SetPixelV
SetPolyFillMode
SetPort
SetPrinter
SetPrinterData
SetPrinterDataEx
SetPriorityClass
SetPrivateObjectSecurity
SetPrivateObjectSecurityEx
SetProcessAffinityMask
SetProcessDefaultLayout
SetProcessPriorityBoost
SetProcessShutdownParameters
SetProcessWindowStation
SetProcessWorkingSetSize
SetProp
SetRect
SetRectEmpty
SetRectRgn
SetROP2
SetScrollInfo
SetScrollPos
SetScrollRange
SetSecurityDescriptorControl
SetSecurityDescriptorDacl
SetSecurityDescriptorGroup
SetSecurityDescriptorOwner
SetSecurityDescriptorRMControl
SetSecurityDescriptorSacl
SetSecurityInfo
SetServiceBits
SetServiceObjectSecurity
SetServiceStatus
SetStdHandle
SetStretchBltMode
SetSwapAreaSize
SetSysColors
SetSysModalWindow
SetSystemCursor

SetSystemPaletteUse
SetSystemPowerState
SetSystemTime
SetSystemTimeAdjustment
SetTapeParameters
SetTapePosition
SetTextAlign
SetTextCharacterExtra
SetTextColor
SetTextJustification
SetThreadAffinityMask
SetThreadContext
SetThreadDesktop
SetThreadExecutionState
SetThreadIdealProcessor
SetThreadLocale
SetThreadPriority
SetThreadPriorityBoost
SetThreadToken
SetTimer
SetTimeZoneInformation
SetTokenInformation
SetUnhandledExceptionFilter
SetupComm
SetupDiCreateDeviceInfoList
SetupDiCreateDeviceInfoListEx
SetupDiCreateDeviceInterfaceRegKey
SetupDiDeleteDeviceInterfaceData
SetupDiDeleteDeviceInterfaceRegKey
SetupDiDestroyDeviceInfoList
SetupDiEnumDeviceInterfaces
SetupDiGetClassDevs
SetupDiGetClassDevsEx
SetupDiGetDeviceInterfaceAllias
SetupDiGetDeviceInterfaceDetail
SetupDiOpenClassRegKeyEx
SetupDiOpenDeviceInterface
SetupDiOpenDeviceInterfaceRegKey
SetupHookProc
SetUserFileEncryptionKey
SetUserObjectInformation
SetUserObjectSecurity
SetViewportExtEx
SetViewportOrgEx
SetVolumeLabel

SetVolumeMountPoint
SetWaitableTimer
SetWindowExtEx
SetWindowLong
SetWindowLongPtr
SetWindowOrgEx
SetWindowPlacement
SetWindowPos
SetwindowRgn
SetWindowsHook
SetWindowsHookEx
SetWindowText
SetWindowWord
SetWinMetaFileBits
SetWorldTransform
ShellProc
ShowCaret
ShowCursor
ShowOenedPopups
ShowScrollBar
ShowWindow
ShowWindowAsync
SignalObjectAndWait
SizeofResource
Sleep
SleepEx
StartDoc
StartDocPrinter
StartPage
StartPagePrinter
StartService
StartServiceCtrlDispatcher
StretchBlt
StretchDIBits
StrokeAndFillPath
StrokePath
SubtractRect
SuspendThread
SwapMouseButton
SwitchDesktop
SwitchToFiber
SwitchToThread
SysMsgProc
SystemParametersInfo

SystemTimeToFileTime
SystemTimeToTzSpecificLocalTime

T Functions
TabbedTextOut
TerminateJobObject
TerminateProcess
TerminateThread
TextOut
Thread32First
Thread32Next
ThreadProc
TileWindow
TimerAPCProc
TimerProc
TlsAlloc
TlsFree
TlsGetValue
TlsSetValue
ToAscii
ToAsciiEx
Toolhelp32ReadProcessMemory
ToUnicode
ToUnicodeEx
TrackMouseEvent
TrackPopupMenu
TrackPopupMenuEx
TransactNamedPipe
TranslateAccelerator
TranslateCharsetInfo
TranslateMDISysAccel
TranslateMessage
TranslateName
TransmitCommChar
TransparentBlt
TryEnterCriticalSection

U Functions
Uint32x32To64
UnhandledExceptionFilter
UnhookWindowsHook
UnhookWindowsHookEx
UnionRect

UnloadKeyboardLayout
UnloadUserProfile
UnlockFile
UnlockFileEx
UnlockResource
UnlockSegment
UnlockServiceDatabase
UnmapViewOfFile
UnpackDDElParam
UnrealizeObject
UnregisterClass
UnregisterDeviceNotification
UnregisterHotKey
UnregisterWait
UnregisterWaitEx
UpdateColors
UpdateLayeredWindow
UpdateResource
UpdateWindow
UserHandleGrantAccess

V Functions
ValidateRect
ValidateRgn
VerFindFile
VerifyVersionInfo
VerInstallFile
VerLanguageName
VerQueryValue
VirtualAlloc
VirtualAllocEx
VirtualFree
VirtualFreeEx
VirtualLock
VirtualProtect
VirtualProtectEx
VirtualQuery
VirtualQueryEx
VirtualUnlock
VkKeyScan
VkKeyScanEx

W Functions

WaitCommEvent
WaitForDebugEvent
WaitForInputIdle
WaitForMultipleObjects
WaitForMultipleObjectsEx
WaitForPrinterChange
WaitForSingleObject
WaitForSingleObjectEx
WaitMessage
WaitNamedPipe
WaitOrTimerCallback
WideCharToMultiByte
WidenPath
WindowFromDC
WindowFromPoint
WindowProc
WinExec
WinMain
WriteConsole
WriteConsoleInput
WriteConsoleOutput
WriteConsoleOutputAttribute
WriteConsoleOutputCharacter
WriteFile
WriteFileEx
WriteFileGather
WritePrinter
WritePrivateProfileSection
WritePrivateProfileString
WritePrivateProfileStruct
WriteProcessMemory
WriteProfileSection
WriteProfileString
WriteTapemark
wsprintf
wvsprintf

Y Functions
Yield

Z Functions
ZeroMemory

Win32 API Functions by Category (95)

1. Access Control
2. Access Control Editor
3. Atom
4. Bitmap
5. Brush
6. Button
7. Caret
8. Client/Server Access
   Control
9. Clipboard
10. Clipping
11. Color
12. Combo Box
13. Common Dialog Box
14. Communication
15. Console
16. Coordinate Space and
    Transformation
17. Cursor
18. Data Decompression
    Library
19. DbgHelp
20. Debugging
21. Device Context
22. Device Input and Output
23. Device Management

24. Dialog Box
25. Dynamic Data Exchange
26. Dynamic Data
    Exchange Management
27. Dynamic Link Library
28. Edit Control
29. Error Handling
30. Event Logging
31. File I/O
32. File Mapping
33. File System
34. Filled Shape
35. Font and Text
36. Handle and Object
37. Hook
38. Icon
39. ImageHlp
40. Input Method Editor
41. Keyboard Accelerator
42. Keyboard Input
43. Line and Curve
44. List Box
45. Low-Level Access Control
46. Mailslot
47. Memory Management
48. Menu

49. Message and Message
    Queue
50. Metafile
51. Mouse Input
52. Multiple Display Monitors
53. Multiple Document
    Interface
54. National Language
    Support
55. Network Management
56. Network DDE
57. Painting and Drawing
58. Path
59. Pen
60. Performance Monitoring
61. Pipe
62. Power Management
63. Printing and Print Spooler
64. Process, Thread and Job
65. PSAPI
66. Rectangle
67. Region
68. Registry
69. Resource
70. Rich Edit Control
71. Scroll Bar

1. Access Control Functions

Function	Description
The following functions are used with access tokens.	
AdjustTokenGroups	Changes the group information in an access token.
AdjustTokenPrivilages	Enables or disables the privilages in an access token. It does not grant new privilages or revoke existing ones.
CheckTokenMembership	Determines whether a specified SID is enabled in a specified access token.
CreateRestrictedToken	Creates a new token that is a restricted version of an existing token. The restricted token can have disabled SIDs, deleted privileges, and a list of restricting SIDs.
DuplicateToken	Creates a new impersonation token that duplicates an existing token.
DuplicateTokenEx	Creates a new primary token or impersonation token that duplicates an existing token.
GetTokenInformation	Retrieves information about a token.
IsTokenRestricted	Determines whether a token has a list of restricting SIDs.
OpenProcessToken	Retrieves a handle to the primary access token for a process.
OpenthreadToken	Retrieves a handle to the impersonation access token for a thread.
SetThreadToken	Assigns or removes an impersonation token for a thread.
SetTokenInformation	Changes a token's owner, primary group, or default DACL.

The following functions are used with privileges.	
AllocateLocallyUniqueId	Allocates a locally unique identifier (LUID).
LookupPrivilegeDisplayName	Retrieves a displayable name representing a specified privilege.
LoopupPrivilegeName	Retrieves the name corresponding to the privilege represented on a specific system by a specified LUID.

LoopupPrivilegeValue	Retrieves the LUID used on a specified system to locally represent the specified privilege name.

The following functions are used with security identifiers (SIDSs).

AllocateAndInitializeSid	Allocates and initializes a SID with the specified number of subauthorities.
ConvertSidToStringSid	Converts a SID to a string format suitable for display, storage, or transport.
ConvertStringSidToSid	Converts a string-format SID to a valid, functional SID.
CopySid	Copies a source SID to a buffer.
EqualPrefixSid	Test two SID prefix values for equality. A SID prefix is the entire SID except for the last subauthority value.
EqualSid	Tests two SIDs for equality. They must match exactly to be considered equal.
FreeSid	Frees a SID previously allocated by using the AllocateAndInitializeSid function.
GetLengthSid	Retrieves the length of a SID.
GetSidIdentifierAuthority	Retrieves a pointer to a SID's identifier authority.
GetSidLengthRequired	Retrieves the size of the buffer required to store a SID with a specified number of subauthorities.
GetSidSubAuthority	Retrieves a pointer to a specified subauthority in a SID.
GetSidSubAuthorityCount	Retrieves the number of subauthorities in a SID.
InitializeSid	Initializes a SID structure.
IsValidSid	Tests the validity of a SID by verifying that the revision number is within a known range and that the number of subauthorities is less than the maximum.
LookupAccountName	Retrieves the SID corresponding to a specified account name.
LookupAccountSid	Retrieves the account name corresponding to a specified SID.

The following functions are used with security descriptors

ConvertSecurityDescriptorToStringSecurityDescriptor	Converts a security descriptor to a string format.
ConvertStringSecurityDescriptorToSecurityDescriptor	Converts a string-format security descriptor into a valid, functional security descriptor.
GetNamedSecurityInfo	Retrieves a copy of the security descriptor for an object specified by name.
GetSecurityDescriptroControl	Retrieves a security descriptor's control and revision information.
GetSecurityDescriptorRMControl	Retrieves the resource manager control bits.
GetSecurityInfo	Retrieves a copy of the security descriptor for an object specified by a handle.

SetNamedSecurityInfo	Sets specified security information in the security descriptor of a specified object.
SetSecurityDescriptorControl	Sets the control bits of a security descriptor.
SetSecurityDescriptorRMControl	Sets the resource manager control bits.
SetSecurityInfo	Sets specified security information in the security descriptor of a specified object.

The following functions are used to manipulate access-control lists.

BuildExplicitAccessWithName	Initializes an EXPLICIT_ACCESS structure.
BuildTrusteeWithName	Initializes a TRUSTEE structure. The caller specifies the trustee name.
BuildTrusteeWithObjectsAndName	Initializes a TRUSTEE structure with the specified object-specific ACE information.
BuildTrusteeWithObjectsAndSid	Initializes a TRUSTEE structure with the specified object-specific ACE information.
BuildTrusteeWithSid	Initializes a TRUSTEE structure. The caller specifies the security identifier of the trustee.
GetAuditedPermissionFromAcl	Retrieves the audited access rights for a specified trustee.
GetEffectiveRightsFromAcl	Retrieves the effective access rights that an ACL grants to a specified trustee.
GetExplicitEntriesFromAcl	Retrieves an array of structures that describe the ACEs in an ACL.
GetTrusteeForm	Retrieves the trustee from a TRUSTEE structure.
GetTrusteeName	Retrieves the trustee name from a TRUSTEE structure.
GetTrusteeType	Retrieves the trustee type from a TRUSTEE structure.
SetEntriesInAcl	Creates a new ACL by merging new access-control of audit-control information into an existing ACL.

2. Access Control Editor Functions

The following functions are used with the access control editor.

| CreateSecurityPage | Creates a basic security property page that enables the user to view and edit the access rights allowed or denied by the ACEs in an object's DACL. |
| EditSecurity | Displays a property sheet that contains a basic security property page. |

3. Atom Functions

AddAtom	Adds a character string to the local atom table.
DeleteAtom	Decrements the reference count of a local string atom.
FindAtom	Searches the local atom table for the specified character string.

GetAtomName	Retrieves a copy of the character string associated with the specified local atom.
GlobalAddAtom	Adds a character string to the global atom table.
GlobalDeleteAtom	Decrements the reference count of a global string atom.
GlobalFindAtom	Searches the global atom table for the specified character string.
GlobalGetAtomName	Retrieves a copy of the character string associated with the specified global atom.
InitAtomTable	Initializes the local atom table.

4. Bitmap Functions

AlphaBlend	Displays a bitmap with transparent or semitransparent pixels.
BitBlt	Performs a bit-block transfer.
CreateBitmap	Creates a bitmap
CreateBitmapIndirect	Creates a bitmap.
CreateCompatibleBitmap	Creates a bitmap compatible with a device.
CreateDIBitmap	Creates a device-dependent bitmap (DDB) from a DIB.
CreateDIBSection	Creates a DIB that applications can write to directly.
ExtFloodFill	Fills an area of the display surface with the current brush.
GetBitmapDimensionEx	Gets the dimensions of a bitmap.
GetDIBColorTable	Retrieves RGB color values from a DIB section.
GetDIBits	Copies a bitmap into a buffer.
GetPixel	Gets the RGB color value of the pixel at a given coordinate.
GetStretchBltMode	Gets the current stretching mode.
GradientFill	Fills rectangle and triangle structures.
LoadBitmap	Loads a bitmap from a module's executable file.
MaskBlt	Combines the color data in the source and destination bitmaps.
PlgBlt	Performs a bit-block transfer.
SetBitmapDimensionEx	Sets the preferred dimensions to a bitmap.
SetDIBColorTable	Sets RGB values in a DIB.
SetDIBits	Sets the pixels in a bitmap using color data from a DIB.
SetDIBitsToDevice	Sets the pixels in a rectangle using color data from a DIB.
SetPixel	Sets the color for a pixel.
SetPixelV	Sets a pixel to the best approximation of a color.
SetStretchBltMode	Sets the bitmap stretching mode.
StretchBlt	Copies a bitmap and stretches or compresses it.
StretchDIBits	Copies the color data in a DIB.
TransparentBlt	Performs a bit-block transfer of color data.

5. Brush Functions

CreateBrushIndirect	Creates a brush with a specified style, color, and pattern.
CreateDIBPatternBrushPt	Creates a brush with the pattern from a DIB.
CreateHatchBrush	Creates a brush with a hatch pattern and color.
CreatePatternBrush	Creates a brush with a bitmap pattern.
CreateSolidBrush	Creates a brush with a solid color.
GetBrushOrgEx	Gets the brush origin for a device context.
GetSysColorBrush	Gets a handle for a brush that corresponds to a color index.
PatBlt	Paints a rectangle.
SetBrushOrgEx	Sets the brush origin for a device context.

6. Button Functions

CheckDlgButton	Changes the check state of a button control.
CheckRadioButton	Adds a check mark to a specified radio button in a group and removes a check mark from all other radio buttons in the group.
IsDlgButtonChecked	Determines whether a button control has a check mark next to it or whether a three-state button control is grayed, checked, or neither.

7. Caret Functions

CreateCaret	Creates a new shape for the system caret and assigns ownership of the caret to the specified window.
DestroyCaret	Destroys the caret's current shape, frees the caret from the window, and removes the caret from the screen.
GetCaretBlinkTime	Retrieves the time required to invert the caret's pixels.
GetCaretPos	Copies the caret's position to the specified POINT structure.
HideCaret	Removes the caret from the screen.
SetCaretBlinkTime	Sets the caret blink time to the specified number of milliseconds.
SetCaretPos	Moves the caret to the specified coordinates.
ShowCaret	Makes the caret visible on the screen at the caret's current position.

8. Client/Server Access Control Functions

The following functions are used by servers to impersonate clients.

CreateProcessAsUser	Windows NT 3.51 and later
CreateProcesswithLogonW	Windows 2000
ImpersonalLoggedOnUser	Windows NT 3.51 and later
ImpersonateNamedPipeClient	Windows NT 3.51 and later

ImpersonateSelf	Windows NT 3.51 and later
LogonUser	Windows NT 3.51 and later
RevertToSelf	Windows NT 3.1 and later

The following functions are used by servers to check and set the security descriptors on private objects.

AccessCheck	Windows NT 3.1 and later
AccessCheckAndAuditAlarm	Windows NT 3.1 and later
AccessCheckByType	Windows 2000
AccessCheckByTypeAndAuditAlarm	Windows 2000
AccessCheckByTyperesultList	Windows 2000
AccessCheckByTypeResultListAndAuditAlarm	Windows 2000
AccessCheckByTypeResultListAndAuditAlarmByHandle	Windows 2000
AreAllAccessesGranted	Windows NT 3.1 and later
AreAnyAccessesGranted	Windows NT 3.1 and later
BuildSecurityDescriptor	Windows NT 4.0 and later
ConvertToAutoInheritPrivateObjectSecurity	Windows 2000
CreatePrivateObjectSecurity	Windows NT 3.1 and later
CreatePrivateObjectSecurityEx	Windows 2000
DestroyPrivateObjectSecurity	Windows NT 3.1 and later
GetPrivateObjectSecurity	Windows NT 3.1 and later
LookupSecurityDescriptorParts	Windows NT 4.0 and later
MapGenericMask	Windows NT 3.1 and later
PrivilegeCheck	Windows NT 3.1 and later
SetPrivateObjectSecurity	Windows NT 3.1 and later
SetPrivateObjectSecurityEx	Windows 2000

The following functions are used by servers to generate audit messages in the security event log.

ObjectCloseAuditAlarm	Windows NT 3.1 and later
ObjectPrivilegeAuditAlarm	Windows NT 3.1 and later
PrivilegedServiceAuditAlarm	Windows NT 3.1 and later

9. Clipboard Functions

ChangeClipboardChain	Removes a specified window from the chain of clipboard viewers.
CloseClipboard	Closes the clipboard.
CountClipboardFormats	Retrieves the number of different data formats currently on the clipboard.

EmptyClipboard	Empties the clipboard and frees handles to data in the clipboard.
EnumClipboardFormats	Enumerates the data formats currently available on the clipboard.
GetClipboardData	Retrieves data from the clipboard in a specified format.
GetClipboardFormatName	Retrieves from the clipboard the name of the specified registered format.
GetClipboardOwner	Retrieves the window handle of the current owner of the clipboard.
GetClipboardSequenceNumber	Retrieves the clipboard sequence number for the current window station.
GetClipboardViewer	Retrieves the handle to the first window in the clipboard viewer chain.
GetOpenClipboardWindow	Retrieves the handle to the window that currently has the clipboard open.
GetPriorityClipboardFormat	Retrieves the first available clipboard format in the specified list.
Is ClipboardFormatAvailable	Determines whether the clipboard contains data in the specified format.
OpenClipboard	Opens the clipboard for examination and prevents other applications from modifying the clipboard content.
RegisterClipboardFormat	Registers a new clipboard format.
SetClipboardData	Places data on the clipboard in a specified clipboard format.
SetClipboardViewer	Adds the specified window to the chain of clipboard viewers.

10. Clipping Functions

ExcludeClipRect	Creates a new clipping region that consists of the existing clipping region minus the specified rectangle.
ExtSelectClipRgn	Combines the specified region with the current clipping region using the specified mode.
GetClipBox	Retrieves the dimensions of the tightest bounding rectangle that can be drawn around the current visible area on the device.
GetClipRgn	Retrieves a handle identifying the current application-defined clipping region for the specified device context.
GetMetaRgn	Retrieves the current meta region for the specified device context.
GetRandomRgn	Copies the system clipping region of a specified device context to a specific region.
IntersectClipRect	Creates a new clipping region from the intersection of the current clipping region and the specified rectangle.
OffsetClipRgn	Moves the clipping region of a device context by the specified offsets.

PtVisible	Determines whether the specified point is within the clipping region of a device context.
RectVisible	Determines whether any part of the specified rectangle lies within the clipping region of a device context.
SelectClipPath	Selects the current path as a clipping region for a device context, combining the new region with any existing clipping region by using the specified mode.
SelectClipRgn	Selects a region as the current clipping region for the specified device context.
SetMetaRgn	Intersects the current clipping region for the specified device context with the current metaregion and saves the combined region as the new metaregion for the specified device context.

11. Color Functions

AnimatePalette	Replaces entries in the specified logical palette.
CreateHalftonePalette	Creates a halftone palette for the specified device context (DC).
CreatePalette	Creates a logical palette.
GetColorAdjustment	Retrieves the color adjustment values for the specified DC.
GetNearestColor	Retrieves a color value identifying a color from the system palette that will be displayed when the specified color value is used.
GetNearestPaletteIndex	Retrieves the index for the entry in the specified logical palette most closely matching a specified color value.
GetpaletteEntries	Retrieves a specified range of palette entries from the given logical palette.
GetSystemPaletteEntries	Retrieves a range of palette entries from the system palette that is associated with the specified DC.
GetSystemPaletteUse	Retrieves the current state of the system (physical) palette for the specified DC.
RealizePalette	Maps palette entries from the current logical palette to the system palette.
ResizePalette	Increases or decreases the size of a logical palette based on the specified value.
SelectPalette	Selects the specified logical palette into a device context.
SetColorAdjustment	Sets the color adjustment values for a DC using the specified values.
SetPaletteEntries	Sets RGB (red, green, blue) color values and flags in a range of entries in a logical palette.
SetSystemPaletteUse static colors.	Allows an application to specify whether the system palette contains 2 or 20
UnrealizeObject	Resets the origin of a brush or resets a logical palette.
UpdateColors	Updates the client area of the specified device context by remapping the current colors in the client area to the currently realized logical palette.

12. Combo Box Functions

DlgDirListComboBox	Replaces the contents of a combo box with the names of specified subdirectories and files.
DlgDirSelectComboBoxEx	Retrieves the current selection from a combo box filled by using the DlgDirListComboBox function.
GetComboBoxInfo	Retrieves information about a specified combo box.

13. Common Dialog Box Functions

ChooseColor	Creates a Color dialog box that enables the user to select a color.
ChooseFont	Creates a Font dialog box that enables the user to choose attributes for a logical font.
CommDlgExtendedError	Returns a common dialog box error code.
FindText	Creates a system-defined modeless Find dialog box that lets the user specify a string to search for and options to use when searching for text in a document.
GetFileTitle	Retrieves the name of the specified file.
GetOpenFileName	Creates an Open dialog box that lets the user specify the drive, directory, and the name of a file or set of files to open.
GetSaveFileName	Creates a Save dialog box that lets the user specify the drive, directory, and name of a file to save.
PageSetupDlg	Creates a Page Setup dialog box that enables the user to specify the attributes of a printed page.
PrintDlg	Displays a Print dialog box.
PrintDlgEx	Displays a Print property sheet that enables the user to specify the properties of a particular print job.
ReplaceText	Creates a system-defined modeless dialog box that lets the user specify a string to search for and a replacement string, as well as options to control the find and replace operations.

14. Communication Functions

BuildCommDCB	Fills a specified DCB structure with values specified in a device-control string.
BuildCommDCBAndTimeouts	Translates a device-definition string into appropriate device-control block codes and places them into a device-control block.
ClearCommBreak	Restores character transmission for a specified communications device and places the transmission line in a nonbreak state.
ClearCommError	Retrieves information about a communications error and reports the current status of a communication device.

CommConfigDialog	Displays a driver-supplied configuration dialog box.
EscapeCommFunction	Directs a specified communications device to perform an extended function.
GetCommConfig	Retrieves the current configuration of a communications device.
GetCommMask	Retrieves the value of the event mask for a specified communications device.
GetCommModemStatus	Retrieves modem control-register values.
GetCommProperties	Retrieves information about the communications properties for a specified communications device.
GetCommState	Retrieves the current control settings for a specified communications device.
GetCommTimeouts	Retrieves the time-out parameters for all read and write operations on a specified communications device.
GetDefaultCommConfig	Retrieves the default configuration for the specified communications device.
PurgeComm	Discards all characters from the output or input buffer of a specified communications resource.
SetCommBreak	Suspends character transmission for a specified communications device and places the transmission line in a break state.
SetCommConfig	Sets the current configuration of a communications device.
SetCommMask	Specifies a set of events to be monitored for a communications device.
SetCommState	Configures a communications device according to the specifications in a device-control block.
SetCommTimeouts	Sets the time-out parameters for all read and write operations on a specified communications device.
SetDefaultCommConfig	Sets the default configuration for a communications device.
SetupComm	Initializes the communications parameters for a specified communications device.
TransmitCommChar	Transmits a specified character ahead of any pending data in the output buffer of the specified communications device.
WaitCommEvent	Waits for an event to occur for a specified communication device.

15. Console Functions

AllocConsole	Allocates a new console for the calling process.
CreateConsoleScreenBuffer	Creates a console screen buffer.
FillconsoleOutputAttribute	Sets the text and background color attributes for a specified number of character cells.

FillConsoleOutputCharacter	Writes a character to the screen buffer a specified number of times.
FlushConsoleInputBuffer	Flushes the console input buffer.
FreeConsole	Detaches the calling process from its console.
GenerateConsoleCtrlEvent	Sends a specified signal to a console process group that shares the console associated with the calling process.
GetConsoleCP	Retrieves the input code page used by the console associated with the calling process.
GetConsoleCursorInfo	Retrieves information about the size and visibility of the cursor for the specified console screen buffer.
GetConsoleMode	Retrieves the current input mode of a console's input buffer or the current output mode of a console screen buffer.
GetConsoleOutputCP	Retrieves the output code page used by the console associated with the calling process.
GetConsoleScreenBufferInfo	Retrieves information about the specified console screen buffer.
GetConsoleTitle	Retrieves the title bar string for the current console window.
GetLargestConsoleWindowSize	Retrieves the size of the largest possible console window.
GetNumberOfConsoleInputEvents	Retrieves the number of unread input records in the console's input buffer.
GetNumberOfConsoleMouseButtons	Retrieves the number of buttons on the mouse used by the current console.
GetStdHandle	Retrieves a handle for the standard input, standard output, or standard error device.
HandlerRoutine	An application-defined function used with the SetConsoleCtrlHandler function.
PeekConsoleInput	Reads data from the specified console input buffer without removing it from the buffer.
ReadConsole	Reads character input from the console input buffer and removes it from the buffer.
ReadConsoleInput	Reads data from a console input buffer and removes it from the buffer.
ReadConsoleOutput	Reads character and color attribute data from a rectangular block of character cells in a console screen buffer.
ReadConsoleOutputAttribute	Copies a specified number of foreground and background color attributes from consecutive cells of a console screen buffer.
ReadConsoleOutputCharacter	Copies a number of characters from consecutive cells of a console screen buffer.
ReadConsoleOutputAttribute	Copies a specified number of foreground and background color attributes form consecutive cells of a console screen buffer.

ReadConsoleOutputCharacter	Copies a number of characters from consecutive cells of a console screen buffer.
ScrollConsoleScreenBuffer	Moves a block of data in a screen buffer.
SetConsoleActiveScreenBuffer	Sets the specified screen buffer to be the currently displayed console screen buffer.
SetConsoleCP	Sets the input code page used by the console associated with the calling process.
SetConsoleCtrlHandler	Adds or removes an application-defined HandlerRoutine from the list of handler functions for the calling process.
SetConsoleCursorInfo	Sets the size and visibility of the cursor for the specified console screen buffer.
SetConsoleCursorPosition	Sets the cursor position in the specified console screen buffer.
SetConsoleMode	Sets the input mode of a console's input buffer or the output mode of a console screen buffer.
SetConsoleOutputCP	Sets the output code page used by the console associated with the calling process.
SetConsoleScreenBufferSize	Changes the size of the specified console screen buffer.
SetConsoleTextAttribute	Sets the foreground (text) and background color attributes of characters written to the screen buffer.
SetConsoleTitle	Sets the title bar string for the current console window.
SetConsoleWindowInfo	Sets the current size and position of a console screen buffer's window.
SetStdHandle	Sets the handle for the standard input, standard output, or standard error device.
WriteConsole	Writes a character string to a console screen buffer beginning at the current cursor location.
WriteConsoleInput	Writes data directly to the console input buffer.
WriteConsoleOutput	Writes character and color attribute data to a specified rectangular block of character cells in a console screen buffer.
WriteConsoleOutputAttribute	Copies a number of foreground and background color attributes to consecutive cells of a console screen buffer.
WriteConsoleOutputCharacter	Copies a number of characters to consecutive cells of a console screen buffer.

16. Coordinate Space and Transformation Functions

ClientToScreen	Converts the client-area coordinates of a specified point to screen coordinates.
CombineTransform	Concatenates two world-space to page-space transformations.
DPtoLP	Converts device coordinates into logical coordinates.

GetCurrentPositionEx	Retrieves the current position in logical coordinates.
GetGraphicsMode	Retrieves the current graphics mode for the specified device context.
GetMapMode	Retrieves the current mapping mode.
GetViewportExtEx	Retrieves the x-extent and y-extent of the current viewport for the specified device context.
GetViewportOrgEx	Retrieves the x-coordinates and y-coordinates of the viewport origin for the specified device context.
GetWindowExtEx	Retrieves the x-extent and y-extent of the window for the specified device context.
GetWindowOrgEx	Retrieves the x-coordinates and y-coordinates of the window origin for the specified device context.
GetWorldTransform	Retrieves the current world-space to page-space transformation.
LptoDP	Converts logical coordinates into device coordinates.
MapWindowPoints	Converts (maps) a set of points from a coordinate space relative to one window to a coordinate space relative to another window.
ModifyWorldTransform	Changes the world transformation for a device context using the specified mode.
OffsetViewportOrgEx	Modifies the viewport origin for a device context using the specified horizontal and vertical offsets.
OffsetWindowOrgEx	Modifies the window origin for a device context using the specified horizontal and vertical offsets.
ScaleViewportExtEx	Modifies the viewport for a device context using the ratios formed by the specified multiplicands and divisors.
ScalewindowExtEx	Modifies the window for a device context using the ratios formed by the specified multiplicands and divisors.
ScreenToClient	Converts the screen coordinates of a specified point on the screen to client coordinates.
SetGraphicsMode	Sets the graphics mode for the specified device context.
SetMapMode	Sets the mapping mode of the specified device context.
SetViewportExtEx	Sets the horizontal and vertical extents of the viewport for a device context by using the specified value.
SetViewportOrgEx	Specifies which device point maps to the window origin (0,0).
SetWindowExtEx	Sets the horizontal and vertical extents of the window for a device context by using the specified values.
SetWindowOrgEx	Specifies which window point maps to the viewport origin (0,0).
SetworldTransform	Sets a two-dimensional linear transformation between world space and page space for the specified device context.

17. Cursor Functions

ClipCursor	Confines the cursor to a rectangular area on the screen.
CopyCursor	Copies the specified cursor.
CreateCursor	Creates a cursor having the specified size, bit patterns, and hot spot.
DestroyCursor	Destroys a cursor.
GetClipCursor	Retrieves the screen coordinates of the rectangular area to which the cursor is confined.
GetCursor	Retrieves a handle to the current cursor.
GetCursorInfo	Retrieves information about the global cursor.
GetCursorPos	Retrieves the cursor's position.
LoadCursor	Loads a cursor resource from an executable file.
LoadCursorFromFile	Creates a cursor based on data contained in a file.
SetCursor	Sets the cursor shape.
SetCursorPos	Moves the cursor to the specified screen coordinates.
SetSystemCursor	Enables an application to customize the system cursors.
ShowCursor	Displays or hides the cursor.

18. Data Decompression Library Functions

GetExpandedName	Retrieves the original name of a compressed file.
LZClose	Closes a file that was opened by using LZOpenFile.
LZCopy	Copies a source file to a destination file. If the source file is compressed with the Microsoft File Compression Utility (COMPRESS.EXE), this function creates a decompressed destination file.
LZInit	Allocates memory for the internal data structures required to decompress files, and then creates and initializes them.
LZOpenFile	Creates, opens, reopens, or deletes the specified file.
LZRead	Reads (at most) the specified number of bytes from a file and copies them into a buffer.
LZSeek	Moves a file pointer a number of bytes from a starting position.

19. DbgHelp Functions

General

ImagehlpApiVersion

ImagehlpApiVersionEx

MakeSureDirectoryPathExists

SearchTreeForFile

Debugger

The debugging service functions are the functions most suited for use by a debugger or the debugging code in an application. These functions can be used in concert with the symbol handler functions for easier use.

EnumeratedLoadedModules

EnumLoadModulesProc

FindDebugFileProc

FindDebugInfoFile

FindDebugInfoFileEx

FindExecutableImage

FindExecutableImageEx

FindExeFileProc

FunctionTableAccessProc

GetModuleBaseProc

ReadProcessMemoryProc

StackWalk

TranslateAddressProc

UnDecorateSymbolName

Image Access

The image access functions access the data in an executable image. The functions provide high-level access to the base of images and very specific to the most common parts of an image's data.

GetTimestampForLoadedLibrary

ImageDirectoryEntryToData

ImageDirectoryEntryToDataEx

ImageNtHeader

ImageRvaToSection

ImageRvaToVa

Symbol Handler

The symbol handler functions give applications easy and portable access to the symbolic debugging information of an image. These functions should be used exclusively to ensure access to symbolic information. This is necessary because these functions isolate the application from the symbol format.

SymbolRegisteredCallback

SymbolRegisteredFunctionEntryCallback

SymCleanup

SymEnumerateModules

SymEnumerateSymbols

SymEnumModulesCallback

SymEnumSymbolsCallback

SymFunctionTableAccess

SymGetLineFromAddr

SymGetLineFromName

SymGetLineNext

SymGetLinePrev

SymGetModuleBase

SymGetModuleInfo

SymGetModuleInfoEx

SymGetOptions

SymGetSearchPath

SymGetSymbolInfo

SymGetSymFromAddr

SymGetSymFromName

SymGetSymNext

SymGetSymPrev

SymInitialize

SymLoadModule

SymMatchFileName

SymRegisterCallback

SymRegisterFunctionEntryCallback

SymSetOptions

SymSetSearchPath

SymTypeNameCallback

SymUnDName

SymUnloadModule

20. Debugging Functions

ContinueDebugEvent	Enables a debugger to continue a thread that previously reported a debugging event.
DebugActiveProcess	Enables a debugger to attach to an active process and debug it.
DebugBreak	Causes a breakpoint exception to occur in the current process.
FatalExit	Transfers execution control to the debugger.
FlushInstructionCache	Flushes the instruction cache for the specified process.

GetThreadContext	Retrieves the context of the specified thread.
GetThreadSelectorEntry	Retrieves a descriptor table entry for the specified selector and thread.
IsDebuggerPresent	Determines whether the calling process is running under the context of a debugger.
OutputDebugString	Sends a string to the debugger for display.
ReadProcessMemory	Reads data from an area of memory in a specified process.
SetThreadContext	Sets the context for the specified thread.
WaitForDebugEvent	Waits for a debugging event to occur in a process being debugged.
WriteProcessMemory	Writes data to an area of memory in a specified process.

21. Device Context Functions

CancelDC	Cancels any pending operation on the specified device context.
ChangeDisplaySettings	Changes the settings of the default display device to the specified graphics mode.
ChangeDisplaySettingsEx	Changes the settings of the specified display device to the specified graphics mode.
CreateCompatibleDC	Creates a memory device context compatible with the specified device.
CreateDC	Creates a device context for a device using the specified name.
CreateIC	Creates an information context for the specified device.
DeleteDC	Deletes the specified device context.
DeleteObject	Deletes a logical pen, brush, font, bitmap, region, or palette, freeing all system resources associated with the object.
DeviceCapabilities	Retrieves the capabilities of a printer device driver.
DrawEscape	Provides drawing capabilities of the specified video display that are not directly available through the graphics device interface.
EnumDisplayDevices	Retrieves information about the display devices in a system.
EnumDisplaySettings	Retrieves information about one of the graphics modes for a display device.
EnumDisplaySettingsEx	Retrieves information about one of the graphics modes for a display device.
EnumObjects	Enumerates the pens or brushes available for the specified device context.
EnumObjectsProc	An application-defined callback function used with the EnumObjects function.
GetCurrentObject	Retrieves a handle to an object of the specified type that has been selected into the specified device context.

GetDC	Retrieves a handle to a display device context for the client area of a specified window or for the entire screen.
CreateCompatibleDC	Creates a memory device context compatible with the specified device.
CreateDC	Creates a device context for a device using the specified name.
CreateIC	Creates an information context for the specified device.
DeleteDC	Deletes the specified device context.
DeleteObject	Deletes a logical pen, brush, font, bitmap, region, or palette, freeing all system resources associated with the object.
DeviceCapabilities	Retrieves the capabilities of a printer device driver.
DrawEscape	Provides drawing capabilities of the specified video display that are not directly available through the graphics device interface.
EnumDisplayDevices	Retrieves information about the display devices in a system.
EnumDisplaySettings	Retrieves information about one of the graphics modes for a display device.
EnumDisplaySettingsEx	Retrieves information about one of the graphics modes for a display device.
EnumObjects	Enumerates the pens or brushes available for the specified device context.
EnumObjectsProc	An application-defined callback function used with the EnumObjects function.
GetCurrentObject	Retrieves a handle to an object of the specified type that has been selected into the specified device context.
GetDC	Retrieves a handle to a display device context for the client area of a specified window or for the entire screen.
GetDCBrushColor	Retrieves the current brush color for the specified device context.
GetDCEx	Retrieves a handle to a display device context for the client area of a specified window or for the entire screen.
GetDCOrgEx	Retrieves the final translation origin for a specified device context.
GetDCPenColor	Retrieves the current pen color for the specified device context.
GetDeviceCaps	Retrieves device-specific information for the specified device.
GetObject	Retrieves information for the specified graphics object.
GetObjectType	Retrieves the type of the specified object.
GetStockObject	Retrieves a handle to one of the stock pens, brushes, fonts, or palettes.
ReleaseDC	Releases a device context, freeing it for use by other applications.

ResetDC	Updates the specified printer or plotter device context using the specified information.
RestoreDC	Restores a device context to the specified state.
SaveDC	Saves the current state of the specified device context by copying data describing selected objects and graphic modes to a context stack.
SelectObject	Selects an object into the specified device context.
SetDCBrushColor	Sets the current device context brush color to the specified color value.
SetDCPenColor	Sets the current device context pen color to the specified color value.

22. Device Input and Output Functions

DeviceIoControl	Sends a control code directly to a specified device driver.

23. Device Management Functions

RegisterDeviceNotification	Specifies the device or type of device for which a window will receive notifications.
SetupDiCreateDeviceInfoList	Creates an empty device information set.
SetupDiCreateDeviceInfoListEx	Creates an empty device information set for a local or remote computer.
SetupDiCreateDeviceInterfaceRegKey	Creates a registry key for storing information about a device interface instance.
SetupDiDeleteDeviceInterfaceData	Deletes a device interface from a device information set.
SetupDiDeleteDeviceInterfaceRegKey	Deletes the registry subkey used by applications and drivers to store information specific to a device interface instance.
SetupDiDestroyDeviceInfoList	Destroys a device information set and frees all associated memory.
SetupDiEnumDeviceInterfaces	Retrieves a context structure for a device interface of a device information set.
SetupDiGetClassDevs	Retrieves a device information set that contains all devices of a specified class.
SetupDiGetClassDevsEx	Retrieves a device information set that contains all devices of a specified class on a local or remote computer.
SetupDiGetDeviceInterfaceAlias	Retrieves an alias for the specified device interface.
SetupDiGetDeviceInterfaceDetail	Retrieves detailed information about a specified device interface.
SetupDiOpenClassRegKeyEx	Opens the registry key for the device setup or interface class, or a subkey for a specific class.
SetupDiOpenDeviceInterface	Retrieves information about an existing device interface and adds it to the specified device information set.

SetupDiOpenDeviceInterfaceRegKey	Opens the registry subkey that applications and drivers use to store information specific to a device interface instance.
UnregisterDeviceNotification	Closes the specified device notification handle.

24. Dialog Box Functions

CreateDialog	Creates a modeless dialog box from a dialog box template resource.
CreateDialogIndirect	Creates a modeless dialog box from a dialog box template in memory.
CreateDialogIndirectParam	Creates a modeless dialog box from a dialog box template in memory.
CreateDialogParam	Creates a modeless dialog box from a dialog box template resource.
DefDlgProc	Calls the default dialog box window procedure to provide default processing for any window messages that a dialog box with a private window class does not process.
DialogBox	Creates a modal dialog box from a dialog box template resource.
DialogBoxIndirect	Creates a modal dialog box from a dialog box template in memory.
DialogBoxIndirectParam	Creates a modal dialog box from a dialog box template in memory.
DialogBoxParam	Creates a modal dialog box from a dialog box template resource.
DialogProc	An application-defined callback function used with the CreateDialog and DialogBox families of functions.
EndDialog	Destroys a modal dialog box.
GetDialogBaseUnits	Retrieves the system's dialog base units.
GetDlgCtrlID	Retrieves the identifier of the specified control
GetDlgItem	Retrieves a handle to a control in the specified dialog box.
GetDlgItemInt	Translates the text of a specified control in a dialog box into an integer value.
GetDlgItemText	Retrieves the title or text associated with a control in a dialog box.
GetNextDlgGroupItem	Retrieves a handle to the first control in a group of controls that precedes (or follows) the specified control.
GetNextDlgTabItem	Retrieves a handle to the first control that has the WS_TABSTOP style that precedes (or follows) the specified control.
IsDialogMessage	Determines whether a message is intended for the specified dialog box.

MapDialogRect	Converts the specified dialog box units to screen units (pixels).
MessageBox	Creates, displays, and operates a message box.
MessageBoxEx	Creates, displays, and operates a message box.
MessageBoxIndirect	Creates, displays, and operates a message box.
SendDlgItemMessage	Sends a message to the specified control in a dialog box.
SetDlgItemInt	Sets the text of a control in a dialog box to the string representation of a specified integer value.
SetDlgItemText	Sets the title or text of a control in a dialog box.

25. Dynamic Data Exchange Functions

DdeSetQualityOfService	Specifies the quality of service a raw DDE application desires for future DDE conversations it initiates.
FreeDDElParam	Frees the memory specified by the lParam parameter of a posted DDE message.
ImpersonateDdeClientWindow	Enables a DDE server application to impersonate a DDE client application's security context.
PackDDElParam	Packs a DDE lParam value into an internal structure used for sharing DDE data between processes.
ReuseDDElParam	Enables an application to reuse a packed DDE lParam paramter.
UnpackDDElParam	Unpacks a DDE lParam value received from a posted DDE message.

26. Dynamic Data Exchange Management Functions

DdeAbandonTransaction	Abandons the specified asynchronous transaction and releases all resources associated with the transaction.
DdeAccessData	Provides access to the data in the specified dynamic data exchange (DDE) object.
DdeAddData	Adds data to the specified dynamic data exchange (DDE) object.
DdeCallBack	An application-defined callback function used with the DDEML functions.
DdeClientTransaction	Begins a data transaction between a client and a server.
DdeCmpStringHandles	Compares the values of two string handles.
DdeConnect	Establishes a conversation with a server application that supports the specified service name and topic name pair.
DdeConnectList	Establishes a conversation with all server applications that support the specified service name and topic name pair.

DdeCreateDataHandle	Creates a DDE object and fills the object with data from the specified buffer.
DdeCreateStringHandle	Creates a handle that identifies the specified string.
DdeDisconnect	Terminates a DDE conversation.
DdeDisconnectList	Destroys the specified conversation list and terminates all conversations associated with the list.
DdeEnableCallback	Enables or disables transactions for a specific conversation or for all conversations currently established by the calling application.
DdeFreeDataHandle	Frees a DDE object and deletes the data handle associated with the object.
DdeFreeStringHandle	Frees a string handle in the calling application.
DdeGetData	Copies data from the specified DDE object to the specified local buffer.
DdeGetLastError	Retrieves the most recent error code set by the failure of a DDEML function.
DdeImpersonateClient	Impersonates a DDE client application in a DDE client conversation.
DdeInitialize	Registers an application with DDEML.
DdeKeepStringHandle	Increments the usage count associated with the specified handle.
DdeNameService	Registers or unregisters the service names a DDE server supports.
DdePostAdvise	Causes the system to send an XTYPE_ADVREQ transaction the calling (server) application's dynamic data exchange (DDE) callback function for each client with an active advise loop on the specified topic and item.
DdeQueryConvInfo	Retrieves information about a DDE transaction and about the conversation in which the transaction takes place.
DdeQueryNextServer	Retrieves the next conversation handle in the specified conversation list.
DdeQueryString	Copies text associated with a string handle into a buffer.
DdeReconnect	Enables a client DDEML application to attempt to reestablish a conversation with a service that has terminated a conversation with the client.
DdeSetUserHandle	Associates an application-defined value with a conversation handle or a transaction identifier.
DdeUnaccessData	Unaccesses a DDE object.
DdeUninitialize	Frees all DDEML resources associated with the calling application.

27. Dynamic-Link Library Functions

DisableThreadLibraryCalls	Disables thread attach and thread detach notifications for the specified DLL.
DllMain	An optional entry point into a DLL.
FreeLibrary	Decrements the reference count of the loaded DLL. When the reference count reaches zero, the module is unmapped from the address space of the calling process.
FreeLibraryAndExitThread	Decrements the reference count of a loaded DLL by one, and then calls ExitThread to terminate the calling thread.
GetModuleFileName	Retrieves the full path and file name for the file containing the specified module.
GetModuleHandle	Retrieves a module handle for the specified module.
GetProcAddress	Retrieves the address of the specified exported DLL function.
LoadLibrary	Maps the specified executable module into the address space of the calling process.
LoadLibraryEx	Maps the specified executable module into the address space of the calling process.

28. Edit Control Functions

EditWordBreakProc	An application-defined callback function used with the EM_SET-WORDBREAKPROC message.

29. Error Handling Functions

Beep	Generates simple tones on the speaker.
FatalAppExit	Displays a message box and terminates the application when the message box is closed.
FlashWindow	Flashes the specified window one time.
FlashWindowEx	Flashes the specified window.
FormatMessage	Formats a message string.
GetLastError	Retrieves the calling thread's last-error code value.
MessageBeep	Plays a waveform sound.
SetErrorMode	Controls whether the system will handle the specified types of serious errors, or whether the process will handle them.
SetLastError	Sets the last-error code for the calling thread.
SetLastErrorEx	Sets the last-error code for the calling thread.

30. Event Logging Functions

BackupEventLog	Saves the specified event log to a backup file.
ClearEventLog	Clears the specified event log, and optionally saves the current copy of the logfile to a backup file.
CloseEventLog	Closes a read handle to the specified event log.
DeregisterEventSource	Closes a write handle to the specified event log.
GetEventLogInformation	Retrieves information about the specified event log.
GetNumberOfEventLogRecords	Retrieves the number of records in the specified event log.
GetOldesEventLogRecord	Retrieves the absolute record number of the oldest record in the specified event log.
NotifyChangeEventLog	Enables an application to receive notification when an event is written to the specified event logfile.
OpenBackupEventLog	Opens a handle to a backup event log.
OpenEventLog	Opens a handle to an event log.
ReadEventLog	Reads a whole number of entries from the specified event log.
RegisterEventSource	Retrieves a registered handle to an event log.
ReportEvent	Writes an entry at the end of the specified event log.

31. File I/O Functions

AreFileApisANSI	Determines whether the file I/O functions are using the ANSI or OEM character set code page.
CancelIo	Cancels all pending I/O operations that were issued by the calling thread from the specified file handle.
CloseHandle	Closes an open object handle.
CopyFile	Copies an existing file to a new file.
CopyFileEx	Copies an existing file to a new file.
CopyProgressRoutine	An application-defined callback function used with CopyFileEx and MoveFileWithProgress.
CreateDirectory	Creates a new directory.
CreateDiretoryEx	Creates a new directory with the attributes of a specified template directory.
CreateFile	Creates or opens a file object.
CreateIoCompletionPort	Creates an I/O completion port or associates an instance of an opened file with a newly created or an existing I/O completion port.
DefineDosDevice	Defines, redefines, or deletes MS-DOS device names.

DeleteFile	Deletes an existing file.
FileIOCompletionRoutine	An application-defined callback function used with ReadFileEx and WriteFileEx.
FindClose	Closes the specified search handle.
FindCloseChangeNotification	Stops change notification handle monitoring.
FindFirstChangeNotification	Creates a change notification handle.
FindFirstFile	Searches a directory for a file whose name matches the specified file name.
FindFirstFileEx	Searches a directory for a file whose name and attributes match those specified.
FindNextChangeNotification	Requests that the operating system signal a change notification handle the next time it detects an appropriate change.
FindNextFile	Continues a file search.
FlushFileBuffers	Clears the buffers for the specified file and causes all buffered data to be written to the file.
GetBinaryType	Determines whether a file is executable.
GetCurrentDirectory	Retrieves the current directory for the current process.
GetDiskFreeSpace	Retrieves information about the specified disk, including the amount of free space on the disk.
GetDiskFreeSpaceEx	Retrieves information about the specified disk, including the amount of free space on the disk.
GetDriveType	Determines whether a disk drive is a removable, fixed, CD-ROM, RAM disk, or network drive.
GetFileAttributes	Retrieves attributes for a specified file or directory.
GetFileAttributesEx	Retrieves attributes for a specified file or directory.
GetFileInformationByHandle	Retrieves file information for a specified file.
GetFileSize	Retrieves the size of a specified file.
GetFileSizeEx	Retrieves the size of a specified file.
GetFileType	Retrieves the file type of the specified file.
GetFullPathName	Retrieves the full path and file name of a specified file.
GetLogicalDrives	Returns a bitmask representing the currently available disk drives.
GetLogicalDriveStrings	Fills a buffer with strings that specify valid drives in the system.
GetLongPathName	Converts the specified path to its long form.
GetQueuedCompletionStatus	Attempts to dequeue an I/O completion packet from a specified I/O completion port.
GetShortPathName	Retrieves the short path form of a specified input path.
GetTempFileName	Creates a name for a temporary file.

GetTempPath	Retrieves the path of the directory designated for temporary files.
Int32x32To64	Multiplies two signed 32-bit integers.
Int64ShllMod32	Performs a left logical shift operation on an unsigned 64-bit integer value.
Int64ShraMod32	Performs a right arithmetic shift operation on a signed 64-bit integer value.
Int64ShrlMod32	Performs a right logical shift operation on an unsigned 64-bit integer value.
LockFile	Locks a region in an open file.
LockFileEx	Locks a region in an open file for shared or exclusive access.
MoveFile	Moves an existing file or a directory.
MoveFileEx	Moves an existing file or a directory.
MoveFilewithProgress	Moves a file or directory.
MulDiv	Multiplies two 32-bit values and then divides the 64-bit result by a third 32-bit value.
PostQueuedCompletionStatus	Posts an I/O completion packet to an I/O completion port.
QueryDosDevice	Retrieves information about MS-DOS device names.
ReadDirectoryChangesW	Retrieves information describing the changes occurring within a directory.
ReadFile	Reads data from a file, starting at the specified position.
ReadFileEx	Reads data from a file asynchronously.
ReadFileScatter	Reads data from a file and stores the data into a set of buffers.
RemoveDirectory	Deletes an existing empty directory.
ReplaceFile	Replaces one file with another file.
SearchPath	Searches for the specified file.
SetCurrentDirectory	Changes the current directory for the current process.
SetEndOfFile	Moves the end-of-file position for the specified file.
SetFileApisToANSI	Causes the file I/O functions to use the ANSI character set code page.
SetFileApisToOEM	Causes the file I/O functions to use the OEM character set code page.
SetFileAttributes	Sets a file's attributes.
SetFilePointer	Moves the file pointer of an open file.
SetFilePointerEx	Moves the file pointer of an open file.
SetFileSecurity	Sets the security of a file or directory object.
SetVolumeLabel	Sets the label of a file system volume.

Uint32x32To64	Multiplies two unsigned 32-bit integers, returning an unsigned 64-bit integer result.
UnlockFile	Unlocks a previously locked region in an open file.
UnlockFileEx	Unlocks a previously locked region in an open file.
WriteFile	Writes data to a file.
WriteFileEx	Writes data to a file asynchronously.
WriteFileGather	Gathers data from a set of buffers and writes the data to a file.

32. File Mapping Functions

CreateFileMapping	Creates or opens a named or unnamed file-mapping object for the specified file.
FlushViewOfFile	Writes to the disk a byte range within a mapped view of a file.
MapViewOfFile	Maps a view of a file into the address space of the calling process.
MapViewOfFileEx	Maps a view of a file into the address space of the calling process.
OpenFileMapping	Opens a named file-mapping object.
UnmapViewOfFile	Unmaps a mapped view of a file from the calling process's address space.

33. File System Functions

The following functions are used with file systems.

CreateHardLink	Establishes an NTFS hard link between an existing file and a new file.
GetCompressedFileSize	Retrieves the actual number of bytes of disk storage used to store a specified file.
GetDiskFreeSpace	Retrieves information about the specified disk, including the amount of free space on the disk.
GetDiskFreeSpaceEx	Retrieves information about the specified disk, including the amount of free space on the disk.
GetFileSize	Retrieves the size of a specified file.
GetFileSizeEx	Retrieves the size of a specified file.
GetLogicalDrives	Returns a bitmask representing the currently available disk drives.
GetLogicalDriveStrings	Fills a buffer with strings that specify valid drives in the system.
GetVolumeInformation	Retrieves information about a file system and volume.
SetVolumeLabel	Sets the label of a file system volume.

The following functions are used with the encrypted file system.

AddUsersToEncryptedFile	Adds user keys to a specified encrypted file.
DecrypFile	Decrypts an encrypted file or directory.
EncrypFile	Encrypts a file or directory.
EncryptionDisables	Disables or enables encryption of the indicated directory and the files in it.
FileEncryptionStatus	Retrieves the encryption status of the specified file.
FreeEncryptionCertificateHashList	Frees a certificate hash list.
QueryRecoveryAgentsOnEncryptedFile	Retrieves a list of recovery agents for the specified file.
QueryUsersOnEncryptedFile	Retrieves a list of users for the specified file.
RemoveUsersFromEncryptedFile	Removes specified certificate hashes from a specified file.
SetUserFileEncryptionKey	Sets the user's current key to the specified certificate

The following functions are used with volume mount points.

DeleteVolumeMountPoint	Unmounts the volume from the specified volume mount point.
FindFirstVolume	Returns the name of a volume on a computer.
FindFirstVolumeMountPoint	Returns the name of a volume mount point on the specified volume.
FindNextVolume	Continues a volume search started by a call to FindFirstVolume.
FindNextVolumeMountPoint	Continues a volume mount point search started by a call to FindFirstVolumeMountPoint.
FindVolumeClose	Closes the specified volume search handle.
FindVolumeMountPointClose	Closes the specified mount-point search handle.
GetVolumeNameForVolumeMountPoint	Takes a volume mount point or root directory and returns the corresponding unique volume name.
GetVolumePathName	Returns the volume mount point at which the specified path is mounted.
SetVolumeMountPoint	Mounts the specified volume at the specified volume mount point.

34. Filled Shape Functions

Chord	Draws an area bounded by an ellipse and a line segment.
Ellipse	Draws an ellipse.
FillRect	Fills a rectangle using a brush.
FrameRect	Draws a border around a rectangle using a brush.
InvertRect	Inverts the color values of the pixels in a rectangle.

Pie	Draws a pie-shaped wedge bounded by an ellipse and two radials.
Polygon	Draws a polygon.
PolyPolygon	Draws a series of closed polygons.
Rectangle	Draws a rectangle.
RoundRect	Draws a rectangle with rounded corners.

35. Font and Text Functions

AddFontMemResourceEx	Adds an embedded font to the system font table.
AddFontResource	Adds a font resource to the system font table.
AddFontResourceEx	Adds a private or non-enumerable font to the system font table.
CreateFont	Creates a logical font.
CreateFontIndirect	Creates a logical font from a structure.
CreateFontIndirectEx	Creates a logical font from a structure.
CreateScalableFontResource	Creates a font resource file for a scalable font.
DrawText	Draws formatted text in a rectangle.
DrawTextEx	Draws formatted text in rectangle.
EnumFontFameExProc	An application-defined callback function used with EnumFontFamiliesEx to process fonts.
EnumFontFamiliesEx	Enumerates all fonts in the system with certain characteristics.
ExtTextOut	Draws a character string.
GetAspectRatioFilterEx	Gets the setting for the aspect-ratio filter.
GetCharABCWidths	Gets the widths of consecutive characters from the TrueType font.
GetCharABCWidthFloat	Gets the widths of consecutive characters from the current font.
GetCharABCWidthsI	Gets the widths of consecutive glyph indices or from an array of glyph indices from the TrueType font.
GetCharacterPlacement	Gets information about a character string.
GetCharWidth32	Gets the widths of consecutive characters from the current font.
GetCharWidthFloat	Gets the fractional widths of consecutive characters from the current font.
GetCharWidthI	Gets the widths of consecutive glyph indices or an array of glyph indices from the current font.
GetFontData	Gets metric data for a TrueType font.
GetFontLanguageInfo	Returns information about the selected font for a display context.

GetFontUnicodeRanges	Tells which Unicode characters are supported by a font.
GetGlyphIndices	Translates a string into an array of glyph indices.
GetGlyphOutline	Gets the outline or bitmap for a character in the TrueType font.
GetKerningPairs	Gets the character-kerning pairs for a font.
GetOutlineTextMetrics	Gets text metrics for TrueType fonts.
GetRasterizerCaps	Tells whether TrueType fonts are installed.
GetTabbedTextExtent	Computes the width and height of a character string, including tabs.
GetTextAlign	Gets the text-alignment setting for a device context.
GetTextCharacterExtra	Gets the current intercharacter spacing for a device context.
GetTextColor	Gets the text color for a device context.
GetTextExtentExPoint	Gets the number of characters in a string that will fit within a space.
GetTextExtentExPointI	Gets the number of glyph indices that will fit within a space.
GetTextExtentPoint32	Computes the width and height of a string of text.
GetTextExtentPointI	Computes the width and height of an array of glyph indices.
GetTextFace	Gets the name of the font that is selected into a device context.
GetTextMetrics	Fills a buffer with the metrics for a font.
PolyTextOut	Draws several strings using the font and text colors in a device context.
RemoveFontMemResourceEx	Removes a font whose source was embedded in a document from the system font table.
RemoveFontResource	Removes the fonts in a file from the system font table.
RemovefontResourceEx	Removes a private or non-enumerable font from the system font table.
SetMapperFlags	Alters the algorithm used to map logical fonts to physical fonts.
SetTextAlign	Sets the text-alignment flags for a device context.
SetTextCharacterExtra	Sets the intercharacter spacing.
SetTextColor	Sets the text color for a device context.
SetTextJustification	Specifies the amount of space the system should add to the break characters in a string.
TabbedTextOut	Writes a character string at a location, expanding tabs to specified values.
TextOut	Writes a character string at a location.

36. Handle and Object Functions

CloseHandle	Closes an open object handle.
DuplicateHandle	Duplicates an object handle.
GetHandleInformation	Retrieves certain properties of an object handle.
SetHandleInformation	Sets certain properties of an object handle.

37. Hook Functions

CallMsgFilter	Passes the specified message and hook code to the hook procedures associated with the WH_SYSMSGFILTER hook.
CallNextHookEx	Passes the hook information to the next hook procedure in the current hook chain.
CallWndProc	An application-defined or library-defined callback function used with the SeWindowsHookEx function.
CallWndRetProc	An application-defined or library-defined callback function used with the SetWindowsHookEx function.
CBTProc	An application-defined or library-defined callback function used with the SetWindowsHookEx function.
DebugProc	An application-defined or library-defined callback function used with the SetWindowsHookEx function.
ForegroundIdleProc	An application-defined or library-defined callback function used with the SetWindowsHookEx function.
GetMsgProc	An application-defined or library-defined callback function used with the SetWindowsHookEx function.
JournalPlaybackProc	An application-defined or library-defined callback function used with SetWindowsHookEx function.
JournalRecordProc	An application-defined or library-defined callback function used with the SetWindowsHookEx function.
KeyboardProc	An application-defined or library-defined callback function used with the SetwindowsHookEx function.
LowLevelKeyboardProc	An application-defined or library-define callback function used with the SetWindowsHookEx function.
LowLevelMouseProc	An application-defined or library-defined callback function used with the SetWindowsHookEx function.
MessageProc	An application-defined or library-defined callback function used with the SetWindowsHookEx function.
MouseProc	An application-defined or library-defined callback function used with the SeWindowsHookEx function.
SetWindowsHookEx	Installs an application-defined hook procedure into a hook chain.

ShellProc	An application-defined or library-defined callback function used with the SetWindowsHookEx function.
SysMsgProc	A library-defined callback function used with the SetWindowsHookEx function.
UnhookWindowsHookEx	Removes a hook procedure installed in a hook chain by the SetWindowsHookEx function.

38. Icon Functions

CopyIcon	Copies an icon from another module.
CreateIcon	Creates an icon with a specified size, color, and bit pattern.
CreateIconFromResource	Creates an icon or cursor from resource bits.
CreateIconFromResourceEx	Creates an icon or cursor from resource bits.
CreateIconIndirect	Creates an icon or cursor from an ICONINFO structure.
DestroyIcon	Destroys an icon.
DrawIcon	Draws an icon.
DrawIconEx	Draws an icon or cursor, performing raster operations, and stretching or compressing the icon or cursor.
DuplicateIcon	Creates a duplicate of a specified icon.
ExtractAssociatedIcon	Gets a handle to an indexed icon in a file or an icon found in an executable file.
ExtractIcon	Gets a handle to an icon from an executable file, dynamic-link library (DLL), or icon file.
ExtractIconEx	Gets an array of handles to large or small icons extracted from an executable file, dynamic-link library (DLL), or icon file.
GetIconInfo	Gets information about an icon or cursor.
LoadIcon	Loads an icon from the executable file associated with an application.
LookupIconIdFromDirectory	Searches for an icon or cursor that best fits the current display device.
LookupIconIdFromDirectoryEx	Searches for an icon or cursor that best fits the current display device.

39. ImageHlp Functions

ImageAcces—The image access functions access the data in an executable image. The functions provide high-level access to the base images and very specific access to the most common parts of an image's data.

GetImageConfigInformation

GetImageUnusedHeaderBytes

ImageLoad

ImageUnload

MapAndLoad

SetImageConfigInformation

UnMapAndLoad

Image Integrity—The image integrity functions manage the set of certificates in an image file.

DigestFunction

ImageAddCertificate

ImageEnumerateCertificates

ImageGetCertificateData

ImageGetCertificateHeader

ImageGetDigestStream

ImageRemoveCertificate

Image Modification—The image modification functions allow you to change the executable image.

BindImage

BindImageEx

CheckSumMappedFile

MapFileAndCheckSum

ReBaseImage

SplitSymbols

StatusRoutine

TouchFileTimes

UpdateDebugInfoFile

UpdateDebugInfoFileEx

40. Input Method Editor Functions

EnumInputContext

EnumRegisterWordProc

ImmAssociateContext

ImmAssociateContextEx

ImmConfigureIME

ImmCreateContext

ImmDestroyContext

ImmDisableIME

ImmEnumInputContext

ImmEnumRegisterWord

ImmEscape

ImmGetCandidateList

ImmGetCandidateListCount

ImmGetCandidateWindow

ImmGetCompositionFont

ImmGetCompositionString

ImmGetCompositionWindow

ImmGetContext

ImmGetConversionList

ImmGetConversionStatus

ImmGetDefaultIMEWnd

ImmGetDescription

ImmGetGuideLine

ImmGetIMEFileName

ImmGetImeMenuItems

ImmGetOpenStatus

ImmGetProperty

ImmGetRegisterWordStyle

ImmGetStatusWindowPos

ImmGetVirtualKey

ImmInstallIME

ImmIsIME

ImmIsUIMessage

ImmNotifyIME

ImmRegisterWord

ImmReleaseContext

ImmSetCandidateWindow

ImmSetCompositionFont

ImmSetCompositionString

ImmSetCompositionWindow

ImmSetConversionStatus

ImmSetOpenStatus

ImmSetStatusWindowPos

ImmSimulateHotKey

ImmUnregisterWord

41. Keyboard Accelerator Functions

CopyAcceleratorTable	Copies the specified accelerator table.
CreateAcceleratorTable	Creates an accelerator table.
DestroyAcceleratorTable	Destroys an accelerator table.
LoadAccelerators	Loads the specified accelerator table.
TranslateAccelerator	Processes accelerator keys for menu commands.

42. Keyboard Input Functions

ActivateKeyboardLayout	Sets the input locale identifier for the calling thread or the current process.
BlockInput	Blocks keyboard and mouse input events from reaching applications.
EnableWindow	Enables or disables mouse and keyboard input to the specified window or control.
GetActiveWindow	Retrieves the window handle to the active window attached to the calling thread's message queue.
GetAsyncKeyState	Determines whether a key is up or down at the time the function is called, and whether the key was pressed after a previous call to GetAsyncKeyState.
GetFocus	Retrieves the handle to the window that has the keyboard focus.
GetKeyboardLayout	Retrieves the active input locale identifier for the specified thread.
GetKeyboardLayoutList	Retrieves the input locale identifiers corresponding to the current set of input locales in the system.
GetKeyboardLayoutName	Retrieves the name of the active input locale identifier.
GetKeyboardState	Copies the status of the 256 virtual keys to the specified buffer.
GetKeyNameText	Retrieves a string that represents the name of a key.
GetKeyState	Retrieves the status of the specified virtual key.
GetLastInputInfo	Retrieves the time of the last input event.
IsWindowEnabled	Determines whether the specified window is enabled for mouse and keyboard input.
keybd_event	Synthesizes a keystroke.
LoadKeyboardLayout	Loads a new input locale identifier.
MapVirtualKey	Translates (maps) a virtual-key code into a scan code or character value, or translates a scan code into a virtual-key code.
OemKeyScan	Maps OEM ASCII codes 0 through 0x0FF into the OEM scan codes and shift states.

RegisterHotKey	Defines a system-wide hot key.
SendInput	Synthesizes keystrokes, mouse motions, and button clicks.
SetActiveWindow	Activates a window.
SetFocus	Sets the keyboard focus to the specified window.
SetKeyboardState	Copies a 256-byte array of keyboard key states into the calling thread's keyboard input-state table.
ToAscii	Translates the specified virtual-key code and keyboard state to the corresponding character or characters.
ToAsciiEx	Translates the specified virtual-key code and keyboard state to the corresponding character or characters.
ToUnicode	Translates the specified virtual-key code and keyboard state to the corresponding Unicode character or characters.
ToUnicodeEx	Translates the specified virtual-key code and keyboard state to the corresponding Unicode character or characters.
UnloadKeyboardLayout	Unloads an input locale identifier.
UnregisterHotKey	Frees a hot key previously registered by the calling thread.
VkKeyScan	Translates a character to the corresponding virtual-key code and shift state for the current keyboard.
VkKeyScanEx	Translates a character to the corresponding virtual-key code and shift state.

43. Line and Curve Functions

AngleArc	Draws a line segment and an arc.
Arc	Draws an elliptical arc.
ArcTo	Draws an elliptical arc.
GetArcDirection	Retrieves the current arc direction for the specified device context.
LineDDA	Determines which pixels should be highlighted for a line defined by the specified starting and ending points.
LineDDAProc	An application-defined callback function used with the LineDDA function.
LineTo	Draws a line from the current position up to, but not including, the specified point.
MoveToEx	Updates the current position to the specified point and optionally returns the previous position.
PolyBezier	Draws one or more Bezier curves.
PolyBezierTo	Draws one or more Bezier curves.
PolyDraw	Draws a set of line segments and Bezier curves.

Polyline	Draws a series of line segments by connecting the points in the specified array.
PolylineTo	Draws one or more straight lines.
PolyPolyline	Draws multiple series of connected line segments.
SetArcDirection	Sets the drawing direction to be used for arc and rectangle functions.

44. List Box Functions

DlgDirList	Replaces the contents of a list box with the names of the subdirectories and files in a specified directory.
DlgDirSelectEx	Retrieves the current selection from a single-selection list box.
GetListBoxInfo	Retrieves information about the specified list box.

45. Low-Level Access Control Functions

The following low-level functions are used to manipulate security descriptors.

GetNamedSecurityInfo	Retrieves a copy of the security descriptor for an object specified by name.
GetKernelObjectSecurity	Retrieves a copy of the security descriptor protecting a kernel object.
GetPrinter	Retrieves information about a specified printer.
GetSecurityDescriptorDacl	Retrieves a pointer to the discretionary access-control list (ACL) in a specified security descriptor.
GetSecurityDescriptorGroup	Retrieves the primary group information from a security descriptor.
GetSecurityDescriptorLength	Retrieves the length, in bytes, of a structurally valid security descriptor.
GetSecurityDescriptorOwner	Retrieves the owner information from a security descriptor.
GetSecurityDescriptorSacl	Retrieves a pointer to the system access-control list (ACL) in a specified security descriptor.
GetUserObjectSecurity	Retrieves security information for the specified user object.
InitializeSecurityDescriptor	Initializes a new security descriptor.
IsValidSecurityDescriptor	Determines whether the components of a security descriptor are valid.
MakeAbsoluteSD	Creates a security descriptor in absolute format by using a security descriptor in self-relative format as a template.
MakeSelfRelativeSD	Creates a security descriptor in self-relative format by using a security descriptor in absolute format as a template.
NetShareGetInfo	Retrieves information about a particular shared resource on a server.

NetShareSetInfo	Sets the parameters of a shared resource.
QueryServiceObjectSecurity	Retrieves a copy of the security descriptor associated with a service object.
RegGetKeySecurity	Retrieves a copy of the security descriptor protecting the specified open registry key.
RegSetKeySecurity	Sets the security of an open registry key.
SetFileSecurityInfo	Sets the security of a file or directory object. The caller identifies the object by name.
SetKernelObjectSecurity	Sets the security of a kernel object. For example, this can be process, thread, or event.
SetPrinter	Sets the data for a specified printer or sets the state of the specified printer by pausing printing, resuming printing, or clearing all print jobs.
SetSecurityDescriptorDacl	Sets information in a discretionary access-control list (ACL).
SetSecurityDescriptorGroup	Sets the primary group information of an absolute-format security descriptor, replacing any primary group information already present in the security descriptor.
SetSecurityDescriptorOwner descriptor.	Sets the owner information of an absolute-format security
SetSecurityDescriptorSacl	Sets information in a system access-control list (ACL).
SetServiceObjectSecurityInfo	Sets specified security information in the security descriptor of a specified object.
SetUserObjectSecurity	Sets the security of a user object.

The following low-level functions are use to manipulate ACEs and ACLs.

AddAccessAllowedAce	Adds an access-allowed ACE to an ACL. The access is granted to a specified SID.
AddAccessAllowedAceEx	Adds an access-allowed ACE to the end of a DACL.
AddAccessAllowedObjectAce	Adds an access-allowed ACE to the end of a DACL.
AddAccessDeniedAce	Adds an access-denied ACE to an ACL.
AddAccessDeniedAceEx	Adds an access-denied ACE to the end of a DACL.
AddAccessDeniedObjectAce	Adds an access-denied ACE to the end of a DACL.
AddAce	Adds one or more ACEs to a specified ACL. An ACE is an access-control entry.
AddAuditAccessAce	Adds a system audit ACE to a system ACL.
AddAuditAccessAceEx	Adds a system-audit ACE to the end of a SACL.
AddAuditAccessObjectAce	Adds a system-audit ACE to the end of a SACL.
DeleteAce	Deletes an ACE from an ACL.
FindFirstFreeAce	Retrieves a pointer to the first free byte in an access-control list (ACL).

GetAce	Obtains a pointer to an ACE in an ACL.
GetAclInformation	Retrieves information about an access-control list (ACL).
InitializeAcl	Creates a new ACL structure.
IsValidAcl	Validates an access-control list (ACL).
SetAclInformation	Sets information about an access-control list (ACL).

46. MailSlot Functions

CreateMailslot	Creates a mailslot with the specified name.
GetMailslotInfo	Retrieves information about the specified mailslot.
SetMailslotInfo	Sets the time-out value used by the specified mailslot for a read operation.

47. Memory Management Functions

The following functions are used in memory management.

CopyMemory	Copies a block of memory from one location to another.
FillMemory	Fills a block of memory with a specified value.
GetWriteWatch	Retrieves the addresses of the pages that have been written to in a region of virtual memory.
GlobalMemoryStatus	Obtains information about the system's current usage of both physical and virtual memory.
GlobalMemoryStatusEx	Obtains information about the system's current usage of both physical and virtual memory.
IsBadCodePtr	Determines whether the calling process has read access to the memory at the specified address.
IsBadReadPtr	Verifies that the calling process has read access to the specified range of memory.
IsBadStringPtr	Verifies that the calling process has read access to a range of memory pointed to by a string pointer.
IsBadWritePtr	Verifies that the calling process has write access to the specified range of memory.
MoveMemory	Moves a block of memory from one location to another.
ResetWriteWatch	Resets the write-tracking state for a region of virtual memory.
ZeroMemory	Fills a block of memory with zeros.

The following are the AWE functions.

AllocateUserPhysicalPages	Allocates physical memory pages to be mapped and unmapped within any AWE region of the process.

FreeUserPhysicalPages	Frees physical memory pages previously allocated with AllocateUserPhysicalPages.
MapUserPhysicalPages	Maps previously allocated physical memory pages at the specified address within an AWE region.
MapUserPhysicalPagesScatter	Maps previously allocated physical memory pages at the specified address within an AWE region.

The following are the global and local functions. These functions are slower than other memory management functions and do not provide as many features. Therefore, new applications should use the heap functions. However, the global functions are still used with DDE and the clipboard functions.

GlobalAlloc	Allocates the specified number of bytes from the heap.
GlobalDiscard	Discards the specified global memory block.
GlobalFlags	Returns information about the specified global memory object.
GlobalFree	Frees the specified global memory object.
GlobalHandle	Retrieves the handle associated with the specified pointer to a global memory block.
GlobalLock	Locks a global memory object and returns a pointer to the first byte of the object's memory block.
GlobalReAlloc	Changes the size or attributes of a specified global memory object.
GlobalSize	Retrieves the current size of the specified global memory object.
GlobalUnlock	Decrements the lock count associated with a memory object.
LocalAlloc	Allocates the specified number of bytes from the heap.
LocalDiscard	Discards the specified local memory object.
LocalFlags	Returns information about the specified local memory object.
LocalFree	Frees the specified local memory object.
LocalHandle	Retrieves the handle associated with the specified pointer to a local memory object.
LocalLock	Locks a local memory object and returns a pointer to the first byte of the object's memory block
LocalReAlloc	Changes the size or the attributes of a specified local memory object.
LocalSize	Returns the current size of the specified local memory object.
LocalUnlock	Decrements the lock count associated with a memory object.

The following are the heap functions.

GetProcessHeap	Obtains a handle to the heap of the calling process.
GetProcessHeaps	Obtains handles to all of the heaps that are valid for the calling process.

HeapAlloc	Allocates a block of memory from a heap.
HeapCompact	Attempts to compact a specified heap.
HeapCreate	Creates a heap object.
HeapDestroy	Destroys the specified heap object.
HeapFree	Frees a memory block allocated from a heap.
HeapLock	Attempts to acquire the lock associated with a specified heap.
HeapReAlloc	Reallocates a block of memory from a heap.
HeapSize	Returns the size of a memory block allocated from a heap.
HeapUnlock	Releases ownership of the lock associated with a specified heap.
HeapValidate	Attempts to validate a specified heap.
HeapWalk	Enumerates the memory blocks in a specified heap.

The following are the virtual memory functions.

VirtualAlloc	Reserves or commits a region of pages in the virtual address space of the calling process.
VirtualAllocEx	Reserves or commits a region of pages in the virtual address space of the calling process.
VirtualFree	Releases or decommits a region of pages within the virtual address space of the calling process.
VirtualFreeEx	Releases or decommits a region memory within the virtual address space of a specified process.
VirtualLock	Locks the specified region of the process's virtual address space into physical memory.
VirtualProtect	Changes the access protection on a region of committed pages in the virtual address space of the calling process.
VirtualProtectEx	Changes the access protection on a region of committed pages in the virtual address space of the calling process.
VirtualQuery	Provides information about a range of pages in the virtual address space of the calling process.
VirtualQueryEx	Provides information about a range of pages in the virtual address space of the calling process.
VirtualUnlock	Unlocks a specified range of pages in the virtual address space of a process.

48. Menu Functions

AppendMenu	Appends an item to various menus and submenus.
CheckMenuItem	Checks or clears a menu item.
CheckMenuRadioItem	Checks a specified menu item and makes it a radio item.

CreateMenu	Creates a menu.
CreatePopupMenu	Creates a drop-down menu, submenu, or shortcut menu.
DeleteMenu	Deletes a menu item.
DestroyMenu	Deletes a menu.
DrawMenuBar	Redraws a menu bar.
EnableMenuItem	Enables, disables, or grays a menu item.
EndMenu	Ends the calling thread's active menu.
GetMenu	Gets a handle to the menu.
GetMenuBarInfo	Gets information about a menu bar.
GetMenuCheckMarkDimensions	Returns the dimensions of the default check-mark bitmap.
GetMenuDefaultItem	Gets the default menu item on a menu.
GetMenuInfo	Gets information about a menu.
GetMenuItemCount	Gets the number of items in a menu.
GetMenuItemID	Gets the identifier of a menu item.
GetMenuItemInfo	Gets information about a menu item.
GetMenuItemRect	Gets the bounding rectangle for a menu item.
GetMenuState	Gets the menu flags associated with a menu item.
GetMenuString	Copies the text string of a menu item into a buffer.
GetSubMenu	Gets a handle to the drop-down menu or submenu activated by a menu item.
GetSystemMenu	Allows a copying or modifying of a window menu.
HilliteMenuItem	Highlights or removes the highlighting from an item in a menu bar.
InsertMenu	Inserts a new menu item into a menu.
InsertMenuItem	Inserts a new menu item in a menu.
IsMenu	Determines when a handle is a menu handle.
LoadMenu	Loads a menu resource.
LoadMenuIndirect	Loads a specified menu template.
MenuItemFromPoint	Determines which menu item is at a specified location.
ModifyMenu	Changes an existing menu item.
RemoveMenu	Deletes a menu item or detaches a submenu from a menu.
SetMenu	Assigns a new menu to a window.
SetMenuDefaultItem	Sets the default menu item for a menu.
SetMenuInfo	Sets information for a menu.
SetMenuItemBitmaps	Associates a bitmap with a menu item.
SetMenuItemInfo	Changes information about a menu item.

| TrackPopupMenu | Displays a shortcut menu at a location and tracks item selection on a menu. |
| TrackPopupMenuEx | Displays a shortcut menu at a location and tracks item selection on a shortcut menu. |

49. Message and Message Queue Functions

BroadcastSystemMessage	Sends a message to the specified recipients.
DispatchMessage	Dispatches a message to a window procedure.
GetInputState	Determines whether there are mouse-button or keyboard messages in the calling thread's message queue.
GetMessage	Retrieves a message from the calling thread's message queue.
GetMessageExtraInfo	Retrieves the extra message information for the current thread.
GetMessagePos	Retrieves the position of the cursor for the last message retrieved by GetMessage.
GetMessageTime	Retrieves the message time for the last message retrieved by GetMessage.
GetQueueStatus	Indicates the type of messages found in the calling thread's message queue.
InSendMessage	Determines whether the current window procedure is processing a message that was sent from another thread.
InSendMessageEx	Determines whether the current window procedure is processing a message that was sent from another thread.
PeekMessage	Dispatches incoming sent messages, checks the thread message queue for a posted message, and retrieves the message (if any exits).
PostMessage	Posts a message in the message queue associated with the thread that created the specified window and returns without waiting for the thread to process the message.
PostQuitMessage	Indicates to the system that a thread has made a request to teminate (quit).
PostThreadMessage	Posts a message to the message queue of the specified thread.
RegisterWindowMessage	Defines a new window message that is guaranteed to be unique throughout the system.
ReplyMessage	Replies to a message sent through the SendMessage function without returning control to the function that called SendMessage.
SendAsynProc	An application-defined callback function used with the SendMessageCallback function.
SendMessage	Sends the specified message to a window or windows.

SendMessageCallback	Sends the specified message to a window or windows. It calls the window procedure for the specified window and returns immediately.
SendMessageTimeout	Sends the specified message to a window or windows. The function calls the window procedure for the specified window and, if the specified window belongs to a different thread, does not return until the window procedure has processed the message or the specified time-out period has elapsed.
SetMessageExtraInfo	Sets the extra message information for the current thread.
TranslateMessage	Translates virtual-key messages into character messages.
WaitMessage	Yields control to other threads when a thread has no other messages in its message queue.

50. Metafile Functions

CloseEnhMetaFile	Closes an enhanced-metafile device context.
CopyEnhMetaFile	Copies the contents of an enhanced-format metafile to a specified file.
CreateEnhMetaFile	Creates a device context for an enhanced-format metafile.
DeleteEnhMetaFile	Deletes an enhanced-format metafile or an enhanced-format metafile handle.
EnhMetaFileProc	An application-defined callback function used with the EnumEnhMetaFile function.
EnumEnhMetaFile	Enumerates the records within an enhanced-format metafile.
GdiComment	Copies a comment from a buffer into a specified enhanced-format metafile.
GetEnhMetaFile	Creates a handle that identifies the enhanced-format metafile stored in the specified file.
GetEnhMetaFileBits	Retrieves the contents of the specified enhanced-format metafile and copies then into a buffer.
GetEnhMetaFileDescription	Retrieves an optional text description from an enhanced-format metafile and copies the string to the specified buffer.
GetEnhMetaFileHeader	Retrieves the record containing the header for the specified enhanced-format metafile.
GetEnhMetaFilePaletteEntries	Retrieves optional palette entries from the specified enhanced metafile.
GetWinMetaFileBits	Converts the enhanced-format records from a metafile into Windows-format records.
PlayEnhMetaFile	Displays the picture stored in the specified enhanced-format metafile.
PlayEnhMetaFileRecord	Plays an enhanced-metafile record by executing the graphics device interface (GDI) functions identified by the record.

| SetEnhMetaFileBits | Creates a memory-based enhanced-format metafile from the specified data. |
| SetWinMetaFileBits | Converts a metafile from the older Windows format to the new enhanced format. |

51. Mouse Input Functions

DragDetect	Captures the mouse and tracks its movement until the user performs one or more specified actions.
GetCapture	Gets a handle to the window that has captured the mouse.
GetDoubleClickTime	Gets the double-click time for the mouse.
GetMouseMovePointsEx	Gets the previous coordinates of the mouse or pen.
GetLastInputInfo	Gets the time of the last input event.
mouse_event	Synthesizes mouse motion and button clicks.
ReleaseCapture	Releases the mouse capture and restores mouse input processing.
SetCapture	Sets the mouse capture to a window.
SetDoubleClickTime	Set the double-click time for the mouse.
SwapMouseButton	Reverses the left and right mouse buttons.
TrackMouseEvent or _TrackMouseEvent	Posts messages when a mouse leaves a window or hovers over a window.

52. Multiple Display Monitors Functions

EnumDisplayMonitors	Enumerates display monitors that intersect a region formed by the intersection of a specified clipping rectangle and the visible region of a device context.
GetMonitorInfo	Retrieves information about a display monitor.
MonitorEnumProc	An application-defined callback function that is called by the EnumDisplayMonitors function.
MonitorFromPoint	Retrieves a handle to the display monitor that contains a specified point.
MonitorFromRect	Retrieves a handle to the display monitor that has the largest area of intersection with a specified rectangle.
MonitorFromWindow	Retrieves a handle to the display monitor that has the largest area of intersection with the bounding rectangle of a specified window.

53. Multiple Document Interface Functions

CreateMDIWindow	Creates a multiple document interface (MDI) window.
DefFrameProc	Provides default processing for any window message that the window procedure of a multiple document interface (MDI) frame window does not process.
DefMDIChildProc	Provides default processing for any window message that the window procedure of a multiple document interface (MDI) child window does not process.
TranslateMDISysAccel	Processes accelerator keystrokes for window menu commands of the multiple document interface (MDI) child window associated with the specified MDI client window.

54. National Language Support Functions

ConvertDefaultLocal

EnumCalendarInfo

EnumCalendarInfoEx

EnumCalendarInfoProc

EnumCalendarInfoProcEx

EnumCodePagesProc

EnumDateFormats

EnumDateFormatsEx

EnumDateFormatsProc

EnumDateFormatsProcEx

EnumLanguageGroupLocales

EnumLanguageGroupLocalesProc

EnumLanguageGroupsProc

EnumLocalesProc

EnumSystemCodePages

EnumSystemLanguageGroups

EnumSystemLocales

EnumTimeFormats

EnumTimeFormatsProc

EnumUILanguages

EnumUILanguagesProc

GetACP

GetCalendarInfo

GetCPInfo

GetCPInfoEx

GetCurrencyFormat

GetDateFormat

GetLocaleInfo

GetNumberFormat

GetOEMCP

GetSystemDefaultLangID

GetSystemDefaultLCID

GetSystemDefaultUILanguage

GetThreadLocale

GetTimeFormat

GetUserDefaultLangID

GetUserDefaultLCID

GetUserDefaultUILanguage

IsValidCodePage

IsValidLanguageGroup

IsValidLocale

LCMapString

SetCalendarInfo

SetLocaleInfo

SetThreadLocale

55. Network Management Functions

The network management functions can be grouped as follows.

Alert Functions

NetAlertRaise

NetAlertRaiseEx

API Buffer Functions

NetApiBufferAllocate

NetApiBufferFree

NetApiBufferReallocate

NetApiBufferSize

Directory Service Functions

NetGetJoinableOUs

NetGetJoinInformation

NetJoinDomain

NetRenameMachineInDomain

NetUnjoinDomain

NetValidateName

Distributed File System (DFS) Functions

NetDfsAdd

NetDfsAddFtRoot

NetDfsAddStdRoot

NetDfsAddStdRootForced

NetDfsEnum

NetDfsGetClientInfo

NetDfsGetInfo

NetDfsMangerInitialize

NetDfsRemove

NetDfsRemoveFtRoot

NetDfsRemoveFtRootForced

NetDfsRemoveStdRoot

NetDfsSetClientInfo

NetDfsSetInfo

Get Functions

NetGetAnyDCName

NetGetDCName

NetGetDisplayInformationIndex

NetQueryDisplayInformation

Group Functions

NetGroupAdd

NetGroupAddUser

NetGroupDel

NetGroupDelUser

NetGroupEnum

NetGroupGetInfo

NetGroupGetUsers

NetGroupSetInfo

NetGroupSetUsers

Local Group Functions

NetLocalGroupAdd

NetLocalGroupAddMembers

NetLocalGroupDel

NetLocalGroupDelMembers

NetLocalGroupEnum

NetLocalGroupGetInfo

NetLocalGroupGetMembers

NetLocalGroupSetInfo

NetLocalGroupSetMembers

MessageFunctions

NetMessageBufferSend

NetMessageNameAdd

NetMessageNameDel

NetMessageNameEnum

NetMessageNameGetInfo

NetFile Functions

NetFileClose

NetFileClose2

NetFileEnum

NetFileGetInfo

RemoteUtilityFunctions

NetRemoteComputerSupports

NetRemoteTOD

Replicator Functions

NetReplExportDirAdd

NetReplExportDirDel

NetReplExportDirEnum

NetReplExportDirGetInfo

NetReplExportDirLock

NetReplExportDirSetInfo

NetReplExportDirUnlock

NetReplGetInfo

NetReplImportDirAdd

NetReplImportDirDel

NetReplImportDirEnum

NetReplImportDirGetInfo

NetReplImportDirLock

NetReplImportDirUnlock

NetReplSetInfo

Schedule Functions

NetScheduleJobAdd

NetScheduleJobDel

NetScheduleJobEnum

NetScheduleJobGetInfo

Server Functions

NetServerDiskEnum

NetServerEnum

NetServerGetInfo

NetServerSetInfo

Server and Workstation Transport Functions

NetServerComputerNameAdd

NetServerComputerNameDel

NetServerTransportAdd

NetServerTransportAddEx

NetServerTransportDel

NetServerTransportEnum

NetWkstaTransportAdd

NetWkstaTransportDel

NetWkstaTransportEnum

Session Functions

NetSessionDel

NetSessionEnum

NetSessionGetInfo

Share Functions

NetConnectionEnum

NetShareAdd

NetShareCheck

NetShareDel

NetShareEnum

NetShareGetInfo

NetShareSetInfo

Statistics Functions

NetStatisticsGet

Use Functions

NetUseAdd

NetUseDel

NetUseEnum

NetUseGetInfo

User Functions

NetUserAdd

NetUserChangePassword

NetUserDel

NetUserEnum

NetUserGetGroups

NetUserGetInfo

NetUserGetLocalGroups

NetUserSetGroups

NetUserSetInfo

User Modals Functions

NetUserModalsGet

NetUserModalsSet

Workstation and Workstation User Functions

NetWkstaGetInfo

NetWkstaSetInfo

NetWkstaUserGetInfo

NetWkstaUserSetInfo

NetWkstaUserEnum

Windows Networking Functions

MultinetGetConnectionPerformance

WNetAddConnection2

WNetAddConnection3

WNetCancelConnection

WNetCancelConnection2

WnetCloseEnum

WNetConnectionDialog

WNetConnectionDialog1

WNetDisconnectDialog

WNetDisconnectDialog1

WNetEnumResource

WNetGetConnection

WNetGetLastError

WNetGetNetworkInformation

WNetGetProviderName

WNetGetResouceInformation

WNetGetResourceParent

WNetGetUniversalName

WNetGetUser

WNetOpenEnum

WNetUseConnection

56. Network DDE Functions

NDdeGetErrorString	Converts an error code returned by a network DDE function into an error string that explains the returned error code.
NDdeGetShareSecurity	Retrieves the security descriptor associated with the DDE share.
NDdeGetTrustedShare	Retrieves the options associated with a DDE share that is in the server user's list of trusted shares.
NDdeIsValidAppTopicList	Determines whether an application and topic string ("AppName｜TopicName") use the proper syntax.
NDdeIsValidShareName	Determines whether a share name use the proper syntax.
NDdeSetShareSecurity	Sets the security descriptor associated with the DDE share.
NDdeSetTrustedShare	Grants the specified DDE share trusted status within the current user's context.
NDdeShareAdd	Creates and adds a new DDE share to the DDE share database manager (DSDM).
NDdeShareDel	Deletes a DDE share from the DSDM.
NDdeShareEnum	Retrieves the list of available DDE share
NDdeShareGetInfo	Retrieves DDE share information.
NDdeShareSetInfo	Sets DDE share information.
NDdeTrustedShareEnum	Retrieves the names of all network DDE shares that are trusted in the context of the calling process.

57. Painting and Drawing Functions

BeginPaint	Prepares a window for painting.
DrawAnimatedRects	Draws a rectangle and animates it to indicate icon or window activity.
DrawCaption	Draws a window caption.
DrawEdge	Draws one or more edges of rectangle.
DrawFocusRect	Draws a rectangle in the style that indicates the rectangle has the focus.
DrawFrameControl	Draws a frame control.
DrawState	Displays an image and applies a visual effect to indicate a state.
DrawStateProc	A callback function that renders a complex image for DrawState.
EndPaint	Marks the end of painting in a window.
ExcludeUpdateRgn	Prevents drawing within invalid areas of a window.
GdiFlush	Flushes the calling thread's current batch.
GdiGetBatchLimit	Returns the maximum number of function calls that can be accumulated in the calling thread's current batch.

GdiSetBatchLimit	Sets the maximum number of function calls that can be accumulated in the calling thread's current batch.
GetBkColor	Returns the background color for a device context.
GetBkMode	Returns the background mix mode for a device context.
GetBoundsRect	Gets the accumulated bounding rectangle for a device context.
GetROP2	Gets the foreground mix mode of a device context.
GetUpdateRect	Gets the coordinates of the smallest rectangle that encloses the update region of a window.
GetUpdateRgn	Gets the update region of a window.
GetWindowDC	Gets the device context for a window, including title bar, menus, and scroll bars.
GetWindowRgn	Gets a copy of the window region of a window.
GrayString	Draws gray text at a location.
InvalidateRect	Adds a rectangle to a window's update region.
InvalidateRgn	Invalidates the client area within a region.
LockWindowUpdate	Disables or reenables drawing in a window.
OutputProc	A callback function used with the GrayString function. It is used to draw a string.
PaintDesktop	Fills the clipping region in a device context with a pattern.
RedrawWindow	Updates a region in a window's client area.
SetBkColor	Sets the background to a color value.
SetBkMode	Sets the background mix mode of a device context.
SetBoundsRect	Controls the accumulation of bounding rectangle information for a device context.
SetROP2	Sets the foreground mix mode.
SetWindowRgn	Sets the window region of a window.
UpdateWindow	Updates the client area of window.
ValidateRect	Validates the client area within a rectangle.
ValidateRgn	Validates the client area within a region.
WindowFromDC	Returns a handle to the window associated with a device context.

58. Path Functions

AbortPath	Closes and discards any paths in the specified device context.
BeginPath	Opens a path bracket in the specified device context.
CloseFigure	Closes an open figure in a path.
EndPath	Closes a path bracket and selects the path defined by the bracket into the specified device context.

FillPath	Closes any open figures in the current path and fills the path's interior by using the current brush and polygon-filling mode.
FlattenPath	Transforms any curves in the path that is selected into the current device context (DC), turning each curve into a sequence of lines.
GetMiterLimit	Retrieves the miter limit for the specified device context.
GetPath	Retrieves the coordinates defining the endpoints of lines and the control points of curves found in the path that is selected into the specified device context.
PathToRegion	Creates a region from the path that is selected into the specified device context.
SetMiterLimit	Sets the limit for the length of miter joins for the specified device context.
StrokeAndFillPath	Closes any open figures in a path, strokes the outline of the path by using the current pen, and fills its interior by using the current brush.
StrokePath	Renders the specified path by using the current pen.
WidenPath	Redefines the current path as the area that would be painted if the path were stroked using the pen currently selected into the given device context.

59. Pen Functions

CreatePen	Creates a logical pen that has the specified style, width, and color.
CreatePenIndirect	Creates a logical cosmetic pen that has the style, width, and color specified in a structure.
ExtCreatePen	Creates a logical cosmetic or geometric pen that has the specified style, width, and brush attributes.

60. Performance Monitoring Functions

CounterPathCallBack

PdhAddCounter

PdhBrowseCounters

PdhCalculateCounterFromRawValue

PdhCloseLog

PdhCloseQuery

PdhCollectQueryData

PdhCollectQueryDataEx

PdhComputerCounterStatistics

PdhConnectMachine

PdhEnumMachines

PdhEnumObjectItems

PdhEnumObjects

PdhExpandCounterPath

PdhExpandWildCardPath

PdhFormatFromRawValue

PdhGetCounterInfo

PdhGetCounterTimeBase

PdhGetDataSourceTimeRange

PdhGetDefaultPerfCounter

PdhGetDefaultPerfObject

PdhGetDllVersion

PdhGetFormattedCounterArray

PdhGetFormattedCounterValue

PdhGetLogFileSize

PdhGetRawCounterArray

PdhGetRawCounterValue

PdhIsRealTimeQuery

PdhLookupPerfIndexByName

PdhLookupPerfNameByIndex

PdhMakeCounterPath

PdhOpenLog

PdhOpenQuery

PdhParseCounterPath

PdhParseInstanceName

PdhReadRawLogRecord

PdhRemoveCounter

PdhSelectDataSource

PdhSetcounterScaleFactor

PdhSetDefaultRealTimeDataSource

PdhSetQueryTimeRange

PdhUpdateLog

PdhUpdateLogFileCatalog

PdhValidatePath

61. Pipe Functions

CallNamedPipe	Connects to a message-type pip, writes to and reads from the pipe, and then closes the pipe.
ConnectNamedPipe	Enables a named pipe server process to wait for a client process to connect to an instance of a named pipe.
CreateNamePipe	Creates an instance of a named pipe and returns a handle for subsequent pipe operations.
CreatePipe	Creates an anonymous pipe.
DisconnectNamedPipe	Disconnects the server end of a named pipe instance from a client process.
GetNamedPipeHandleState	Retrieves information about a specified named pipe.
GetNamedPipeInfo	Retrieves information about the specified named pipe.
PeekNamedPipe	Copies data from a named or anonymous pipe into a buffer without removing it from the pipe.
SetNamedPipeHandleState	Sets the read mode and the blocking mode of the specified named pipe.
TransactNamedPipe	Combines the functions that write a message to and read a message from the specified named pipe into a single network operation.
WaitNamedPipe	Waits until either a time-out interval elapses or an instance of the specified named pipe is available for a connection.

62. Power Management Functions

GetDevicePowerState	Retrieves the current power state of the specified device.
GetSystemPowerStatus	Retrieves the power status of the system.
IsSystemResumeAutomatic	Indicates the current state of the computer.
RequestWakeupLatency	Specifies roughly how quickly the computer should enter the working state.
SetSystemPowerState	Suspends the system by shutting power down.
SetThreadExecutionState	Enables applications to inform the system that it is in use.

63. Printing and Print Spooler Functions

The following functions are used to print.

AbortDoc

DeviceCapabilities

EndDoc

EndPage

Escape

ExtEscape

SetAbortProc

StartDoc

StartPage

The following functions are used to access the print spooler.

Abort Printer	EndDocPrinter
AbortProc	EndPagePrinter
AddForm	EnumForms
AddJob	EnumJobs
AddMonitor	EnumMonitors
AddPort	EnumPorts
AddPrinter	EnumPrinterData
AddPrinterConnection	EnumPrinterDataEx
AddPrinterDriver	EnumPrinterDrivers
AddPrinterDriverEx	EnumPrinterKey
AddPrintProcessor	EnumPrinter
AddPrintProvidor	EnumPrintProcessorDatatypes
AdvancedDocumentProperties	EnumPrintProcessors
ClosePrinter	FindClosePrinterChangeNotification
ConfigurePort	FindFirstPrinterChangeNotification
ConnectToPrinterDlg	FindNextPrinterChangeNotification
DeleteForm	FlushPrinter
DeleteMonitor	FreePrinterNotifyInfo
DeletePort	GetDefaultPrinter
DeletePrinter	GetForm
DeletePrinterConnection	GetJob
DeletePrinterData	GetPrinter
DeletePrinterDataEx	GetPrinterData
DeletePrinterDriver	GetPrinterDataEx
DeletePrinterDriverEx	GetPrinterDriver
DeletePrinterKey	GetPrinterDriverDirectory
DeletePrintProcessor	GetPrintProcessorDirectory
DeletePrintProvidor	OpenPrinter
DocumentProperties	PrinterProperties

ReadPrinter	SetPrinter
ResetPrinter	SetPrinterData
ScheduleJob	SetPrinterDataEx
SetDefaultPrinter	StartDocPrinter
SetForm	StartPagePrinter
SetJob	WritePrinter
SetPort	

64. Process, Thread, and Job Functions

The following functions are used with processes.

CommandLineToArgvW	Parses a Unicode command-line string.
CreateProcess	Creates a new process and its primary thread.
CreateProcessAsUser	Creates a new process and its primary thread. The new process runs in the security context of the specified user.
CreateProcesswithLogonW	Creates a new process and its primary thread. The new process then runs the specified executable file in the security context of the specified credentials (user, domain, and password).
ExitProcess	Ends a process and all its threads.
FreeEnvironmentStrings	Frees a block of environment strings.
GetCommandLine	Retrieves the command-line string for the current process.
GetCurrentProcess	Retrieves a pseudo handle for the current process.
GetCurrentProcessId	Retrieves the process identifier of the calling process.
GetEnvironmentStrings	Retrieves the environment block for the current process.
GetEnvironmentVariable	Retrieves the value of the specified variable from the environment block of the calling process.
GetExitCodeProcess	Retrieves the termination status of the specified process.
GetGuiResources	Retrieves the count of handles to graphical user interface (GUI) objects in use by the specified process.
GetPriorityClass	Retrieves the priority class for the specified process.
GetProcessAffinityMask	Retrieves a process affinity mask for the specified process and the system affinity mask for the system.
GetProcessIoCounters	Retrieves accounting information for all I/O operations performed by the specified process.
GetProcessPriorityBoost	Retrieves the priority boost control state of the specified process.
GetProcessShutdownParameters	Retrieves shutdown parameters for the currently calling process.
GetProcessTimes	Retrieves timing information about the specified process.

GetProcessVersion	Retrieves the major and minor version numbers of the system on which the specified process expects to run.
GetProcessWorkingSetSize	Retrieves the minimum and maximum working set sizes of the specified process.
GetStartupInfo	Retrieves the contents of the STARTUPINFO structure that was specified when the calling process was created.
OpenProcess	Opens an existing process object.
SetEnvironmentVariable	Sets the value of an environment variable for the current process.
SetProcessAffinityMask	Sets a processor affinity mask for the threads of a specified process.
SetProcessPriorityBoost	Disables the ability of the system to temporarily boost the priority of the threads of the specified process.
SetProcessShutdownparameters	Sets shutdown parameters for the currently calling process.
SetProcessWorkingSetSize	Sets the minimum and maximum working set sizes for the specified process.
TerminateProcess	Terminates the specified process and all of its threads.

The following functions are used with threads.

AttachThreadInput	Attaches the input processing mechanism of one thread to that of another thread.
CreateRemoteThread	Creates a thread that runs in the virtual address space of another process.
CreateThread	Creates a thread to execute within the virtual address space of the calling process.
ExitThread	Ends a thread.
GetCurrentThread	Retrieves a pseudo handle for the current thread.
GetCurrentThreadId	Retrieves the thread identifier of the calling thread.
GetExitCodeThread	Retrieves the termination status of the specified thread.
GetThreadPriority	Retrieves the priority value for the specified thread.
GetThreadPriorityBoost	Retrieves the priority boost control state of the specified thread.
GetThreadTimes	Retrieves timing information for the specified thread.
OpenThread	Opens an existing thread object.
ResumeThread	Decrements a thread's suspend count.
SetThreadAffinityMask	Sets a processor affinity mask for the specified thread.
SetThreadIdealProcessor	Specifies a preferred processor for a thread.
SetThreadPriority	Sets the priority value for the specified thread.
SetThreadPriorityBoost	Disables the ability of the system to temporarily boost the priority of a thread.

Sleep	Suspends the execution of the current thread for a specified interval.
SleepEx	Suspends the current thread until the specified condition is met.
SuspendThread	Suspends the specified thread.
SwitchToThread	Causes the calling thread to yield execution to another thread that is ready to run on the current processor.
TerminateThread	Terminates a thread.
ThreadProc	An application-defined function that serves as the starting address for a thread.
TisAlloc	Allocates a thread local storage (TLS) index.
TisFree	Releases a TLS index.
TisGetValue	Retrieves the value in the calling thread's TLS slot for a specified TLS index.
TlsSetValue	Stores a value in the calling thread's TLS slot for a specified TLS index.
WaitForInputIdle	Waits until the specified process is waiting for user input with no input pending, or until the time-out interval has elapsed.

The following functions are used with job objects

AssignProcessToJobObject	Associates a process with an existing job object.
CreateJobObject	Creates or opens a job object.
OpenJobObject	Opens an existing job object.
QueryInformationJobObject	Retrieves limit and job state information from the job object.
SetInformationJobObject	Set limits for a job object.
TerminateJobObject	Terminates all processes currently associated with the job.
UserHandleGrantAccess	Grants or denies access to a handle to a User object to a job that has a user-interface restriction.

The following functions are used in thread pooling.

BindI.CompletionCallback	Binds the specified file handle to the thread pool's I/O completion port.
QueueUserWorkItem	Queues a work item to a worker thread in the thread pool.

65. PSAPI Functions (process status APIs)

EmptyWorkingSet

EnumDeviceDrivers

EnumProcesses

EnumProcessModules

GetDeviceDriverBaseName

GetDeviceDriverFileName

GetMappedFileName

GetModuleBaseName

GetModuleFileNameEx

GetModuleInformation

GetProcessMemoryInfo

GetWsChanges

InitializeProcessForWsWatch

QueryWorkingSet

66. Rectangle Functions

CopyRect	Copies the coordinates of one rectangle to another.
EqualRect	Determines whether the two specified rectangles are equal by comparing the coordinates of their upper-left and lower-right corners.
InflatRect	Increases or decreases the width and height of the specified rectangle.
IntersectRect	Calculates the intersection of two source rectangles and places the coordinates of the intersection rectangle into the destination rectangle.
IsRectEmpty	Determines whether the specified rectangle is empty.
OffsetRect	Moves the specified rectangle by the specified offsets.
PtInRect	Determines whether the specified point lies within the specified rectangle.
SetRect	Sets the coordinates of the specified rectangle.
SetRectEmpty	Creates an empty rectangle in which all coordinates are set to zero.
SubtractRect	Determines the coordinates of a rectangle formed by subtracting one rectangle from another.
UnionRect	Creates the union of two rectangles.

67. Region Functions

CombineRgn	Combines two regions and stores the result in a third region.
CreateEllipticRgn	Creates an elliptical region.
CreateEllipticRgnIndirect	Creates an elliptical region.
CreatePolygonRgn	Creates a polygonal region.

CreatePolyPolygonRgn	Creates a region consisting of a series of polygons.
CreateRectRgn	Creates a rectangular region.
CreateRectRgnIndirect	Creates a rectangular region.
CreateRoundRectRgn	Creates a rectangular region with rounded corners.
EqualRgn	Checks the two specified regions to determine whether they are identical.
ExtCreateRegion	Creates a region from the specified region and transformation data.
FillRgn	Fills a region by using the specified brush.
FrameRgn	Draws a border around the specified region by using the specified brush.
GetPolyFillMode	Retrieves the current polygon fill mode.
GetRegionData	Fills the specified buffer with data describing a region.
GetRgnBox	Retrieves the bounding rectangle of the specified region.
InvertRgn	Inverts the colors in the specified region.
OffsetRgn	Moves a region by the specified offsets.
PaintRgn	Paints the specified region by using the brush currently selected into the device context.
PtInRegion	Determines whether the specified point is inside the specified region.
RectInRegion	Determines whether any part of the specified rectangle is within the boundaries of a region.
SetPolyFillMode	Sets the polygon fill mode for functions that fill polygons.
SetRectRgn	Converts a region into a rectangular region with the specified coordinates.

68. Registry Function

RegCloseKey	Releases a handle to the specified registry key.
RegConnectRegistry	Establishes a connection to a predefined registry handle on another computer.
RegCreateKeyEx	Creates the specified registry key.
RegDeleteKey	Deletes a subkey.
RegDeleteValue	Removes a named value from the specified registry key.
RegDisablePredefinedCache	Disables the predefined registry handle table of HKEY_CURRENT_USER for the specified process.
RegEnumKeyEx	Enumerates subkeys of the specified open registry key.
RegEnumValue	Enumerates the values for the specified open registry key.

RegFlushKey	Writes all the attributes of the specified open registry key into the registry.
RegGetKeySecurity	Retrieves a copy of the security descriptor protecting the specified open registry key.
RegLoadKey	Creates a subkey under HKEY_USERS or HKEY_LOCAL_MACHINE and stores registration information from a specified file into that subkey.
RegNotifyChangeKeyValue	Notifies the caller about changes to the attributes or contents of a specified registry key.
RegOpenCurrentUser	Retrieves a handle to the HKEY_CURRENT_USER key for the user the current thread is impersonating.
RegOpenKeyEx	Opens the specified registry key.
RegOpenUserClassesRoot	Retrieves a handle to the HKEY_CLASSES_ROOT key for the specified user.
RegOverridePredefKey	Maps a predefined registry key to a specified registry key.
RegQueryInfoKey	Retrieves information about the specified registry key.
RegQueryMultipleValues	Retrieves the type and data for a list of value names associated with an open registry key.
RegQueryValueEx	Retrieves the type and data for a specified value name associated with an open registry key.
RegReplaceKey	Replaces the file backing a registry key and all its subkeys with another file.
RegRestoreKey	Reads the registry information in a specified file and copies it over the specified key.
RegSaveKey	Saves the specified key and all of its subkeys and values to a new file.
RegSetKeySecurity	Sets the security of an open registry key.
RegSetValueEx	Sets the data and type of a specified value under a registry key.
RegUnLoadKey	Unloads the specified registry key and its subkeys from the registry.

69. Resource Functions

BeginUpdateResource	Returns a handle that can be used by UpdateResource to add, delete, or replace resources.
CopyImage	Creates a new icon, cursor, or bitmap and copies the attributes of the old one to the new one.
EndUpdateResource	Ends a resource update in an executable file.

EnumResLangProc	An application-defined callback function used with EnumResourceLanguages.
EnumResNameProc	An application-defined callback function used with EnumResourceNames.
EnumResourceLanguages	Searches for resources of a specified type and name and passes the language to a callback function.
EnumResourceNames	Searches for resources of a specified type and passes the name or the ID to a callback function.
EnumResourceTypes	Searches for resources and passes each type to a callback function.
EnumResTypeProc	An application-defined callback function used with EnumResourceTypes.
FindResource	Finds a resource with a specified type and name.
FindResourceEx	Finds a resource with a specified type, name, and language.
LoadImage	Loads an icon, cursor, or bitmap.
LoadResource	Loads a resource into global memory.
LockResource	Locks a resource in memory.
SizeofResource	Returns the size of a resource.
UpdateResource	Adds, deletes, or replaces a resource.

70. Rich Edit Control Functions

This section groups messages, notification messages, and structures associated with rich edit controls. Some of these application programming interface (API) elements are also used with edit controls.

Formatting

BIDIOPTIONS

CHARFORMAT

EM_GETAUTOURLDETECT

EM_GETBIDIOPTIONS

EM_GETCHARFORMAT

EM_GETPARAFORMAT

EM_GETRECT

EM_GETTYPOGRAPHYOPTIONS

EM_SETBIDIOPTIONS

EM_SETBKGNDCOLOR

EM_SETCHARFORMAT

EM_SETEVENTMASK

EM_SETFONTSIZE

EM_SETLANGOPTIONS

EM_SETPALETTE

EM_SETPARAFORMAT

EM_SETRECT

EM_SETTYPOGRAPHYOPTIONS

PARAFORMAT

PARAFORMAT2

Selection and Hit Testing

CHARRANGE

EM_CHARFROMPOS

EM_EXGETSEL

EM_EXSETSEL

EM_GETFIRSTVISIBLELINE

EM_GETSEL

EM_HIDESELECTION

EM_POSFROMCHAR

EM_SELECTIONTYPE

EM_SETSEL

EN_SELCHANGE

SELCHANGE

Text Operations

EM_EXLIMITTEXT

EM_FINDTEXT

EM_FINDTEXTEX

EM_FINDTEXTEXW

EM_FINDTEXTW

EM_GETLIMITTEXT

EM_GETTEXTEX

EM_GETTEXLENGTHEX

EM_GETTEXTMODE

EM_GETTEXTRANGE

EM_REPLACESEL

EM_SETLIMITTEXT

EM_SETTEXTEX

EM_SETTEXTMODE

FINDTEXT

FINDTEXTEX

GETTEXTEX

GETTEXTLENGTHEX

SETTEXTEX

TEXTRANGE

Word and Line Breaks

EM_EXLINEFROMCHAR

EM_FINDWORDBREAK

EM_GETWORDBREAKPROC

EM_SETWORDBREAKPROC

EM_GETWORDBREAKPROCEX

EM_SETWORDBREAKPROCEX

EditWordBreakProcEx

Lines and Scrolling

EM_GETLINE

EM_GETLINECOUNT

EM_GETSCROLLPOS

EM_GETTHUMB

EM_LINEFROMCHAR

EM_LINEINDEX

EM_LINELENGTH

EM_LINESCROLL

EM_SCROLL

EM_SCROLLCARET

EM_SETSCROLLPOS

EM_SHOWSCROLLBAR

Editing Operations

EM_CANPASTE

EM_CANREDO

EM_CANUNDO

EM_EMPTYUNDOBUFFER

EM_GETEDITSTYLE

EM_GETREDONAME

EM_GETUNDONAME

EM_PASTESPECIAL

EM_RECONVERSION

EM_REDO

EM_SETUNDOLIMIT

EM_STOPGROUPTYPING

EM_UNDO

REPASTESPECIAL

Streams

EDITSTREAM

EM_STREAMIN

EM_STREAMOUT

Printing

EM_DISPLAYBAND

EM_FORMATRANGE

EM_SETTARGETDEVICE

FORMATRANGE

Bottomless Rich Edit Controls

EM_REQUESTRESIZE

EN_REQUESTRESIZE

REQRESIZE

Interfaces

EM_GETOLEINTERFACE

EM_SETOLECALLBACK

EN_OLEOPFAILED

ENOLEOPFAILED

IrichEditOle

IrichEditOleCallback

REOBJECT

Miscellaneous

EM_GETEVENTMASK

EM_GETIMECOLOR

EM_GETIMECOMPMODE

EM_GETIMEOPTIONS

EM_GETLANGOPTIONS

EM_GETMODIFY

EM_GETOPTIONS

EM_GETPUNCTUATION

EM_GETWORDWRAPMODE

EM_GETZOOM

EM_SETEVENTMASK

EM_SETIMECOLOR

EM_SETTIMEOPTIONS

EM_SETMODIFY

EM_SETOPTIONS

EM_SETPUNCTUATION

EM_SETREADONLY

EM_SETWORDWRAPMODE

EM_SETZOOM

EN_CHANGE

EN_CORRECTTEXT

EN_DROPFILES

EN_ERRSPACE

EN_HSCROLL

EN_IMECHANGE

EN_KILLFOCUS

EN_LINK

EN_MAXTEXT

EN_MSGFILTER

EN_PROTECTED

EN_SAVECLIPBOARD

EN_SETFOCUS

EN_STOPNOUNDO

EN_UPDATE

EN_VSCROLL

COMPCOLOR

ENCORRECTTEXT

ENDROPFILES

ENLINK

ENPROTECTED

ENSAVECLIPBOARD

MSGFILTER

PUNCTUATION

Rich Edit Callback Functions

EditStreamCallBack	An application defined-callback function used with the EM_STREAMIN and EM_STREADMOUT messages.
EditWordBreakProcEx	An application-defined callback function used with the EM_SET-WORDBREAKPROCEX message.

Rich Edit Interfaces

The rich edit control supports the client functionality defined by COM. The control provides full support for most COM client features. It does not support linking to its contents. The client is responsible for dialogs and error messages, managing storage for COM objects, and document and application-window level in-place activation support. The client can use the EM_GETOLEINTERFACE message to obtain an IRichEditOle interface from the rich edit control, which allows it to manage objects. The client uses the EM_SETOLECALLBACK message to register an IrichEditOleCallback interface that the control uses to obtain the required interfaces and storage.

IRichEditOle	An interface used by the client of a rich text edit control to carry out OLE-related operations.
IRichEditOleCallback	An interface used by a rich text edit control to retrieve OLE-related information from its client.

71. Scroll Bar Functions

EnableScrollBar	Enables or disables one or both scroll bar arrows.
GetScrollBarInfo	Retrieves information about the specified scroll bar.
GetScrollInfo	Retrieves the parameters of a scroll bar.
GetScrollPos	Retrieves the current position of the scroll box.
GetScrollRange	Retrieves the current minimum and maximum scroll box positions.
ScrollDC	Scrolls a rectangle of bits horizontally and vertically.
ScrollWindow	Scrolls the contents of the specified window's client area.
ScrollWindowEx	Scrolls the contents of the specified window's client area.
SetScrollInfo	Sets the parameter of a scroll bar.
SetScrollPos	Sets the position of the scroll box.
SetScrollRange	Sets the minimum and maximum scroll box position.
ShowScrollBar	Shows or hides the specified scroll bar.

72. Service Functions

The following functions are used by services and programs that control or configure services.

ChangeServiceConfig	Changes the configuration parameters of a service.
ChangeServiceConfig2	Changes the optional configuration parameters of a service.

CloseServiceHandle	Closes the specified handle to a service control manager object or a service object.
ControlService	Sends a control code to a service.
CreateService	Creates a service object and adds it to the specified service control manager database.
DeleteService	Marks the specified service for deletion from the service control manager database.
EnumDependentServices	Retrieves the name and status of each service that depends on the specified service.
EnumServicesStatus	Enumerates services in the specified service control manager database.
EnumServicesStatusEx	Enumerates services in the specified service control manager database based on the specified information level.
GetServiceDisplayName	Retrieves the display name of the specified service.
GetServiceKeyName	Retrieves the service name of the specified service.
Handler	An application-defined callback function used with the RegisterServiceCtrlHandler function.
HandlerEx	An application-defined callback function used with the RegisterServiceCtrlHandlerEx function.
LockServiceDatabase	Requests ownership of the service control manager database lock.
NotifyBootConfigStatus	Reports the boot status to the service control manager.
OpenSCManager	Establishes a connection to the service control manager on the specified computer and opens the specified service control manager database.
OpenService	Opens an existing service.
QueryServiceConfig	Retrieves the configuration parameters of the specified service.
QueryServiceConfig2	Retrieves the optional configuration parameters of the specified service.
QueryServiceLockStatus	Retrieves the lock status of the specified service control manager database.
QueryServiceObjectSecurity	Retrieves a copy of the security descriptor associated with a service object.
QueryServiceStatus	Retrieves the current status of the specified service.
QueryServiceStatusEx	Retrieves the current status of the specified service based on the specified information level.
RegisterServiceCtrlHandler	Registers a function to handle service control requests for an application.
RegisterServiceCtrlHandlerEx	Registers a function to handle service control requests for an application.

ServiceMain	An application-defined function that serves as the entry point for a service.
SetServiceBits	Registers a service type with the service control manager and the Server service.
SetServiceObjectSecurity	Sets the security descriptor of a service object.
SetServiceStatus	Updates the service control manager's status information for the calling service.
StartService	Starts a service.
StartServiceCtrlDispatcher	Connects the main thread of a service process to the service control manager.
UnlockServiceDatabase	Unlocks a service control manager database by releasing the specified lock.

73. Static Control Messages

STM_GETICON

STM_GETIMAGE

STM_SETICON

STM_SETIMAGE

STN_CLICKED

STN_DBLCLK

STN_DISABLE

STN_ENABLE

WM_CTLCOLORSTATIC

74. String Functions

CharLower	Converts a character string or a single character to lowercase.
CharLowerBuff	Converts uppercase characters in a buffer to lowercase characters.
CharNext	Retrieves a pointer to the next character in a string.
CharNextExA	Retrieves the pointer to the next character in a string.
CharPrev	Retrieves a pointer to the preceding character in a string.
CharPrevExA	Retrieves the pointer to the preceding character in a string.
CharToOem	Translates a string into the OEM-defined character set.
CharToOemBuff	Translates a specified number of characters in a string into the OEM-defined character set.

CharUpper	Converts a character string or a single character to uppercase.
CharUpperBuff	Converts lowercase characters in a buffer to uppercase characters.
CompareString	Compares two character strings, using the specified locale.
FoldString	Maps one string to another, performing a specified transformation option.
GetStringTypeA	Retrieves character-type information for the characters in the specified source string.
GetStringTypeEx	Retrieves character-type information for the characters in the specified source string.
GetStringTypeW	Retrieves character-type information for the characters in the specified source string.
IsCharAlpha	Determines whether a character is an alphabetic character.
IsCharAlphaNumeric	Determines whether a character is either an alphabetic or a numeric character.
IsCharLower	Determines whether a character is lowercase.
IsCharUpper	Determines whether a character is uppercase.
LoadString	Loads a string resource from the executable file associated with a specified module.
lstrcat	Appends one string to another.
lstrcmp	Compares two character strings
lstrcmpi	Compares two character strings.
lstrcpy	Copies a string to a buffer.
lstrcpyn	Copies a specified number of characters from a source string into a buffer.
lstrlen	Retrieves the lengh of the specified string (not including the terminating null character).
MultiByteToWideChar	Maps a character string to a wide-character (Unicode) string.
OemToChar	Translates a string from the OEM-defined character set into either an ANSI or a wide-character string.
OemToCharBuff	Translates a specified number of characters in a string from the OEM-defined character set into either an ANSI or a wide-character string.
WideCharToMultiByte	Maps a wide-character string to a new character string.
wsprintf	Formats and stores a series of characters and values in a buffer.
Wvsprintf	Formats and stores a series of characters and values in a buffer.

75. Structured Exception Handling Functions

AbnormatTermination	Indicates whether the _try block of a termination handler terminated normally.
GetExceptionCode	Retrieves a code that identifies the type of exception that occurred.
GetExceptionInformation	Retrieves a machine-independent description of an exception, and information about the machine state that existed for the thread when the exception occurred.
RaiseException	Raises an exception in the calling thread.
SetUnhandledExceptionFilter	Enables an application to supersede the top-level exception handler of each thread and process.
UnhandledExceptionFileter	Passes unhandled exception to the debugger, if the process is being debugged.

76. Synchronization Functions

The following functions are used in synchronization.

APCProc	An application-defined callback function used with the QueueUserAPC function.
GetOverlappedResult	Retrieves the results of an overlapped operation.
QueueUserAPC	Adds a user-mode asynchronous procedure call (APC) object to the APC queue of the specified thread.

The following functions are used in Critical-Section.

DeleteCriticalSection	Releases all resources used by an unowned critical section object.
EnterCriticalSection	Waits for ownership of the specified critical section object.
InitializeCriticalSection	Initializes a critical section object.
InitializeCriticalSectionAndSpinCount	Initializes a critical section object and sets the spin count for the critical section.
LeaveCriticalSection	Releases ownership of the specified critical section object.
SetCriticalSectionSpinCount	Sets the spin count for the specified critical section.
TryEnterCriticalSection	Attempts to enter a critical section without blocking.

The following functions are used with Events.

CreateEvent	Creates or opens a named or unnamed event object.
OpenEvent	Opens an existing named event object.

PulseEvent	Sets the specified event object to the signaled state and then resets it to the nonsignaled state after releasing the appropriate number of waiting threads.
ResetEvent	Sets the specified event object to the nonsignaled state.
SetEvent	Sets the specified event object to the signaled state.

The following functions are used with Interlocked.

InterlockedCompareExchange	Performs an atomic comparison of the specified values and exchanges the values, based on the outcome of the comparison.
InterlockedCompareExchangePointer	Performs an atomic comparison of the specified values, based on the outcome of the comparison.
InterlockedDecrement	Decrements (decreases by one) the value of the specified variables and checks the resulting value.
InterlockedExchanged	Atomically exchanges a pair of values.
InterlockedExchangeAdd	Performs an atomic addition of an increment value to an addend variable.
InterlockedExchangePointer	Atomically exchanges a pair of values.
InterlockedIncrement	Increments (increases by one) the value of the specified variable and checks the resulting value.

The following functions are used with Mutex.

CreateMutex	Creates or opens a named or unnamed mutex object.
OpenMutex	Opens an existing named mutex object.
ReleaseMutex	Releases ownership of the specified mutex object.

The following functions are used with Semaphore.

CreateSemaphore	Creates or opens a named or unnamed semaphore object.
OpenSemaphore	Opens an existing named semaphore object.
ReleaseSemaphore	Increases the count of the specified semaphore object by a specified amount.

The following functions are used with Timer-Queue Timer.

ChangeTimerQueueTimer	Updates a timer-queue timer.
CreateTimerQueue	Creates a queue for timers.
CreateTimerQueueTimer	Creates a timer-queue timer.
DeleteTimerQueue	Deletes a timer queue.
DeleteTimerQueueEx	Deletes a timer queue.
DeleteTimerQueueTimer	Cancels a timer-queue timer.

The following functions are used with Wait Function.

MsgWaitForMultipleObjects	Returns when the specified criteria for the specified objects is met.
MsgWaitForMultipleObjectsEx	Returns when the specified criteria for the specified objects is met.
RegisterWaitForSingleObject	Directs a wait thread in the thread pool to wait on the object.
SignalObjectAndWait	Allows the caller to atomically signal an object and wait on another object.
UnregisterWait	Cancels a registered wait operation.
UnregisterWaitEx	Cancels a registered wait operation.
WaitForMultipleObjects	Returns when the specified criteria for the specified objects is met.
WaitForMultipleObjectsEx	Returns when the specified criteria for the specified objects is met.
WaitForSingleObject	Returns when the specified criteria for the specified object is met.
WaitForSingleObjectEx	Returns when the specified criteria for the specified object is met.
WaitOrTimerCallback	Returns when the specified criteria is met.

The following functions are used with Waitable Timer.

CancelWaitableTimer	Sets the specified waitable timer to the inactive state.
CreateWaitableTimer	Creates or opens a waitable timer object.
OpenWaitableTimer	Opens an existing named waitable timer object.
SetWaitableTimer	Activates the specified waitable timer.
TimerAPCProc	Application-defined timer completion routine used with the SetWaitableTimer function.

77. System Information Functions

DnsHostnameToComputerName	Converts a DNS name to a NetBIOS name.
ExpandEnvironmentStrings	Replaces environment-variable strings with their defined values.
GetComputerName	Gets the NetBIOS name of the local computer.
GetComputerNameEx	Gets the NetBIOS or DNS name of the local computer.
GetComputerObjectName	Gets the local computer's name in a specified format.
GetCurrentHwProfile	Gets the current hardware profile for the local computer.
GetKeyboardType	Gets information about the current keyboard.
GetSysColor	Gets the current color of a display element.
GetSystemDirectory	Gets the path of the system directory.

GetSystemInfo	Gets information about the current system.
GetSystemMetrics	Gets system metrics and configuration settings.
GetSystemWindowsDirectory	Gets the path of the shared Windows directory on a multiuser system.
GetUserName	Gets the user name of the current thread.
GetUserNameEx	Gets the name of the user or other security principal associated with the calling thread. You can specify the format of the returned name.
GetVersion	Gets the version number of the operating system.
GetWindowsDirectory	Gets the path of the Windows directory.
IsProcessorFeaturePresent	Determines whether a processor feature is supported by the current computer.
SetComputerName	Stores a new NetBIOS name for the local computer.
SetComputerNameEx	Stores a new NetBIOS or DNS name for the local computer.
SetSysColors	Sets the colors for one or more display elements.
SystemParametersInfo	Queries or sets system-wide parameters.
TranslateName	Converts a directory service object name from one format to another.
VerifyVersionInfo	Compares a set of version requirements to the values for the current operating system.
VerifyVersionInfo	Compares a set of version requirements to the values for the current operating system.
VerSetConditionMask	Builds the condition mask for the VerifyVersionInfo function.

78. System Shutdown Functions

AbortSystemShutdown

ExitWindows

ExitWindowEx

InitiateSystemShutdown

InitiateSystemShutdownEx

LockWorkstation

79. Tape Backup Functions

BackupRead	Reads data associated with a specified file or directory into a buffer.
BackupSeek	Seeks forward in a data stream.
BackupWrite	Writes a stream of data from a buffer to a specified file or directory.

CreateTapePartition	Reformats a tape.
EraseTape	Erases all or part of a tape.
GetTapeParameters	Retrieves information that describes the tape or the tape drive.
GetTapePosition	Retrieves the current address of the tape.
GetTapeStatus	Determines whether the tape device is ready to process tape commands.
PrepareTape	Prepares the tape to be accessed or removed.
SetTapeParameters	Specifies the block size of a tape or configures the tape device.
SetTapePosition	Sets the tape position on the specified device.
WriteTapemark	Writes a specified number of filemarks, setmarks, short filemarks, or long filemarks to a tape device.

80. Terminal Services API Functions

ProcessIDToSessionId	Retrieves the Terminal Services session associated with a specified process.
VirtualChannelClose	Closes the client end of a virtual channel.
VirtualChannelEntry	An application-defined entry point for the client-side DLL of an application that uses Terminal Services virtual channels.
VirtualChannelInit	Initializes a client DLL's access to Terminal Services virtual channels.
VirtualChannelInitEvent	An application-defined callback function that Terminal Services calls to notify the client DLL of virtual channel events.
VirtualChannelOpen	Opens the client end of a virtual channel.
VirtualChannelOpenEvent	An application-defined callback function that Terminal Services calls to notify the client DLL of events for a specific virtual channel.
VirtualChannelWrite	Sends data from the client end of a virtual channel to a partner application on the server end.
WTSCloseServer	Closes an open handle to a terminal server.
WTSDisconnectSession	Disconnects the logged-on user from the specified Terminal Services session without closing the session.
WTSEnumerateProcesses	Retrieves information about the active processes on a specified terminal server.
WTSEnumerateSessions	Retrieves a list of sessions on a specified terminal server.
WTSFreeMemory	Frees memory allocated by a Terminal Services function.
WTSLogoffSession	Logs off a specified Terminal Services session.
WTSOpenServer	Opens a handle to the specified terminal server.
WTSQuerySessionInformation	Retrieves session information for the specified session on the specified terminal server.

WTSQueryUserConfig	Retrieves configuration information for the specified user on the specified domain controller or terminal server.
WTSSendMessage	Displays a message box on the client desktop of a specified Terminal Services session.
WTSSetUserConfig	Modifies configuration information for the specified user on the specified domain controller or terminal server.
WTSShutdownSystem	Shuts down (and optionally reboots) the specified terminal server.
WTSTerminateProcess	Terminates the specified process on the specified terminal server.
WTSVirtualChannelClose	Closes an open virtual channel handle.
WTSVirtualChannelOpen	Opens a handle to the server end of a specified virtual channel.
WTSVirtualChannelPurgeInput	Purges all queued input data sent from the client to the server on a specified virtual channel.
WTSVirtualChannelPurgeOutput	Purges all queued output data sent from the server to the client on a specified virtual channel.
WTSVirtualChannelRead	Reads data from the server end of a virtual channel.
WTSVirtualChannelWrite	Writes data to the server end of a virtual channel.
WTSWaitSystemEvent	Waits for a Terminal Services event before returning to the caller.

81. Text Object Model Interfaces

ITextDocument	Retrieves the active selection and range objects for any story in the document.
ITextFont	Encapsulates the functionality of the Microsoft Word Font dialog box.
ITestPara	Encapsulates the functionality of the Microsoft Word Paragraph dialog box.
ITextRange	Enables an application to select text in a story and then examine or change the text.
ITextSelection	A text selection is a text range with selection highlighting. It is associated with some kind of view, and has some UI-oriented methods that allow one to emulate keyboard input.
ITextStoryRanges	Enumerates the stories in an ITextDocument object.

82. Time Functions

CompareFileTime	Compares two 64-bit file times.
DosDateTimeToFileTime	Converts MS-DOS date and time values to a 64-bit file time.
FileTimeToDosDateTime	Converts a 64-bit file time to MS-DOS date and time values.

FileTimeToLocalFileTime	Converts a UTC file time to a local file time.
FileTimeToSystemTime	Converts a 64-bit file time to system time format.
GetFileTime	Retrieves the date and time that a file was created, last accessed, and last modified.
GetLocalTime	Retrieves the current local date and time.
GetSystemTime	Retrieves the current system date and time in UTC format.
GetSystemTimeAdjustment	Determines whether the system is applying periodic time adjustments to its time-of-day clock.
GetSystemTimeAsFileTime	Retrieves the current system date and time in UTC format.
GetTickCount	Retrieves the number of milliseconds that have elapsed since the system was started.
GetTimeZoneInformation	Retrieves the current time-zone parameters.
LocalFileTimeToFileTime	Converts a local file time to a file time based on UTC.
SetFileTime	Sets the date and time that a file was created, last accessed, or last modified.
SetLocalTime	Sets the current local time and date.
SetSystemTime	Sets the current system time and date.
SetSystemTimeAdjustment	Enables or disables periodic time adjustments to the system's time-of-day clock.
SetTimeZoneInformation	Sets the current time-zone parameters.
SystemTimeToFileTime	Converts a system time to a file time.
SystemTimeToTzSpecificLocalTime	Converts a UTC time to a specified time zone's corresponding local time.

83. Timer Functions

KillTimer	Destroys the specified timer.
QueryPerformanceCounter	Retrieves the current value of the high-resolution performance counter.
QueryPerformanceFrequency	Retrieves the frequency of the high-resolution performance counter.
SetTimer	Creates a timer with the specified time-out value.
TimerProc	An application-defined callback function that processes WM_TIMER messages.

84. Tool Help Functions

CreateToolhelp32Snapshot

Heap32First

Heap32ListFirst

Heap32ListNext

Heap32Next

Module32First

Module32Next

Process32First

Process32Next

Thread32First

Thread32Next

Toolhelp32ReadProcessMemory

85. Unicode and Character Set Functions

GetTextCharset

GetTextCharsetInfo

IsDBCSLeadByte

IsDBCSLLeadByteEx

IsTextUnicode

MultiByteToWideChar

TranslateCharsetInfo

WideCharToMultiByte

86. Uniscribe Functions

This section describes complex script processing functions.

ScriptApplyDigitSubstitution	Applies digit substitution settings.
ScriptApplyLogicalWidth	Takes an array of advance widths for a run and generates an array of glyph widths.
ScriptBreak	Returns information for determining line breaks.
ScriptCacheGetHeight	Returns information about the currently cached font.
ScriptCPtoX	Returns the x offset of a run to either the leading or the trailing edge of a logical character cluster.
ScriptFreeCache	Frees a SCRIPT_CACHE structure.
ScriptGetCMap	Returns the glyph indices of the characters of a string according to the cmap table.
ScriptGetFontProperties	Returns information from the font cache.
ScriptGetGlyphABCWidth	Returns the ABC width of a glyph.

ScriptGetLogicalWidths	Converts the glyph advance widths into logical widths.
ScriptGetProperties	Returns information about the current scripts.
ScriptIsComplex	Determines whether a string requires complex script processing.
ScriptItemize	Breaks a string into individually shapeable items.
ScriptJustify	Creates an advance widths table to allow text justification.
ScriptLayout	Converts an array of run-embedding levels into a map of visual-to-logical position, and/or logical-to-visual position.
ScriptPlace	Takes the glyphs and visual attributes of a run and generates glyph-advanced width and two-dimensional offset information.
ScriptRecordDigitSubstitution	Reads the National Language Support (NLS) native-digit and digit-substitution settings and then records them in the SCRIPT_DIGITSUBSTITUTE structure.
ScriptShape	Takes a run and generates its glyphs and visual attributes.
ScriptStringAnalyse	Analyzes a plain text string.
ScriptStringCPtoX	Returns the x-coordinate for the leading or trailing edge of a character position.
ScriptStringFree	Frees a SCRIPT_STRING_ANALYSIS structure.
ScriptStringGetLogicalWidths	Converts visual widths into logical widths.
ScriptStringGetOrder	Creates an array that maps an original character position to a glyph position.
ScriptStringOut	Displays a string generated by a prior call to ScriptStringAnalyse and optionally adds highlighting.
ScriptString_pcOutChars	Returns a pointer to the length of a string after clipping.
ScriptString_pLogAttr	Returns a pointer to a logical attributes buffer for an analyzed string.
ScriptString_pSize	Returns a pointer to a SIZE structure for an analyzed string.
ScriptStringValidate	Checks the SCRIPT_STRING_ANALYSIS structure for invalid sequences.
ScriptStringXtoCP	Converts an x-coordinate to a character position.
ScriptTextOut	Takes the output of both the ScriptShape and ScriptPlace calls and then calls the operating system ExtTextOut function appropriately.
ScriptXtoCP	Converts the x offset of a run to a logical character position and a flag to indicate whether the x position fell in the leading or trailing half of the character.

87. User Profiles Functions

CreateEnvironmentBlock

DeleteProfile

DestroyEnvironmentBlock

ExpandEnvironmentStringsForUser

GetAllUsersProfileDirectory

GetDefaultUserProfileDirectory

GetProfilesDirectory

GetProfileType

GetUserProfileDirectory

LoadUserProfile

UnloadUserProfile

88. Version Information Functions

GetFileVersionInfo	Retrieves version information for the specified file.
GetFileVersionInfoSize	Determines whether the operating system can retrieve version information for a specified file. If version information is available, the function returns the size, in bytes, of that information.
VerFindFile	Determines where to install a file based on whether it locates another version of the file in the system.
VerInstallFile	Attempts to install the specified file based on information returned from the VerFindFile function.
VerLanguageName	Retrieves a description string for the language associated with a specified binary Microsoft language identifier.
VerQueryValue	Retrieves specified version information from the specified version-information resource.

89. Window Functions

AdjustWindowRect	Calculates the required size of the window rectangle, based on the desired client-rectangle size.
AdjustWindowRectEx	Calculates the required size of the window rectangle, based on the desired client-rectangle size.
AllowSetForegroundWindow	Enables a process to set the foreground window using the SetForegroundWindow function.
AnimateWindow	Enables you to produce special effects when showing or hiding windows.
ArrangeIconicWindows	Arranges all minimized (iconic) child windows of the specified parent window.
BeginDeferWindowPos	Allocates memory for a multiple-window-position structure and returns the handle to the structure.
BringWindowToTop	Brings the specified window to the top of the Z order.

CascadeWindows	Cascades the specified child windows of the specified parent window.
ChildWindowFromPoint	Determines which, if any, of the child windows belonging to a parent window contains the specified point.
ChildWindowFromPointEx	Determines which, if any, of the child windows belonging to a parent window contains the specified point.
CloseWindow	Minimizes (but does not destroy) the specified window.
CreateWindow	Creates an overlapped, pop-up, or child window.
CreateWindowEx	Creates an overlapped, pop-up, or child window with an extended window style.
DeferWindowPos	Updates the specifed multiple-window-position structure for the specified window.
DestroyWindow	Destroys the specified window.
EndDeferWindowPos	Updates the position and size of one or more windows.
EnumChildProc	An application-defined callback function used with EnumChildWindows.
EnumChildWindows	Enumerates the child windows that belong to the specified parent window.
EnumTheadWindows	Enumerates all nonchild windows associated with a thread.
EnumThreadWndProc	An application-defined callback function used with EnumThreadWindows.
EnumWindows	Enumerates all top-level windows on the screen.
EnumWindowProc	An application-defined callback function used with EnumWindows or EnumDestopWindows.
FindWindow	Retrieves a handle to the top-level window whose class name and window name match the specified strings.
FindWindowEx	Retrieves a handle to the top-level window whose class name and window name match the specified strings.
GetAltTabInfo	Retrieves status information for the application-switching (ALT+TAB) window.
GetAncestor	Retrieves the handle to the ancestor of the specified window.
GetClientRect	Retrieves the coordinates of a window's client area.
GetDesktopWindow	Returns a handle to the desktop window.
GetForegroundWindow	Returns a handle to the foreground window.
GetGUIThreadInfo	Retrieves information about the active window or a GUI thread.
GetLastActivePopup	Determines which pop-up window was most recently active.
GetLayout	Returns the layout of a device context.
GetNextWindow	Retrieves a handle to the next or previous window in Z order.

GetParent	Retrieves a handle to the specified child window's parent window.
GetProcessDefaultLayout	Gets the default layout used for windows with no parent or owner.
GetTitleBarInfo	Retrieves information about the specified title bar.
GetTopWindow	Retrieves a handle to the child window at the top of the Z order.
GetWindow	Retrieves a handle to a window that has the specified relationship to the specified window.
GetWindowInfo	Retrieves information about the specified window.
GetWindowModuleFileName	Retrieves the full path and file name of the module associated with the specified window handle.
GetWindowPlacement	Retrieves the show state and the restored, minimized, and maximized positions of the specified window.
GetWindowRect	Retrieves the dimensions of the bounding rectangle of the specified window.
GetWindowText	Copies the text of the specified window's title bar.
GetWindowTextLength	Retrieves the length of the specifed window's title bar text.
GetWindowThreadProcessId	Retrieves the identifier of the thread that created the specified window.
IsChild	Tests whether a window is a child window or descendent window of a specified parent window.
IsIconic	Determines whether the specified window is minimized (iconic).
IsWindow	Determines whether the specified window handle identifies an existing window.
IsWindowUnicode	Determines whether the specified window is a Unicode window.
IsWindowVisible	Retrieves the visibility state of the specified window.
IsZoomed	Determines whether a window is maximized (zoomed).
LockSetForegroundWindow	Disables calls to SetForegroundWindow.
MoveWindow	Changes the position and dimensions of the specified window.
OpenIcon	Restores a minimized (iconic) window to its previous size and position.
RealChildWindowFromPoint	Retrieves a handle to the child window at the specified point.
RealGetWindowClass	Retrieves the window type.
SetForegroundWindow	Puts the thread that created the specified window into the foreground and activates the window.
SetLayeredWindowAttributes	Sets the opacity and transparency color key of a layered window.

SetLayout	Changes the layout of a device context.
SetParent	Changes the parent window of the specified child window.
SetProcessDefaultLayout	Sets the default layout used for window with no parent or owner.
SetWindowPlacement	Sets the show state and the restored, minimized, and maximized positions of the specified window.
SetWindowPos	Changes the size, position, and Z order of a window.
SetWindowText	Changes the text of the specified window's title bar.
ShowOwnedPopups	Shows or hides all pop-up windows owned by the specified window.
ShowWindow	Sets the specified window's show state.
ShowWindowAsync	Sets the show state of a window created by a different thread.
TitleWindows	Titles the specified child windows of the specified parent window.
UpdatedLayedWindow	Updates the position, size, shape, content, and translucency of a layered window.
WindowFromPoint	Retrieves a handle to the window that contains the specified point.
WinMain	An entry-point function called by the system as the initial entry point for a Win32-based application.

90. Window Class Functions

GetClassInfo	Retrieves information about a window class.
GetClassInfoEx	Retrieves information about a window class, including a handle to its small icon.
GetClassLong	Retrieves the specified 32-bit value from the WNDCLASSEX structure associated with the specified window.
GetClassLongPtr	Retrieves the specified value from the WNDCLASSEX structure associated with the specified window.
GetClassName	Retrieves the name of the class to which the specified window belongs.
GetWindowLong	Retrieves information about the specified window.
GetWindowLongPtr	Retrieves information about the specified window.
RegisterClass	Registers a window class.
RegisterClassEx	Registers a window class.
SetClassLong	Replaces the specified 32-bit value at the specified offset into the extra class memory or the WNDCLASSEX structure.
SetClassLongPtr	Replaces the specified value at the specified offset into the extra class memory or the WNDCLASSEX structure.

SetWindowLong	Changes an attribute of the specified window.
SetWindowLongPtr	Changes an attribute of the specified window.
Unregister Class	Unregisters a window class.

91. Window Procedure Functions

CallWindowProc	Passes message information to the specified window procedure.
DefWindowProc	Calls the default window procedure to provide default processing for any window messages that an application does not process.
WindowProc	An application-defined function that processes messages sent to a window.

92. Window Property Functions

EnmProps	Enumerates all entries in the property list of a window.
EnumPropsEx	Enumerates all entries in the property list of a window.
GetProp	Retrieves a data handle from the property list of the specified window.
PropEnumProc	An application-defined callback function used with the EnumProps function.
PropEnumProcEx	An application-defined callback function used with the EnumPropsEx function.
RemoveProp	Removes an entry from the property list of the specified window.
SetProp	Adds a new entry or changes an existing entry in the property list of the specified window.

93. Window Station and Desktop Functions

CloseDesktop	Closes an open handle to a desktop object.
CloseWindowStation	Closes an open window station handle.
CreateDesktop	Creates a new desktop on the window station associated with the calling process.
CreateWindowStation	Creates a window station object.
EnumDestopProc	An application-defined callback function used with the EnumDesktops function.
EnumDesktops	Enumerates all desktops in the window station assigned to the calling process.
EnumDestopWindows	Enumerates all windows on a desktop by passing a handle to each window.

EnumWindowStationProc	An application-defined callback function used with the EnumWindowStations function.
EnumWindowStations	Enumerates all window stations in the system.
GetProcess WindowStation	Retrieves a handle to the window station associated with the calling process.
GetThreadDesktop	Retrieves a handle to the desktop associated with a specified thread.
GetUserObjectInformation	Retrieves information about a window station or desktop object.
GetUserObjectSecurity	Retrieves security information for the specified user object.
OpenDesktop	Retrieves a handle to an existing desktop.
OpenInputDesktop	Retrieves a handle to the desktop that receives user input.
OpenWindowStation	Retrieves a handle to an existing window station.
SetProcessWindowStation	Assigns a window station to the calling process.
SetThreadDesktop	Assigns a desktop to the calling thread.
SetUserObjectInformation	Sets information about a window station or desktop object.
SetUserObjectSecurity	Sets the security of a user object.
SwitchDesktop	Makes a desktop visible and acitivates it.

94. Windowless Rich Edit Controls Reference

CreateTextServices	Creates an instance of a text services object.
ItextHost	Used by a text services object to obtain text host services.
ItextServices	Extends the Microsoft Text Object Model to provide extra functionality for windowless operation.

95. Windows Networking Functions

MultinetGetConnectionPerformance

WNetAddConnection2

WNetAddConnection3

WNetCancelConnection

WNetCancelConnection2

WNetCloseEnum

WNetConnectionDialog

WNetConnectionDialog1

WNetDisconnectDialog

WNetDisconnectDialog1

WNetEnumResouce

WNetGetconnection

WNetGetLastError

WNetGetNetworkInformation

WNetGetProviderName

WNetGetResourceInformation

WNetGetResourceParent

WNetGetUniversalName

WNetGetUser

WNetOpenEnum

WnetUseconnection

Win32 Data Types

The data types supported by the Microsoft Win32 APIs are used to define function return values, function and message parameters, and structure members. They define the size and meaning of these elements. The following table contains the following types: character, integer, Boolean, pointer, and handle. The character, integer, and Boolean types are common to most C++ compilers. Most of the pointer-type names begin with a prefix of P or LP. Handles refer to a resource that has been loaded into memory.

Type	Definition
Atom	Atom (a reference to a character string in an atom table).
BOOL	Boolean variable (should be TRUE or FALSE).
BOOLEAN	Boolean variable (should be TRUE or FALSE).
BYTE	Byte (8 bits).
CALLBACK	Calling convention for callback functions.
CHAR	8-bit Windows (ANSI character).
COLORREF	Red, green, blue (RGB) color value (32 bit).
CONST	Variable whose value is to remain constant during execution.
CRITICAL_SECTION	Critical-section object.
CTRYID	Country identifier.
DWORD	32-bit unsigned integer.
DWORD_PTR	Unsigned long type for pointer precision. Use when casting a pointer to a long type to perform pointer arithmetic.

DWORD32	32-bit unsigned integer.
DWORD64	64-bit unsigned integer.
FLOAT	Floating-point variable.
FILE_SEGMENT_ELEMENT	64-bit pointer to a buffer.
HACCEL	Handle to an accelerator table.
HANDLE	Handle to an object.
HBITMAP	Handle to a bitmap.
HBRUSH	Handle to a brush.
HCOLORSPACE	Handle to a logical color space.
HCONV	Handle to a dynamic data exchange (DDE).
HCONVLIST	Handle to a DDE conversation list.
HCURSOR	Handle to a cursor.
HDC	Handle to a device context (DC).
HDDEDATA	Handle to DDE data.
HDESK	Handle to a desktop.
HDROP	Handle to an internal drop structure.
HDWP	Handle to a deferred window position structure.
HENHMETAFILE	Handle to an enhanced metafile.
HFILE	Handle to a file opened by OpenFile, not CreateFile.
HFONT	Handle to a font.
HGDIOBJ	Handle to a GDI object.
HGLOBAL	Handle to a global memory block.
HHOOK	Handle to a hook.
HICON	Handle to an icon.
HIMAGELIST	Handle to an image list.
HIMC	Handle to input context.
HINSTANCE	Handle to an instance.
HKEY	Handle to a registry key.
HKL	Input local identifier.
HLOCAL	Handle to a local memory block.
HMENU	Handle to a menu.
HMETAFILE	Handle to a metafile.
HMODULE	Handle to a module.
HNMONITOR	Handle to a display monitor.
HPALETTE	Handle to a palette.

HPEN	Handle to a pen.
HRGN	Handle to a region.
HRSRC	Handle to a resource.
HSZ	Handle to DDE string.
HWINSTA	Handle to a window station.
HWND	Handle to a window.
INT	32-bit signed integer.
INT_PTR	Signed integral type for pointer precision. Use when casting a pointer to an integer to perform pointer arithmetic.
INT32	32-bit signed integer.
INT64	64-bit signed integer.
IPADDR	IP address. To convert this value to the "a.b.c.d" string form of an IP address, map the high-order byte to a, the low-order to d, and so on.
IPMASK	Subnet mask. Uses the same format as IPADDR.
LANGID	Language identifier.
LCID	Local identifier.
LCSCSTYPE	Color space type.
LCSGAMUTMATCH	Gamut-matching method.
LCTYPE	Local information type.
LONG	32-bit signed integer.
LONG_PTR	Signed long type for pointer precision. Use when casting a pointer to a long to perform pointer arithmetic.
LONG32	32-bit signed integer.
LONG64	64-bit signed integer.
LONGLONG	64-bit signed integer.
LPARAM	Message parameter.
LPBOOL	Pointer to a BOOL.
LPBYTE	Pointer to a BYTE.
LPCOLORREF	Pointer to a COLORREF value.
LPCRITICAL_SECTION	Pointer to a CRITICAL_SECTION.
LPCSTR	Pointer to a constant null-terminated string of 8-bit Windows (ANSI) characters.
LPCTSTR	An LPCWSTR if UNICODE is defined, an LPCSTR otherwise.
LPCVOID	Pointer to a constant of any type.
LPCWSTR	Pointer to a constant null-terminated string of 16-bit Unicode characters.
LPDWORD	Pointer to a DWORD.

LPHANDLE	Pointer to a HANDLE.
LPINT	Pointer to an INT.
LPLONG	Pointer to a LONG.
LPSTR	Pointer to a null-terminated string of 8-bit Windows (ANSI) characters.
LPSTR	An LPWSTR if UNICODE is defined, an LPSTR otherwise.
LPVOID	Pointer to any type.
LPWORD	Pointer to a WORD.
LPWSTR	Pointer to a null-terminated string of 16-bit Unicode characters.
LRESULT	Signed result of message processing.
LUID	Locally unique identifier.
PBOOL	Pointer to a BOOL.
PBOOLEAN	Pointer to a BOOL.
PBYTE	Pointer to a BYTE.
PCHAR	Pointer to a CHAR.
PCRITICAL_SECTION	Pointer to a CRITICAL_SECTION.
PCSTR	Pointer to a constant null-terminated string of 8-bit Windows (ANSI) characters.
PCTSTR	A PCWSTR if UNICODE is defined, a PCSTR otherwise.
PCWCH	Pointer to a constant WCHAR.
PCWSTR	Pointer to a constant null-terminated string of 16-bit Unicode characters.
PDWORD	Pointer to a DWORD.
PFLOAT	Pointer to a FLOAT.
PHANDLE	Pointer to a HANDLE.
PHKEY	Pointer to an HKEY.
PINT	Pointer to an INT.
PLCID	Pointer to an LCID.
PLONG	Pointer to a LONG.
PLUID	Pointer to a LUID.
POINTER_32	32-bit pointer. On a 32-bit system, this is a native pointer. On a 64-bit system, this is a truncated 64-bit pointer.
POINTER_64	64-bit pointer. On a 64-bit system, this is a native pointer. On a 32-bit system, this is a sign-extended 32-bit pointer.
PSHORT	Pointer to a SHORT.
PSTR	Pointer to a null-terminated string of 8-bit Windows (ANSI) characters.
PBYTE	Pointer to a TBYTE.
PTCHAR	Pointer to a TCHAR.

PTSTR	A PWSTR if UNICODE is defined, a PSTR otherwise.
PUCHAR	Pointer to a UCHAR.
PUINT	Pointer to a UINT.
PULONG	Pointer to a ULONG.
PUSHORT	Pointer to a USHORT.
PVOID	Pointer to any type.
PWCHAR	Pointer to a WCHAR.
PWORD	Pointer to a WORD.
PWSTR	Pointer to a null-terminated string of 16-bit Unicode characters.
REGSAM	Security access mask for registry key.
SC_HANDLE	Handle to a service control manager database.
SC_LOCK	Handle to a service control manager database lock.
SERVICE_STATUS_HANDLE	Handle to a service status value.
SHORT	Short integer (16 bits).
SIZE_T	The maximum number of bytes to which a pointer can point. Use for a count that must span the full range of a pointer.
SSIZE_T	Signed SIZE_T.
TBYTE	A WCHAR if UNICODE is defined, a CHAR otherwise.
TCHAR	A WCHAR if UNICODE is defined, a CHAR otherwise.
UCHAR	Unsigned CHAR.
UINT	Unsigned INT.
UINT_PTR	Unsigned INT_PTR.
UINT32	Unsigned INT32.
UINT64	Unsigned INT64.
ULONG	Unsigned LONG.
ULONG_PTR	Unsigned LONG_PTR
ULONG32	Unsigned LONG32.
ULONG64	Unsigned LONG64.
ULONGLONG	64-bit unsigned integer.
UNSIGNED	Unsigned attribute.
USHORT	Unsigned SHORT.
VOID	Any type.
WCHAR	16-bit Unicode character.
WINAPI	Calling convention for the Win32 API.
WORD	16-bit unsigned integer.
WPARAM	Message Parameter.

.NET Framework Namespaces

1. Microsoft.ComServices
2. Microsoft.Win32
3. System
4. System.CodeDOM
5. System.CodeDOM.Compiler
6. System.Collections
7. System.Collections.Bases
8. System.ComponentModel
9. System.ComponentModel.Design
10. System.ComponentModel.Design
11. System.Configuration
12. System.Configuration.Assemblies
13. System.Configuration.Core
14. System.Configuration.Install
15. System.Configuration.Interceptors
16. System.Configuration.Schema
17. System.Configuration.Web
18. System.Core
19. System.Data
20. System.Data.ADO
21. System.Data.Internal
22. System.Data.SQLTypes
23. System.Diagnostics
24. System.Diagnostics.SymbolStore
25. System.DirectoryServices
26. System.Drawing
27. System.Drawing.Drawing2D
28. System.Drawing.Imaging
29. System.Drawing.Printing
30. System.Drawing.Text
31. System.Globalization
32. System.IO
33. System.IO.IsolatedStorage
34. System.Management
35. System.Messaging
36. System.Net
37. System.Net.Sockets
38. System.Reflection
39. System.Reflection.Emit
40. System.Resources
41. System.Runtime.CompilerServices
42. System.Runtime.InteropServices

43. System.Runtime.InteropServices.Expando

44. System.Runtime.Remoting

45. System.Runtime.Remoting.Channels.HTTP

46. System.Runtime.Remoting.Channels.SMTP

47. System.Runtime.Remoting.Channels.TCP

48. System.Runtime.Serialization

49. System.Runtime.Serialization.Formatters

50. System.Runtime.Serialization.Formatters.Binary

51. System.Runtime.Serialization.Formatters.Soap

52. System.Security

53. System.Security.Cryptography

54. System.Security.Cryptography.X509Certificates

55. System.Security.Permissions

56. System.Security.Policy

57. System.Security.Principal

58. System.ServiceProcess

59. System.Text

60. System.Text.RegualarExpressions

61. System.Threading

62. System.Timers

63. System.Web

64. System.Web.Caching

65. System.Web.Configuration

66. System.Web.Security

67. System.Web.Services

68. System.Web.Services.Description

69. System.Web.Services.Discovery

70. System.Web.Services.Protocols

71. System.Web.UI

72. System.Web.UI.Design

73. System.Web.UI.Design.WebControls

74. System.Web.UI.HtmlControls

75. System.Web.UI.WebControls

76. System.Web.Util

77. System.WinForms

78. System.WinForms.ComponentModel

79. System.WinForms.Design

80. System.Xml

81. System.Xml.Serialization

82. System.Xml.Xpath

83. System.Xml.Xsl

Note   In MSDN Library—Visual, if you have Filtered by: set to .NET Framework SDK Documentation and type in Microsoft.ComServices namespace in the Look for: pane it will list all the classes, interfaces, etc. for Microsoft.ComServices. If you now type in **System** namespaces in the Look for: pane it will list all the classes, interfaces, etc. for System. For instance, say if you choose **System.Data.ADO**, it will bring up the information on the classes, interfaces, etc. It also shows the definition of the class for C# and C++. For example, the ADO Command Class definitions are as follows:

```
[C#]
public class ADOCommand : DBCommand
```

```
[C++]
public __gc class ADOCommand : public DBCommand
```

System Namespace

The item 3 above in the .NET Framework Namespaces contains fundamental classes and base classes that define commonly-used value and reference data types, events and event handlers, interfaces, attributes, and processing exceptions. In other words, this is one of namespaces that the developer will be working with most often. Therefore, we will list the classes, interfaces, structures, delegates, and enumerations of this namespace.

Classes

Class	Description
AccessException	The exception that is thrown when an attempt to access a class member fails.
Activator	Contains methods to create types of objects locally or remotely, or obtain references to existing objects.
AppDomain	The Common Language Runtime allows multiple applications to run in a single process.
AppDomainFlags	Represents assembly binding information that can be added to an AppDomain. The members are used with the GetData and SetData methods to identify the AppDomain data to be used.
AppDomainUnloadedException	The exception that is thrown when an attempt is made to access an unloaded AppDomain.
AppDomainUnloadInProgressException	The exception that is thrown when there is an attempt to unload multiple AppDomain objects simultaneously.
ApplicationException	The exception that is thrown when a non-fatal application error occurs.
ArgumentException	The exception that is thrown when one or more arguments being provided to the method are not valid.
ArgumentNullException	Indicates when a null argument is passed to a method that cannot accept it.
ArgumentOutOfRangeException	The exception that is thrown when the value of an argument is outside the allowable range of values as defined by the invoked method.

ArithmeticException	The exception that is thrown when the value from an input or arithmetic operation is infinite or cannot be represented in the result type.
Array	Provides methods for creating, manipulating, searching, and sorting arrays; thereby, serving as the base class for all arrays in the Common Language Runtime.
ArrayTypeMismatchException	The exception that is thrown when an attempt is made to store an element of the wrong type within an array.
Attribute	Base class for custom attributes. Contains convenience methods for accessing custom attributes.
AttributeUsageAttribute	A custom attribute applied to another custom attribute (that is, and "end" attribute) that describes how the end attribute is to behave.
BadImageFormatException	The exception that is thrown when there is an invalid format for a DLL (dynamic link library) or an executable program.
BitConverter	Converts an array of bytes to and from the base data types.
Buffer	Provides access to unmanaged memory.
CallContext	This class exposes the API for the users of call context. All methods in CallContext are static and operate upon the call context in the Thread.
CannotUnloadAppDomainException	The exception that is thrown when an attempt to unload an AppDomain fails.
CLS CompliantAttribute	Indicates whether a program element is compliant with the Common Language Specification.
Console	Provides access to the standard input, standard output, and standard error streams.
ContextBoundObject	Defines the base class for all context-bound classes.
ContextMarshallException	The exception that is thrown when the formal type and marshal style of the object are incompatible.
ContextStaticAttribute	Indicates that a field should be treated as a static relative to the context.
Convert	Converts base data types to other base data types.

CoreException	The exception that is thrown by the runtime.
DBNull	Represents a null value.
Delegate	Represents a delegate, which is a data structure that refers to a static method or to an object instance and an instance method of that object.
DivideByZeroException	The exception that is thrown when an attempt is made to perform a divide-by-zero arithmetic operation.
DuplicateWaitObjectException	The exception that is thrown when an object is listed more than once in a waiting list for thread execution.
Empty	Represents an empty value.
EntryPointNotFoundException	The exception that is thrown when an attempt to load a class fails due to the absence of a starting method.
Enum	Provides the base class for enumerations.
Environment	Provides basic access to environment functionality.
EventArgs	EventArgs is the base class for event data.
Exception	Provides information required to handle and process errors.
ExecutionEngineException	The exception that is thrown when an error internal to the Common Language Runtime occurs.
FieldAccessException	The exception that is thrown when an attempt to access a field fails.
FlagsAttribute	Custom attribute indicating the enum should be treated as a bitfield (or set of flags).
FormatException	The exception that is thrown when the format of an argument does not match the contract of its method.
IndexOutOfRangeException	The exception that is thrown when an attempt is made to access an element of an array with an index that is outside the bounds of the array.
InvalidCastException	The exception that is thrown when an invalid cast occurs.
InvalidOperationException	The exception that is thrown when one of the values defining the state of the object involved in a method invocation or an instruction execution violates a rule, causing the operation to become invalid.

LogicalCallContext	Reserved.
MarshalByRefObject	Base class for Remoting objects that need to be marshal by reference. This includes WellKnown SingleCall and WellKnown Singleton WebService objects and Client Activated Objects.
Math	Provides static methods for trigonometric, logarithmic, and other common mathematical functions. Overloaded methods are provided for use with standard base data types.
MethodAccessException	The exception that is thrown when an attempt to access a method fails.
MissingFieldException	The exception that is thrown when there is an attempt to access a nonexistent field.
MissingMemberException	The exception that is thrown when there is a versioning problem with the dynamic-link libraries (DLLs).
MissingMethodException	The exception that is thrown when there is an attempt to access a nonexistent method.
MulticastDelegate	Represents a multicast delegate, which is a delegate that can have an invocation list with more than one element. All multicast delegates are derived from this class. A delegate that inherits directly from Delegate has an invocation list (a linked list of delegates that are to be invoked when the "invoke" method is called) with one elemen—itself. The Delegate.Combine and Delegate.Remove methods are used to create new invocation lists.
MulticastNotSupportedException	The exception that is thrown when there is an attempt to add multiple callbacks to a delegate that does not support multi-casting.
NonSerializedAttribute	Indicates that a member is not serialized.
NotFiniteNumberException	The exception that is thrown when an infinite number is encountered.
NotImplementedException	The exception that is thrown when a requested method or operation is not implemented.
NotSupportedException	The exception that is thrown when an invoked method is not supported.
NullReferenceException	The exception that is thrown when there is an attempt to dereference a null object reference.

Object	Supports all classes in the .NET Framework class hierarchy and provides low-level services to subclasses. This is the ultimate superclass of all classes in .NET Framework; it is the root of the type hierarchy.
ObsoleteAttribute	Represents an attribute that is attached to members that are not to be used any longer. Message is some human readable explanation of what to use. Error indicates whether the compiler should treat usage of such a method as an error.
OperatingSystem	Contains information about an operating system version. The information includes major version number, minor version numbers, a build number, a platform identifier, and descriptive text about the operating system.
OutOfMemoryException	The exception that is thrown when there is not enough memory to continue the execution of a program.
OverflowException	The exception that is thrown when an arithmetic operation results in an overflow.
ParamArrayAttribute	Indicates an array of parameters in a call should be treated as a variable number of parameters.
Radix	The Radix class provides methods for converting numbers between different counting systems. Counting systems from base 2 (binary) through base 36 are supported.
Random	Represents a pseudo-random-number generator, a device that meets certain statistical requirements and produces what is known as a sequence of pseudo-random numbers.
RankException	The exception that is thrown when an array with the wrong number of dimensions is passed to a method.
SerializableAttribute	Indicates that a class is serializable.
ServicedComponent	Defines the root type for all context bound types.
ServicedComponentException	The class is the exception class for ServicedComponent. An Exception is thrown when something has gone wrong.

StackOverflowException	The exception that is thrown when there is a stack overflow violation.
String	Represents an immutable string of characters.
SystemException	The exception that is thrown when there is an exceptional condition that is considered non-fatal and recoverable.
ThreadStaticAttribute	A custom attribute that indicates a static field should not be shared between threads; that is, each thread has its own instance of the static field.
Type	Represents type declarations: class types, interface types, array types, value types, and enumeration types.
TypeInitializationException	The exception that is thrown when the class initializer throws an exception.
TypeLoadException	The exception that is thrown when type-loading failures occur.
TypeUnloadedException	The exception that is thrown when there is an attempt to access an unloaded class.
UnhandledExceptionEvent	Occurs when there is an exception that was not handled by the application domain.
URI	Provides an object representation of a uniform resource locatorURIFormatException An exception class used when an invalid Uniform Resource Identifier is detected.
ValueType	Provides the base class for value types.
Version	Represents the version number for a Common Language Runtime assembly.
WeakReference	Supports a weak reference.
WeakReferenceException	The exception that is thrown when there is an attempt to access a weak-referenced object after it is destroyed.

Interfaces

Interface	Description
ICloneable	Supports cloning, which creates a new instance of a type with the same value as an existing instance. Only objects that implement ICloneable can be cloned.

IComparable	Defines a generalized comparison function, which a value type or class implements to create a type-specific comparison function.
ICovertible	Describes generalized type conversion and convenience methods, which a value type or class implements to create type-specific conversion and convenience methods.
ICustomFormatter	This interface is implemented by classes with special formatting.
IFormattable	Provides functionality to format the value of an object.
IServiceObjectProvider	Provides a mechanism for retrieving a service object, which is a Type object that provides a service to other objects.

Structures

Structure	Description
ArgIterator	Represents a variable argument list. Use this class to step through the argument list of function that takes a variable number of arguments.
Boolean	This class represents the primitive type, Boolean. Objects of this class can have values of either true or false.
Byte	This value type represents an 8-bit unsigned integer.
Char	Represents a character value.
DateTime	Represents a date and time value.
Decimal	Represents a decimal value.
Double	Represents a double-precision floating point number.
Guid	Represents a globally unique identifier (GUID). GUIDs can be used wherever a unique identifier is required.
Int16	Represents a 16-bit signed integer.
Int32	Represents a 32-bit signed integer.
Int64	Represents a 64-bit signed integer.
RuntimeFieldHandle	The RuntimeFieldHandle is a handle to the internal metadata representation of a field.

RuntimeMethodHandle	The RuntimeMethodHandle is a handle to the internal metadata representation of a method.
RuntimeTypeHandle	The RuntimeTypeHandle is a handle to the internal metadata representation of a type.
Sbyte	Represents an 8-bit signed integer.
Single	Represents a single-precision floating point number.
TimeSpan	Represents a period of time.
TypedReference	Describes objects that contain both a managed pointer to a location and a runtime representation of the type that may be stored at that location.
UInt16	Represents a 16-bit unsigned integer.
UInt32	Represents a 32-bit unsigned integer.
UInt64	Represents a 64-bit unsigned integer.
Void	Indicates that a method has the void return type.

Delegates

Delegate	Description
AsyncCallback	References the method that will complete asynchronously.
CrossAppDomainDelegate	Every subclass of Delegate and MulticastDelegate has a constructor and an Invoke method.
EventHandler	Represents the method that will handle an event of a control.
UnhandledExceptionEventHandler	Exception handler for an event that is not handled by an application domain.

Enumerations

Enumeration	Description
AttributeTargets	Specifies the elements to which it is valid to attach an attribute.
LoaderOptimization	This enumeration is used with the LoaderOptimizationAttribute to specify the loader optimizations used for an executable.

PlatformID   Describes the platforms supported by an
                                  assembly. These flags are used to bind to an
                                  assembly.

TypeCode   Specifies the type code of an object.

The set of classes above are part of the approximately 2042 classes, 272
interfaces, 435 enumerations, 148 delegates, and 88 structures already predefined in the .NET Framework for use in application design.

Attributes

This appendix discusses different aspects of using attributes with Visual C++ 7.0.

Simplifying Tasks with ATL Server Attributes

Uses several Visual C++ attributes to simplify tasks that normally would require map-style programming. ATL Server offers developers a set of classes and templates designed to ease ISAP-based Web application development as well as support Web services using SOAP. This section demonstrates several ATL Server attributes that simplify tasks that normally require map-style programming.

ATL Server Attributes

The four primary ATL Server Attributes of use are:
- request_handler
- tag_name
- soap_handler
- soap_method

As with all ATL attributes, it is important to use the following define statement before including atlbase.h (this is done for you in the wizards in stdafx.h).

#define *ATL_ATTRIBUTES*

Stencil Files

ATL Server supports "stencil" files. Stencil files have a .srf extension. SRF files are static HTML files with tags embedded. These tags are replaced with dynamic information generated in C++ code, such as a table from a database query based upon some query parameter or form variable. The *request_handler* attribute associates a namespace in the .srf with a C++ class. In the code below, the Default namespace maps to Cproject1Handler and mynamespace maps to Cproject2Handler.

The *tag_name* attribute maps tags to class methods. Hello does not use an explicit namespace, so it is handled by the default class, which is CProject1Handler.Hello is in turn mapped to CProject1Handler.OnHello. The same is done for testing.Hello. The following is a sample .srf file at which you will point a browser:

```
{{handler Project1.Dll/Default}}
{{subhandler id=testing code=Project1.Dll/mynamespace}}
<html>
<head>

<head>
<body>

This is a test: {{Hello}}<br>
This is a test: {{testing.Hello}}<br>

<body>
</html>
```

Here is the code behind the .srf file that will handle the Hello tag:

```
[ request_handler("Default") ]
class CProjectHandler
{
public:
    DWORD ValidateAndExchange()
    {
        m_HttpResponse.SetContentType(_T("text/html"));
        return HTTP_SUCCESS;
    }

[ tag_name("Helo") ]
DWORD OnHello()
{
        m_HttpResponse << "Hello World!";
        return HTTP_SUCCESS;
}
```

```
};  // class CProjectHandler
[ request_handler("mynamespace") ]
class CProject2Handler
{
public:
    DWORD ValidateAndExchange()
    {
        m_HttpResponse.SetContentType(_T("text/html"));
        return HTTP_SUCCESS;
    }

    [ tag_name("Hello") ]
    DWORD OnHello()
    {
        m_HttpResponse << "Hello World from mynamespace!";
        return HTTP_SUCCESS;
    }
};  // class CProject2Handler
```

Web Services

ATL Server also supports remote invocation of methods over HTTP. This is called SOAP (Simple Object Access Protocol). In the ATL Server implementation, the *soap_handler* attribute maps a SOAP namespace to a class. The *soap_method* attribute identifies methods in that class that will be exported to the client. The current implementation requires an interface declaring the method and a class implementing that interface. In the following example, the client will end up with a class method named HelloWorld. When that method is called from the client, the proxy code (which needs to be manually generated for now using Sproxy.exe) will perform the remote invocation to this server code and return the proper values.

```
[
uuid("2061889F-88D0-4453-A597-991FA2E2C09"), object
]
__interface IProject2Service
{
[id(1)] HRESULT HelloWorld( [in] BSTR bstrInput, [out, retval] BSTR
*bstrOutput);
};
[
coclass,
request_handler(name="Default", sdl="GenProject2ServiceSDL"),
soap_handler(
```

```
                   name="Project2ServiceService",
                   namespace="urn:Project2Service-service",
                   protocol="soap"),
                   uuid("382C7C4E-D2F1-4ACA-92DD-58C7025212D0",
                   default("Iproject2Service")
]
class CProject2Service : public Iproject2Service
{
public:
    [ soap_method ]
    HRESULT HelloWorld(/*[in]*/ BSTR bstrInput,  /*[out, retval]*/ BSTR
                    *bstrOutput)
     {
        CComBSTR bstrOut(L"Hello ");
        bstrOut += bstrInput;
        bstrOut += L"!";
        *bstrOutput = bstrOut.Detach();

        return S_OK;
     }
};  class CProject2Service
```

Using the DLLImport Attribute

This section demonstrates common usage of the DLLImport attribute. The part discusses the benefits of using DLLImport to make calls to native code from a managed application. The second part focuses on the aspects of marshaling and the DLLImport attribute.

Calling Native Code in the Managed World

The DLLImport attribute is very useful when reusing existing native code in a managed application. For instance, your managed application might need to make calls to the unmanaged Win32 APIs. This common scenario is demonstrated in the following code sample where the MessageBox (located in User32.lib) is called:

```
#using <mscorlib.Dll>
using namespace System::Runtime::InteropServices;     // for
DLLImportAttribute

namespace SysWin32
{
```

```
[DllImport("user32.dll", EntryPoint = "MessageBox", CharSet =
Unicode)]
    int MessageBox(void* hWnd, wchar_t* lpText, wchar_t* lpCaption,
unsigned int uType);
}

void main()
{
    SysWin32::MessageBox( 0, L"Hello world!", L"Greetings", 0 );
}
```

The main point of interest is the line of code containing DllImport. Based on the parameter values, this line of code tells the compiler to declare a function residing in the User32.dll and to treat all strings appearing in the signature (such as parameters or the return value) like Unicode strings. If the EntryPoint argument is missing, the default value is the name of the function. In addition, because the CharSet argument specifies Unicode, the Common Language Runtime will first look for a function called MessageBoxW (W because of the Unicode specification). If the run time does not find this function, it will then look for MessageBox and the corresponding decorated name, depending on the calling convention. The only supported conventions are __cdecl and __stdcall.

Marshalling Nonstructured Parameters from Managed to Native

In addition to using the previous method, you can use another method that marshals the managed parameters (from the managed application) to native parameters in the native DLL. The following code sample demonstrates the marshaling technique:

```
#using <mscorlib.dll>
using namespace System;                  // To bring System::String in
using namespace System::RunTime::InteropServices; // for DllImportAttribute
namespace SysWin32
{
    [DllImport("user32.dll", EntryPoint = "MessageBox", CharSet = Unicode)]
    Int32 MessageBox( Int32 hWnd, String* lpText, String*lpCaption, Uint32 uType);
}

void main()
{
    SysWin32::MessageBox(0, S"Hello world!", S"Greetings", 0);
}
```

When the actual call is made, all parameter strings are automatically converted to wchar_t*, because of the value of the CharSet parameter. Similarly, any parameter types of Int32 are converted to unmanaged int and parameter types of Uint32 are converted to unmanaged unsigned int. The following table provides a guide to the result of converting between native and managed contexts:

Native	Managed Extension for C++
int	Int32
short	Int16
char*	String* (CharSet=Ansi) for [in] parameters, Text::StringBuilder* for [out] parameters or return values.
wchar_t*	String* (CharSet = Unicode) for [in] parameters, Text::StringBuilder* for [out] parameters or return values.
Function pointer (callbacks) Limitation: The function pointer must have __stdcall calling convention Because this is the only type support by DllImport.	Delegate type
Array (eg. Wchar_t*[]) Limitation: The CharSet argument only applies to the root type of the function parameters. Therefore, String* __gc[] is marshaled as wchar_t* [] regardless of the value of CharSet.	Managed array of the corresponding type (such as String* __gc[])

Marshaling Structured Types from Native to Managed

In addition to simple types, the runtime provides a mechanism for marshaling simple structures from a managed context to a native one. Simple structures contain no internal data member pointers, members of structured types, or other elements. For the purposes of this topic, we want to call a function in a native DLL that has the following signature:

```
#include <stdio.h>
struct S
{
      char* str;
      int n;
};
int __cdecl func( struct S* p )
```

```
    {
        printf( "%s\n", p->str );
        return p->n;
    }
```

To create a managed wrapper of this function, we need to apply the StructLayout attribute to the calling class. This attribute determines how the structure is organized when it is marshaled. To ensure the structure is organized using the traditional C format, sequential layout is specified (LayoutKind::Sequential). The resulting code is as follows:

```
#using <mscorlib.dll>

using namespace System;
using namespace System::Runtime::InteropServices;

// CharSet = Ansi (Unicode) means that everything that is a string
// in this structure should be marshaled as Ansi (Unicode) strings
[StructLayout ( LayoutKind::Sequential, CharSet=Ansi )]
__gc class MS         // To be compatible with the type in the native code,
                      // this structure should have the members laid out in
                      // the same order as those in the native struct
{
public:
    String* m_str;
    In32 m_n;
};

[DllImport ("some.dll")]
Int32 func( MS* ptr );
void main()
{
    MS* p = new MS;
    p->m_str = S"Hello native!";
    p->m_n = 7;
    Console::WriteLine(func(p));        // Should print 7
}
```

You can also use the __nogc keyword in the managed application, ensuring that no marshaling takes place:

```
#include <stdlib.h>
#include <string.h>
#using <mscorlib.dll>
using namespace System;
using namespace System::Runtime::InteropServices;
__nogc class UMS
{
```

```
public:
        char* m_str;
        int m_n;
};
[DllImport ("some.dll")]
Int32 func( UMS* ptr );
void main()
{
        USM* p = new UMS;
        p->m_str = strdup("Hello native!");
        p->m_n = 7;
        Console::WriteLine(func(p));            // Should print 7
        free( p-m_str );
        delete p;
}
```

The second scenario is:

```
#include <stdio.h>
struct S
{
        wchar_t* str;
        int n;
};
int __cdecl func( struct S p )
{
        printf( "%S\n", p.str );
        return p.n;
}
```

Observe that the parameter is passed by value. To wrap this call in the managed application, use values instead of __gc types. The resulting code is as follows:

```
#using <mscorlib.dll>
using namespace System;
using namespace System::Runtime::InteropServices;
[StructLayout( LayoutKind::Sequential, CharSet=Unicode )]
__value class VS
{
public:
        String* m_str;
        Int32 m_n;
};
```

```
[DllImport( "some.dll" )]
Int32 func( VS ptr );
void main()
{
    VS v;
    v.m_str = S"Hello native!";
    v.m_n = 7;
                Console::WriteLine(func(v));      // Should print 7 also
}
```

Creating a COM DLL with COM Attributes

This section demonstrates how to quickly develop a simple COM server (an inproc server or DLL) using various attributes. The first part develops the COM server using Notepad and the command-line tools. In the second part, the same COM server is developed using the Visual Studio IDE.

Note	The UUID used in this section is purely for demonstration purposes only. If omitted, the module attribute (and other attributes) will automatically generate one for you.

This section focuses on the following attributes:

coclass	object	threading
dual	out	uuid
emitidl	pointer_default	version
helpstring	progid	vi progid
module	retval	

Creating a COM Server Using Notepad

Attributes were designed to ease the tedium and complexity of traditional COM programming. Using attributes in your applications can automate or simplify several common COM Adding Functionality. In this first part, a simple COM server is developed using Notepad and command-line tools. To use attributes in your applications, you must add support for them by defining several related macros (such as **_ATL_ATTRIBUTES**) and including related header files. Using Notepad, create a new header file called MyIncludes.h and add the following lines of code:

```
#pragma          once
#define          STRICT
#ifndef              _WIN32_WINNT
```

```
#define              _WIN32_WINNT 0x0400
#endif
#define              _ATL_ATTRIBUTES
#define              _ATL_APARTMENT_THREADED
#define              _ATL_NO_AUTOMATIC_NAMESPACE
#include             <atlbase.h>
#include             <atlcom.h>
#include             <atlwin.h>
#include             <atltypes.h>
#include             <atlctl.h>
#include             <atlhost.h>
using namespace ATL;
```

Include files beginning with atl bring in ATL support for the application **_ATL_ATTRIBUTES**, support for attributed ATL programming is also added. The next step is to create a source file that implements the inproc server. Using Notepad, add the following lines of code and save the file as MyServer.cpp:

```
#include "MyIncludes.h"
// The module attributes is specified in order to implement DllMain, DllRegisterServer and
// DllUnregisterServer
[ module(dll, name = "MyServer", helpstring = "MyServer 1.0 Type Library") ];
[ emitid ]
```

Using the module attribute saves you the work of implementing the necessary functions required for a COM inproc server. In addition, you do not need to write an .IDL file or the .DEF file (which exports the functions of your server). This is all done automatically by the module attribute. After saving the text file, build the project using the following commands:

```
cl /LD MyServer.cpp
regsvr32 MyServer.dll
```

If you encounter any errors, make sure you have Visual Studio properly installed and the environment variable defined. Building the project successfully registers the server with the operating system. At this point, the COM server does not expose any functionality to the client. This is because the COM server does not implement any server objects. In the next step, you will add server objects to this server. Add the following code to the existing MyServer.cpp file:

```
///////////////////////////////////////
// Iobject1
[
     object,
     uuid,
     dual,
     helpstring("Iobject1 Interface"),
     pointer_default(unique)
]
__interface Iobject1 : Idispatch
{
     HRESULT GetANum [out, retval]int* pint);
};
///////////////////////////////////////
// Cobject1
[
     coclass,
     threading("apartment'),
     vi_progid("MyServer.Object1"),
     progid("MyServer.Object1.1"),
     version(1.0),
     uuid("15615078-523C-43A0-BE6F-651E78A89213"),
     helpstring("Object1 Class")
]
class ATL_NO_VTABLE Cobject1 : public IObject1
{
public:
     Cobject1()
     {
     }
     HRESULT GetANum(int* pint)
     {
          pInt = 101;
          return S_OK;
     }
     DECLARE_PROTECT_FINAL_CONSTRUCT()
     HRESULT FinalConstruct()
     {
          return S_OK;
     }
     void FinalRelease()
     {
     }
};
```

Before moving on, save your changes and examine the new code. The code creates a simple COM object (Cobject1) that implements a custom interface (Iobject1) with a single method. This method (GetANum) returns the value of a data member (of type int). Save your changes and rebuild the application, using the command from the previous step:

```
cl /LD MyServer.cpp
regsvr32 MyServer.dll
```

To determine if the server works, a test client application must be written. Open Notepad and create a new text file (Comtest.cpp) in the same folder as MyServer.cpp. Add the following code and save your results:

```
#include <iostream>
#include <"atlbase.h"
#import "vc70.tlb" no_namespace
void main()
{
        CoInitialize(NULL);
        CoInitialize(NULL);
        {
                CComPtr<Iunkown> spUnknown;
                spUnknown.CoCreateInstance(__uuidof(CObject));
                CComPtr<IObject1> pI;
                spUnknown.QueryInterface(&pI);
                int res = 0;
                res = pI->GetANum();
                cout << res << end1;
        }
        CoUnitialize();
}
```

In order for the client to know what the server has to offer, you must import the type library of the server by using the #import keyword. Because no specific name was given when the server was created, the compiler generated a type library with a default name (vc70.tlb). The following line in the code shown above imports the library:

```
#import "vc70.tlb" no_namespace
```

When this file is imported into the test application, the client has access to the type information in the COM server. This allows the test application to refer to any types defined within (such as CObject1 and IObject1). Build the test application using the following command:

cl comtest.cpp

Once the application has successfully been built, run the application (by entering "comtest" from the command line) to see the integer value being printed.

Creating a COM Server Using Wizards

In the previous part, you created a simple attributed COM server using Notepad. In this part, you will use the Visual Studio IDE and the various wizards to create the same ATL COM Server.

TO CREATE A SIMPLE ATL COM SERVER:

1. In Visual Studio, click the New Project button.
2. Click the Visual C++ Projects node.
3. In the Name text box, enter MyServer.
4. In the right pane, double-click the ATL Project item. This opens the ATL COM Application Wizard.
5. Click Application Settings.
6. Select the Attributed check box.
7. Click Finish to close the dialog box and generate the project. The result is an inproc ATL COM server without any server objects.
8. Build the resulting project. Building the project successfully registers the server with the operating system. As before, the COM server needs to implement a simple COM object.

TO ADD A SERVER OBJECT:

1. In Solution Explorer, right-click the MyServer project and click Add on the shortcut menu.
2. On the Add shortcut menu, click Class.
3. In the right pane, double-click the ATL Simple Object item. This opens the ATL Simple Object Wizard.
4. In the Short Name text box, enter Object1.
5. Click Finish to accept the remaining default values.
6. On the Class View pane, right-click the IObject1 node and select Add Method from the shortcut menu.
7. Add the GetANum method from the previous section.
8. Rebuild the MyServer project.

As before, a test client application must be created. To create the test client application:

1. Click the New Project button.
2. Select the Win32 Projects node.
3. In the Name text box, enter Comtest.
4. On the right pane, double-click the Win32 Project item. This opens the Win32 Application Wizard.
5. Click Application Settings.
6. Select the Empty Project check box.
7. Click Finish to close the dialog box and generate the project.
8. In Solution Explorer, right-click the Comtest project and click Add on the shortcut menu.
9. On the Add shortcut menu, click New Item.
10. In the Name text box, enter comtest.cpp.
11. On the right pane, double-click the C++ File item.
12. Open the file and add the following code:

```
#include <iostream>
#include "atlbase.h"
#import "..//MyServer//_MyServer.tlb" no_namespace
void main()
{
     CoInitialize(NULL);
     {
          CComPtr<IUnknown> spUnknown;
          spUnknown.CoCreateInstance(__uuidof(CObject1));
          CComPtr<IObject1> pI;
          SpUnknown.QueryInterface(&pI);
          int res = 0;
          res = pI->GetANum();
          cout << res << end1;
     }
     CoUninitialize();
}
```

Save your changes and build the project. After a successful build, run the client application to see the integer value being printed as in the previous section.

Creating a Simple COM Object with Attributes

The following section shows how to create a COM object using Visual C++ attributes and where the project was not created using a Visual C++ Wizard. The following COM object defines an interface and implements a method. Note the use of the following attributes:

- module
- object
- id
- in
- out
- retval

Compile this program using /LD and then use regsv32 to register the .dll.

```
#define WIN32_LEAN_AND_MEAN
#define STRICT
#define _ATL_ATTRIBUTES 1
#include <atlbase.h>
#include <atlcom.h>
#include <stdio.h>

// created idl library block "LibName" and the 4 COM entry points and regis-
tration support code

[module(name=LibName)];
[object]                      // defines a custom interface
__interface IMyInterface {    // auto inheritance from IUnknown

    // idl attributes pass through to idl file
    [id(1), helpstring("MyMethod")] HRESULT MyMethod([in] int i, [out, ret-
val] int* j);
};

[coclass]    // automatically implements IUknown for IMyInterface using ATL
struct CMyClass : IMyInterface {
    HRESULT MyMethod(int i, int* j) {
    *j = i;
    printf("MyMethod(%d)\n", I
    return S_OK;
}
};
```

The following code is a client program that uses the COM object that was created with the previous code sample.

```
#import "al.dll"
using namespace LibName;
#include <stdio.h>

// See these error if you do not use regsvr32 on the dll.

void dump_com_error(_com_error &e) {
    printf("An error!\n");
    printf("\a\tCode = %081x\n", e.Error());
    printf("a\a\tCode meaning = %s\n", e.ErrorMessage());
    _bstr_t bstrSource(e.Source());
    _bstr_t bstrDescription(e.Description());
    printf("\a\tSource = %s\n", (LPCTSTR) bstrSource);
    printf("\a\tDescription = %s\n", (LPCTSTR) bstrDescription);
}


void main() {
    CoInitialize(NULL);

    try {
        IMyInterfacePtr p(__uuidof(CMyClass));
        int j = p->MyMethod(9);
        p = 0;
    }
    catch(_com_error &e) {
        dump_com_error(e);
    }
    CoUninitialize();
}
```

Extending Metadata with Custom Attributes

Custom attributes are a simple way to extend the metadata of any given managed element. They are available in all .NET languages. This section walks through how to use custom attributes from Managed Extensions for C++. The purpose of this feature is to allow for metadata to be user extensible. For example, in MTS 1.0 behavior with respect to transactions, synchronization, load balancing, and so on was specified through custom GUIDs inserted into the type library by using the ODL custom attribute. Hence, a client of an MTS server could determine its characteristics by walking the type library. In .NET, the analog of the type library is metadata, and the analog of the ODL custom attribute is custom attributes. Also, walking the type library is analogous to using reflection the types. The following example illustrates some important features of custom attributes:

```
#using <mscorlib.dll>
using namespace System
using namespace System::Reflection;

public __value enum Access { Read, Write, Execute };

/*    Defining the Job attribute:
      The special "attribute" attribute automatically makes a __gc class a
      custom attribute (class implicity inherits from System::Attributes);
Arguments explained below
*/
[attribute( AttributeTargets::Class, AllowMultiple=true )]
public __gc class Job
{
public:
      __property void set_Priority( int value ) { m_Priority = value; }
      __property int get_Priority () { return m_Priority; }
      /* You can overload constructors to specify Job attribute in different ways */
      Job() { m_Access = Access::Read; }
      Job( Access a ) { m_Access = a; }
      Access m_Access;

protected:
      int m_Priority;
};

__gc __ interface IService
{
      void Run();
};

/*    Using the Job attribute:
      Here we specify that QueryService is to be read only with a priority of
      2. To prevent namespace collisions, all custom attributes implicitly end
      with "Attribute". Job could have been specified as public __gc class
      JobAttribute : public Attribute. In other words, Job and JobAttribute are
      equivalent.
*/
[JobAttribute( Access::Read, Priority=2 )]
```

```
__gc struct QueryService : public IService {
    void Run()
    {
       //....
    }


/*    Because we said AllowMultiple=true, we can add multiple attributes
where it makes sense.
*/
[JobAttribute(Access::Read, Priority=1)]
[JobAttribute(Access::Write, Priority=3)]
__gc struct StatsGenerator : public IService {
    void Run()
    {
       //...
    }
};

int main()
{
    IService* pIS;
    QueryService* pQS = new QueryService;
    StatsGenerator* pSG = new StatsGenerator;
    Console::WriteLine(S"Please enter the service to run");
    Console::Write(S"QueryService or StatsGenerator> ");
    if(Console::Read() ==L'Q')
       pIS = __try_cast<IService*>( pQS );
    else
       pIS = __try_cast<IService*>( pSG );

    // Reflection
    MemberInfo* pMI = pIS->GetType();
    object* pObjs __gc[] = pMI->GetCustomAttributes();

    /* We can now quickly and easily view custom attributes for an Object
through Reflection */
    for( int i=0; i <pObjs->Length; i++)
    {
       Console::Write(S" Service Priority =  ");
       Console::WriteLine(static_cast<Job*>(pObjs[i]->Priority);
       Console::Write(S' Service Access = ");
       Console::WriteLine(static_cast<Job*>(pObjs[I]->m_access);
    }
}
```

This example shows a common usage of the custom attributes: instantiating a server that can fully describe itself to clients. A custom attribute definition specifies where it is syntactically allowed. The above Job attribute is allowed on classes, as indicated by the argument:

[attribute(AttributeTargets::Class)] …
Actually
[attribute(Class)] …
is sufficient as long as there are no name collisions. The definition of Attribute Targets:

```
__value enum AttributeTargets {
        Assembly = 0x1,
        Module = 0x2,
        Class = 0x4,
        Struct = 0x8,
        Enum = 0x10,
        Constructor = 0x20,
        Method = 0x40,
        Property = 0x80,
        Field = 0x100,
        Event = 0x200,
        Interface = 0x400,
        Parameter = 0x800,
        Delegate = 0x1000,
        All = 0x1fff,
        ClassMembers = 0x17fc,
};
```

Show the possible syntactic elements on which a custom attribute can be used. Combination of these values (using logical-OR) may be used. Two other named arguments that the "attribute" attribute takes are:

```
bool AllowMultiple;      // default: false
bool Inherited;          // default: true
```

AllowMultiple was previously demonstrated. If TRUE, then the custom attribute can be specified multiple times on any valid targets. The Inherited named argument specifies whether a custom attribute applied on a base class will show up on reflection of a derived class. The following example illustrates this:

```
#using <mscorlib.dll>
using namespace System;
using namespace System::Reflection;

[attribute( AttributeTargets::Method )]
```

```
__gc class BaseOnlyAttribute {};

[attribute( AttributeTargets::Method, Inherited=true )]
__gc class DerivedTooAttribute {};

__gc __interface Ibase {        // base class
public:
     [BaseOnly, DerivedToo]
     void meth();
};

__gc class Derived : public IBase {      // derived class
public:
     void meth() {};
};

int main()
{
     IBase* pIB = new Derived;

     MemberInfo* pMI = pIB->GetType()->GetMethod( S"meth" );
     Object* pObjs __gc[] = pMI->GetCustomAttributes();

     Console::WriteLine( pObjs->Length );
}
```

should print:

1

Reflection on Derived::meth will show DerivedTooAttribute but not
BaseOnlyAttribute. One last but very important note to remember when creating custom attributes is that the public part of the custom attribute class
must be serializable. This is one of the restrictions imposed by the runtime.
What this means when authoring custom attributes is that named arguments
of your custom attribute are limited to compile-time constants. Think of it as
a sequence of bits appended to your class layout in the metadata.
Example 1

```
__gc struct Deadly {};

[attribute( All )]
__gc struct A
```

```
{
    A( System::Type* ) {}
    A( String* ) {}
    A( int ) {}
};
```

```
[A( __typeof( Deadly ) )]// typeof operator only allowed in custom attribute blocks
struct B {};
```

Example 2

```
[attribute( Class )]
__gc Class A
{
public:
    A( Object* ) {}          // error: illegal type for a custom attribute
private:
    Object* m_obj;           // OK member is private
};
```

Simplifying Operations with Database Attributes

This part demonstrates the use of database attributes to simplify database operations. The basic way to access information from a database is to create a table class and an accessor class for a particular table in the database. The database attributes simplify some of the template declarations that you previously had to do. To demonstrate the use of database attributes, this part shows two equivalent table and accessor class declarations: The first uses attributes, and the second uses OLE DB Templates. Such declaration code is typically placed in a header file named for the table or command object, for example, authors.h. By comparing the two files, you can see how much simpler it is to use attributes. Among the differences are:

- Using attributes, you only have to declare one class: CAuthors, while with templates you have to declare two: CAuthorsNoAttrAccessor and CAuthorsNoAttr.
- The db_source call in the attributed version is equivalent to the OpenDataSource() call in the template declaration.
- The db_table call in the attributed version is equivalent to the following template declaration: class CAuthorsNoAttr : public CTable<CAccess<CAuthorsNoAttrAccess> >.

- The db_column calls in the attributed version are equivalent to the column map(see BEGIN_COLUMN_MAP ...END_COLUMN_MAP) in the template declaration. Note that the db_column calls inject an accessor class declaration for you (equivalent to CAuthorsNoAttrAccessor in the template declaration).

Note that in both the attributed and the templated code, you must set rowset properties using CDBPropSet::AddProperty.

Table and Accessor Declaration Using Attributes

The following code calls db_source and db_table on the table class. db_source specifies the data source and connection to be used. db_table injects the appropriate template code to declare a table class. db_column specify the column map and inject the accessor declaration. Here is the table and access declaration using attributes:

```
///////////////////////////////////////////////////////////////
// Table and accessor declaration using attributes
// authors.h
///////////////////////////////////////////////////////////////

// Table class declaration
[
db_source("Provider=Microsoft.Jet.OLEDB.4.0;User ID=Admin;DataSource=C:\\Inetpub\\iis-
samples\\sdk\\asp\\database\\Authors.mdb");
db_table("Authors")
]
class CAuthors
{
public:
                  DWORD    m_dwAuIDStatus;
                  DWORD    m_dwAuthorStatus;
                  DWORD    m_dwYearBornStatus;
                  DWORD    m_dwAuIDLength;
                  DWORD    m_dwAuthorLength;
                  DWORD    m_dwYearBornLength;
                  [db_column(1, status=m_dwAuIDStatus, length=m_dwAuIdLength)]
LONG m_AuID;
                  [db_column(2, status=m_dwAuthorStatus, length=m_dwAuthorLength)]
TCHAR m_Author[51];
[db_column(3, status=m_dwYearBornStatus, length=m_dwYearnBornLength)] SHORT
 m_YearBorn;
                  void GetRowsetProperties(CDBPropSet* pPropSet)
                  {
                     pPropSet->AddProperty(DBPROP_CANFETCHBACKWARDS, true);
                     pPropSet->AddProperty(DBPROP_CANSCROLLBACKWARDS, true);
                     pPropSet->AddProperty(DBPROP_IrowsetChange, true);
                  }
};
```

Table and Accessor Declaration Using Templates

This section covers the table and accessor declaration using templates.

```
///////////////////////////////////////////////////////////////////////////
// Table and accessor class declaration using templates
// Authors.h
///////////////////////////////////////////////////////////////////////////

// Accessor class declaration
class CAuthorsNoAttrAccessor
{
public:
                   DWORD    m_dwAuIDStatus;
                   DWORD    m_dwAuthorStatus;
                   DWORD    m_dwYearBornStatus;
                   DWORD    m_dwAuIDLength;
                   DWORD    m_dwAuthorLength;
                   DWORD    m_dwYearBornLength;
                   LONG     m_AuID;
                   TCHAR    m_Author[51];
                   SHORT    m_YearBorn;
                   Void GetRowSetProperties(CDBPropSet* pPropSet)
                   {
                      pPropSet->AddProperty(DBPROP_CANFETCHBACKWARDS, true);
                      pPropSet->AddProperty(DBPROP_CANSCROLBACKWARDS, true);
                      pPropSet->AddProperty(DBPROP_IRowsetChange, true);
                   }
                   HRESULT OpenDataSource()
                   {
                      CDataSource _db;
                      HRESULT hr;
Hr = _db.OpenFromInitializationString(L"Provider=Microsoft.Jet.OLEDB.4.0;User
ID=Admin;Data Source=C:\\Inetpub\\iisamples\\sdk\\asp\\database\\Authors.mdb");
                         if(FAILED(hr))
                         {
#ifdef _DEBUG
                            AtlTraceErrorRecords(hr);
#endif
                            return hr;
                         }
                         return m_session.Open(_db);
                   }
                   void CloseDataSource()
                   {
                      m_session.Close();
                   }
                   operator const CSession&()
                   {
                      return m_session;
                   {
```

```cpp
operator const CSession&()
{
    return m_session;
}
CSession m_session;
BEGIN_COLUMN_MAP(CAuthorsNoAttrAccessor)
    COLUMN_ENTRY_LENGTH_STATUS(1, m_AuID, m_dwAuIDLength,
m_dwAuIDStatus)
COLUMN_ENTRY_LENGTH_STATUS(2, m_Author, m_dwAuthorLength, m_dwAuthorStatus)
COLUMN_ENTRY_LENGTH_STATUS(3, m_YearBorn, m_dwYearBornLength,
m_dwYearBornStatus)
    END_COLUMN_MAP()
};
class CAuthorsNoAttr : public CTable<CAccessor<CAuthorsNoAttrAccessor> >
{
public:
    HESULT OpenAll()
    {
        HRESULT hr;
        Hr = OpenDataSource();
        if(FAILED(hr))
            return hr;
        __if_exists(GetRowsetProperties)
        {
            CDBPropSet propset(DBPROPSET_ROWSET);
            __if_exists(HasBookmark)
            {
                propset.AddProperty(DBPROP_IRowsetLocate, true);
            }
            GetRowsetProperties(&propset);
            Return OpenRowset(&propset);
        }
        __if_not_exists(GetRowsetProperties)
        {
            __if_exists(HasBookmark)
            {
                CDBPropSet properset(DBPROPSET_ROWSET);
                propset.AddProperty(DBPROP_IRowsetLocate, true);
                return OpenRowset(&propset);
            }
        }
        return OpenRowset();
    }
    HRESULT OpenRowset(DBPROPSET *pPropSet = NULL)
    {
        HRESULT hr = Open(m_session, "Authors", pPropSet);
#ifdef _DEBUG
        if(FAILED(hr))
            AtlTraceErrorRecords(hr);
#endif
```

```
    return hr;
}
void CloseAll()
{
Close();
CloseDataSource();
}
};
```

Creating an ActiveX Control with Attributes

One strength of programming with attributes is the ease of constructing basic framework of usable code. With this model, designing an ActiveX control is made easier by using attributes. In addition to the attributes themselves, several Visual C++ tools take advantage of attributes. When designing an ActiveX control, the ATL Project Wizard and ATL Object Wizard use attributes to develop a basic framework for an ActiveX control. The procedure consists of the following steps:

- Creating the ActiveX Control Project
- Inserting the full Control Component
- Adding a Property Using Attributes
- Adding an Event Using Attributes

Creating the ActiveX Control Project

The first step is to create the project using the Visual C++ IDE. Because the control uses attributes, you need to add attribute support when using the ATL Project Wizard. The resultant project supports attributes and uses them for basic framework implementation. At this point we would typically generate a project using the ATL Project Wizard and add attribute support by checking Attributed on the Application Setting Page. A Visual C++ DLL project will be generated, hosting the ActiveX control. For the purposes of this discussion, the name of the sample project will be MyAxCtrl.

ATTRIBUTES USED IN THE MYAXCTRL PROJECT

Before inserting the Full Control component, there are a few points to make regarding the usage of attributes. The first item of importance is the inclusion of the ATLPLUS.H file (located in STDAFX.H). This file provides information needed by the compiler to invoke the ATL provider. This is important when implementation for an attribute is needed from the ATL provider. Another important attribute, found in the header file of the module application (MYCTL.H), is emitidl. This attribute informs the compiler that all subsequent

IDL category attributes should be used to generate output in the project's IDL file. At this stage of development, the module attribute is the workhorse of the project. This attribute provides information on various characteristics of the target module. The module attribute specifies the module type as a DLL, a unique ID for the module (making use of the uuid attribute), and a simple name for the module.

Inserting the Full Control Component

The next step is to add the Full Control component to your project. As mentioned previously the ATL Object Wizard provides a variety of frameworked components for insertion into a Visual C++ IDE project. One of these components is the Full Control component, located on the Controls page of the ATL Object Wizard. When creating a sample project just insert the Full Control object, providing a short name, and accept all default values. For example, MyCtl is a short name for a control.

ATTRIBUTES USED IN THE FULL CONTROL COMPONENT

Because the Full Control component makes use of attributes, several new attributes would be present in the project. These attributes implement the control object and the default control interface. In your MYCTL.H file, you would find a new set of attributes (referred to as an attribute block) that implements a control framework attached to the new CMyCtl class. This block contains the following attributes:

> control—Declares a control framework with a toolbar bitmap (identified by toolboxbitmap) and sets the related OLEMISC structure to a default set of flags.
>
> threading—Specifies that the control is safe to be used in an apartment thread. This is done by changing the general reference counting and registration code.
>
> progid—Declares a simple ProgID, used by clients of the new control.
>
> uuid—Declares the CLSID for the control.

The other major element added by the ATL Object Wizard is another attribute block (attached to the IMyCt1 interface), implementing the default interface for the control object. This is the default interface of your control and currently the only implemented interface. The interface is declared in your control's declaration file (in the example, MYCTL.H) and is very simple:

```
Interface IMyCtl: public IDispatch
{
};
```

This code declares a custom interface, IMyCtl, that is derived from the standard IDispatch interface and contains no methods. This block contains the following attributes:

- object—Specifies that the following interface definition is a custom interface and should be placed in the .idl file of the project.
- uuid—Declares the IID for the IMyCtl interface.
- dual—Declares the interface as a dual interface (supporting both early and late binding).
- helpstring—A short description of the control object and its purpose.
- pointer default—Specifies the characteristics of any embedded pointers. In the sample control, unique means that the embedded pointers can be NULL and where there will be no duplicate values.

Adding a Property Using Attributes

Adding a property or method to an ActiveX control becomes a quick and simple exercise when using attributes. This part demonstrates the steps needed to add a simple read-write custom property using attributes and discusses the changes to the control project. Note: Adding a stock property requires similar steps but uses a different attribute: stock_property. This attribute is discussed in more detail later in this part. For demonstration purposes, the sample program adds a custom property, called Data, that gets or sets the current value of a character string. This property will be stored in a data member of the BSTR. To fully implement the custom property, you need to add the property to the control's default interface and to the class implementing the control. You can do this with the property attribute. This attribute implements a standard set of read-write property methods for the control interface. These methods are used by clients of the control to access and set value (in this case a data string), using standard COM procedures.

The first step involves modifying your control's basic interface by adding the property attribute. The sample control uses Data as the name of the property:

```
interface IMyCtl: public IDispatch
{
    [ property ] BSTR Data;
};
```

With this modification, the implementation of your custom Data property is only half finished. You must still modify the control class, using the property attribute to implement the access methods and data member. Modify your control class declaration to match the following:

```
class ATL_No_VTALBE CMyCtl : public IMyCtl
{
public:
    [ property( storage_type= CComBSTR ) ] BSTR Data;
    // Continuation of the class declaration
}
```

With this modification (the addition of the property attribute), the implementation is not complete. Using the property attribute, you have declared storage for a BSTR value, of type CComBstr in your control's implementation class. With a successful build, your control implements a custom property that contains a BSTR data string. The actual value of the property is stored in a protected member called __PropertyName that is added directly to your class. For the sample control, the value is stored in a CComBSTR data member called __Data in this case.

IMPLEMENTING A STOCK PROPERTY

Implementing a stock property is similar to the custom property implementation. The stock_property attribute is used in place of property, but the modifications are almost exact. The main difference between the two implementations is the inclusion of the ATLSTOCK.H include file. Include this file after the include file listing in the header file of the control class. This header file defines several important classes for use with stock properties. If this file is not included in your control's declaration file, you will get several errors after adding the stock_property attribute. For example purposes, the stock Caption property is added to the control. As with the custom property, you need to modify both the interface and the control class itself.

To add the stock Caption property, modify your interface declaration (by adding the stock_property attribute) to match the following:

```
interface IMyCtl : public IDispatch
{
    [ property ] BSTR Data;
    [ stock_property( caption ) ];
};
```

In the declaration for your control class, add the stock_property attribute:

```
class ATL_NO_VTABLE  CMyCtl : public IMyCtl
{
public:
    [ property( storage_type= CComBSTR ) ] BSTR Data;
```

```
[ stock_property( caption ) ];
// Continuation of the class declaration
}
```

After a successful build, your control provides support for the Caption stock property. Note the actual value of the stock property is stored in the m_propCaption data member of the target class.

Adding an Event Using Attributes

Events allow an ActiveX control to communicate important information to its container. A common event for controls is to fire the stock Click event when the user clicks on an ActiveX control. Using attributes, adding an event is a simple matter. This part focuses on adding a custom event to the sample project we have been talking about. The event is fired by the sample when a WM_LBUTTONDOWN message is received by the control. Note stock events are implemented by following the same procedure as a stock property. The main difference is that the stock_event attribute is used instead of the stock_property. Adding an event can be broken down into three steps:

- Declaring the event interface.
- Implementing the ability to fire events from the ActiveX control.
- Firing the event at the proper time (i.e., a mouse click on the control).

DECLARING THE EVENT INTERFACE

Currently, the ActiveX sample control implements one interface: a custom interface used for methods and properties. To fire events, the ActiveX control must implement a separate interface; firing only events. In 7.3 Adding a Property Using Attributes above, you saw that the declaration for the primary interface was simple, consisting mainly of the interface keyword and a class derived from IDispatch. Because an event interface can be thought of as a specialized dispatch interface (specialized in that it only fires events), use the same procedure to declare the control's event interface. The following code sample declares an event interface, called _IMyCtlEvents, that contains one method (MyEvent):

```
[ uuid("FF5D58CB-8EB8-11D2-94A2-006008938FB8"), dispinterface, hidden,
        helpstring("_ImyCtlEvents Interface") ]
interface _IMyCtlEvents : public IDispatch
{
    [ id )1) ] HRESULT MyEvent();
};
```

Note   Previously, you defined an interface (IMyCtl) that was implemented by the control. However, this interface is implemented by clients of the control.

The method is actually the sole event supported by the sample control and will be fired when the control receives a mouse click. In the sample, the cause of the event firing is purely made up. Events can be fired at any time by the ActiveX control. It is up to you to decide when the event is to be fired. Now that the event interface is declared, you need to hook it up to the control that will be firing the events.

IMPLEMENTING EVENT FIRING FOR THE CONTROL

Before an ActiveX control can fire events from an existing interface, the two objects must be related in some way. This is accomplished by making use of an attribute specifically designed for this; fire_events. This attribute relates the event interface and the ActiveX control by establishing a connection point for the target class, associating the event interface with the control.

Note   Connection Points are available as an option in the ATL Object Wizard when inserting a Full Control object.

The following example, using the fire_events attribute, connects the _IMyCtlEvents interface to the sample control class (CMyCtl):

```
[
control( miscstatus="131473", toolboxbitmap = 103 ),
threading( "apartment" ),
progid( "BasicCtrl.MyCtl.1" ),
uuid( "38F8048A-8DDE-11D2-94A2-006008938FB8" ),
stock_property( interface_name= IMyCtl ),
fire_events(interface_name= "_IMyCtlEvents" )
]
class ATL_NO_VTABLE : public IMyCtl
{
      ........
};
```

The only new item in the code sample above is the usage of the fire_events attribute. In the 7.4.3, you will see one possible method for firing the MyEvent event.

Firing the Event

At this point, the sample control implements an event interface, with one event. However, the event will never be fired because the control has set no specific condition to be met before firing MyEvent. For demonstration purposes, a simple message handler will be added to fire the event when the user of the control clicks on the control, using the left mouse button. Once again, attributes provides a quick implementation of this with the message_handler attribute. When applied to the control class method, code is added that handles the specified message; in this case, WM_LBUTTON-DOWN. Immediately following this, the handler function is defined by OnClick. Inside this handler function, the event is fired. The following example demonstrates this:

```
[ message_handler (WM_LBUTTONDOWN) ]
void OnClick(UINT keys, Cpoint ptLocation)
{
     Fire_MyEvent();
}
```

The main point of the preceding code example is the call to Fire_MyEvent. The actual function being called, Fire_MyEvent, was added when the MyEvent event was declared. The new public member function of CMyCtl, Fire_MyEvent, can now be used to fire the actual control event. This naming convention is used with all events implemented by an event interface, using attributes. For example, if your control exposed another event (called Event2), a corresponding member function (called Fire_Event2) would be added to your control class.

Conclusion

After completing the above activities and successfully building the project, a complete ActiveX control with properties and an event is ready for use by ActiveX control clients. In this short discussion, several attributes (module, control, property, stock_property, fire_events, and others) were used to implement an ActiveX control with properties and two events.

   In the past, implementing the standard features of an ActiveX control could be a tedious task. However, using the Attribute Programming Model, the various wizards of Visual C++, and the Visual C++ compiler itself, implementing a basic ActiveX control now requires little effort, and makes use of code that has been tested and optimized by the Visual C++ team.

Debugging Visual C++

*D*ebugging Windows applications is a subject that a whole book can and has been written on. John Robbins' book, "*Debugging Applications*" ISBN 0-7356-0886-5, is an excellent book on the subject of debugging Windows applications. In this appendix we will only touch upon some of the new aspects of using the Visual Studio.NET debugger.

Beginning with Visual Studio.NET, debugging is handled by one debugger at the Visual Studio.NET level. You can perform the following tasks to fix logic errors in your code:

- Debug injected and optimized code.
- Use DebugBreak and Assertions.
- Detect and isolate memory leaks.
- Debug inline assembly code.

First, however, let's cover a few of the more commonly asked questions.

FAQs for Debugging Techniques for Visual C

Q—How can I debug access violations when running my program stand-alone?

A—Use Just-In-Time debugging. If you set the Just-In-Time debugging option before you compile, you can run your program stand-alone until the access violation occurs. Then, in the Access Violation dialog box, you can click Cancel to start the debugger. Also, see the Knowledge Base article Q133174 "How to Locate Where a General Protection (GP) Fault Occurs." You can find Knowledge Base articles on the MSDN Library CD, or at http://search.support.microsoft.com/.

Q—How can I debug an access violation?

A—Use the Call Stack window to work your way back up the call stack, looking for corrupted data being passed as a parameter to a function. If that fails, try setting a breakpoint at a point before the location where the access violation occurs. Check to see if data is good at that point. If so, try stepping your way toward the location where the access violation occurred. If you can identify a single action, such as a menu command that led to the access violation, you can try another techniques: setting a breakpoint between the action (in this case the menu command) and the access violation. You can then look at the state of your program during the moments leading up to the access violation. You can use a combination of these techniques to work forward and backward until you have isolated the location where the access violation occurred.

Q—How can I find out if my pointers are corrupting a memory address?

A—If you think, for instance, that one of your pointers may be corrupting memory at address 0x00408000, then use the Memory window to view memory contents starting at that address. Set a breakpoint on that memory address.

Q—How can I find out where my pointer is getting changed?

A—My pointer halts the program when data at the location pointed to by ptr changes.

Q—If halted in MFC, how can I get back to the function that called MFC?

A—When a program starts drawing erratically, and the Break command in the Debug menu is used to halt the program, you could end up in MFC. Use the Call Stack Window to navigate to the function from which MFC was called.

Q—How can I find out who is passing a wrong parameter value?

A—When you discover that the wrong parameter value is being passed to one of your functions, and the function is called from all over the place, you use the Breakpoints dialog box. Set a location breakpoint at the beginning of the function. Then click Condition, and use the Breakpoints Condition dialog box to enter an expression, such as Var==3ll Stack Window to find the calling function navigate to its source code.

Q—When calling a function hundreds of times, which call failed?

A—If your program fails on a call to a certain function, CnvtV, the program probably calls that function a couple hundred times before it fails. If I set a location breakpoint on CnvtV, the program stops on every call to that function, and I don't want that. I don't know what conditions cause the call to fail, so I can't set a conditional breakpoint. We can set a conditional breakpoint without specifying a condition. Set the Skip Count field to a value so high that it will never be reached. In this case, since you believe the function CnvtV is called a couple hundred times, set Skip Count to 1000 or more. Then run the program and wait for it to fail. When it does, open the Breakpoint dialog box and look at the list of breakpoints. The breakpoint you set on CnvtV appears, followed by the skip count and number of iterations remaining:

At "CnvtV(ParamList)" skip 1000 times (750 remaining)

You now know that the breakpoint was skipped 250 times before the function failed. If you reset the breakpoint with a skip count of 250 and run the program again, the program stops at the call to CnvtV that caused it to fail last time.

Q—Where can I look up Win32 Error Codes?

A—WINERROR.H in the INCLUDE directory of your default system installation contains the error code definitions for the Win32 API functions. You can use the ERRLOOK.EXE utility to retrieve a system error message or module error message. The Error Lookup option is available from the Tools menu. For an overview of error codes, see "Error Handling" in the ActiveX Programmer's Reference in the Win32 SDK.

Using the Debugger

The Visual Studio debugger includes menu items, windows, and dialog boxes. You can obtain help on any window, dialog box, or control by selecting the item and pressing F1. You can use the drag-and-drop to move debug information between interface elements. In this section we will cover the following items:

- Execution Control.
- Attaching to a Running Program or Multiple Programs.
- Breakpoints.
- Inspecting Your Program.
- Handling Exceptions.
- Edit and Continue.
- Using Expressions in the Debugger.

Execution Control

The Visual Studio debugger provides powerful commands for controlling the execution of your application. Using debugger commands, you can:

- Start execution.
- Break execution.

- Stop execution.
- Step through your application.
- Run to a desired location.
- Set the execution point.

STARTING EXECUTION

To start debugging, from the Debug menu, choose Start, Step Into, Step Over, or Run to Cursor. If you choose Start, your application starts up and runs until it reaches a breakpoint. You can break execution at any time to examine values, modify variables, and otherwise examine the state of your program. If you choose Step Into, your application starts up and executes its first statement, then breaks. If the first statement is a function call, execution breaks inside the called function, just before the first statement in that function.

If you choose Step Over, your application starts up and executes its first statement. If that statement is a function call, the application executes the entire function call and execution breaks in the main program just after the call statement. If you choose Run to Cursor, your application starts up and runs until it reaches a breakpoint or the cursor location, whichever comes first. You can set the cursor location in a source window or the Disassembly window. In some cases, a break does not occur. This means that execution never reached the code where the cursor is set.

Your solution may contain more than one project. In that case, you can choose the startup project that will be launched by the Debug menu execution commands. Alternatively, you can start a selected project to start from the Solution Explorer.

BREAKING EXECUTION

When you are debugging an application with the Visual Studio debugger, your application is either running (executing) or it is in break mode. Many debugger features are available only in break mode. The debugger breaks execution of the program when execution reaches a breakpoint or when an exception occurs. You can break execution manually at any time. To break execution of your program manually, from the Debug menu, choose Break. The debugger stops execution of your program, but the program does not exit and you can resume execution at any time. The debugger and your application are said to be in break mode.

Note   If the program cannot be stopped for some reason (for example, the program is executing in kernel mode), the debugger freezes all threads and simulates a break. This is known as a "soft break." If you choose an execution command such as Go or Step after a soft break, the debugger reactivates (thaws) the threads. As a result, you may need to choose the Go or Step command twice for execution to resume. A message box informs you when a soft break has occurred.

If you are debugging multiple programs, a Break command or breakpoint normally affects all programs being debugged. You can change this default if you want to break only the current program. To change break behavior when debugging multiple programs, do the following:

1. From the Tools menu, choose Options.
2. In the Options dialog box, select the Debugging folder.
3. In the Debugging folder, select the General Category.
4. In the General group, select, select or clear In Break Mode, only stop execution of the current program.

STOPPING EXECUTION

Stopping execution means terminating the program you are debugging and ending the debugging session. It should not be confused with breaking execution, which temporarily halts execution of the program you are debugging but leaves the debugging session active. To stop debugging:

- From the Debug menu, choose Stop Debugging. If you want to stop the run you are currently debugging and immediately begin a new run, you can use the Restate command.

To stop debugging and restart, from the Debug menu, choose Restart.

STEPPING

One of the most common debugging procedures is stepping—executing code one unit (statement, line, or machine instruction) at a time. With the Visual Studio debugger, you can choose the step unit you want to use—a language statement, a source line, or a machine instruction. To change the step unit:

- From the Debug menu, choose Step By and select Statement, Line, or Instruction.

The Debug menu provides three commands for stepping through code:

- Step Into.
- Step Over.
- Step Out.

Step Into and Step Over differ in only one respect—the way they handle function calls. Either command instructs the debugger to execute the next unit of code. If the next unit contains a function call, Step Into executes only the call itself, then halts at the first unit of code inside the function. Step Over executes the entire function, then halts, at the first unit outside the function. Use Step Into if you want to look inside the function call. Use Step Over if you want to avoid stepping into functions. On a nested function call,

Step Into, steps into the most deeply nested function. If you use Step Into on a call like Func1(Func2), the debugger steps into the function Func2. If you want to select which nested function to step into, use the Step Into Specific Function command from the shortcut menu.

Use Step Out when you are inside a function call and want to return to the calling function. Step Out resumes execution of your code until the function returns, then breaks, at the return point in the calling function. You cannot access the Step commands if your application is running. Step commands are valid only in break mode or before you start the application. To step into a program that is not yet executing, from the Debug menu, choose Step Into. To step while debugging, the debugger must be in break mode. From the Debug menu, choose Step Into, Step Out, or Step Over.

RUNNING TO A SPECIFIED LOCATION

Sometimes, while debugging, you will want to execute to a certain point in code then break. If you have a breakpoint set at that location, all you have to do is select Start or Continue from the Debug menu. You don't need to set a breakpoint in all cases, however. The Visual Studio debugger provides specific commands—run to the cursor location, and run to a specific function.

RUN TO THE CURSOR LOCATION

You can command the debugger to run your application until it reaches the location where the cursor is set. This location may be in a source window or the Disassembly window. The cursor means the insertion point you set by clicking in the window with the mouse. To run to the cursor in a source window:

1. The debugger must in break mode.
2. In a source file, click on a source line to move the cursor to that point.
3. From the Debug menu, select Run to Cursor. The break location depends on the step unit chosen through the Step By command on the Debug menu. If the step unit is line, execution breaks at the first statement on the line. If the step unit is statement, execution breaks at the statement containing the cursor.

To run to the cursor in the Disassembly window:

1. The debugger must be in break mode.
2. If the Disassembly window is not visible, choose Windows from the Debug menu and select Disassembly.
3. In the Disassembly window, click on a line to move the cursor to that point.
4. From the Debug menu, select Run To Cursor.

RUN TO A SPECIFIED FUNCTION

You can command the debugger to run your application until it reaches a specified function. You can specify the function by name (using the toolbar) or you can choose it from the call stack. To run to a specified function in an open source file:

1. On the standard toolbar, type the function name in the Find box and press Enter. This moves the cursor to the specified function.
2. From the Debug menu, select Run to Cursor.

To run to a function on the call stack:

1. The debugger must be in break mode.
2. Open the Call Stack window, if necessary. (Choose Call Stack from the Debug menu, Windows submenu.)
3. In the Call Stack window, click on a function name to select it.
4. From the Debug menu, choose Run to Cursor.

SETTING THE EXECUTION POINT

In the Visual Studio debugger, you can move the execution point to set the next statement of code (or assembly language instruction) to be executed. An arrowhead in the margin of a source or Disassembly window marks the current location of the execution point. By moving the execution point, you can skip over a portion of code or return to a line previously executed. This can be useful in some situations—for example, if you want to skip a section of code that contains a known bug and continue debugging other sections.

Changing the execution point causes the program counter to jump directly to the new location. Use this command with caution. Be aware:

- Instructions between the old and new execution points are not executed.
- If you move the execution point backwards, intervening instructions are not undone.
- Moving the execution point to another function or scope usually results in call-stack corruption, causing a run-time error or exception. If you try moving the execution point to another scope, the debugger opens a dialog box that gives you a warning and a chance to cancel the operation.

You cannot set the execution point while your application is actively running. To set the next statement, the debugger must be in break mode. To set the next statement to execute:

1. In a source window or Disassembly window, click to select the statement or assembly-language instruction you want to execute next.

2. From the Debug menu, choose Set Next Statement. If the current execution point is in the same source file as the statement you want to set, you can move the execution point by dragging the marker arrow.

To set the next statement to execute (alternative method), in the source window, click the execution point marker (yellow arrowhead) and drag it to a location in the same source file where you want to set the next statement.

Debugging Optimized Code

When optimizing code, the compiler repositions and reorganizes instructions, resulting in more efficient compiled code. Because of this rearrangement, the debugger cannot always identify the source code that corresponds to a set of instructions. For this reason, you should do your debugging using an unoptimized version of your program if at all possible. By default, optimization should be turned off in the Debug configuration of a Visual C++ program and turned on in the Release configuration. Sometimes, however, a bug may appear in an optimized version of a program. In that case, you must debug the optimized code.

To turn on optimization in a Debug build configuration:

- When you create a new project, select the Win32 Debug target. Build and debug the Win32 Debug target until you are ready to build a Win32 Release target. The compiler does not optimize the Win32 Debug target.

-or-

- Use the /Od compiler option on the command line, and remove any other /O? compiler options.

-or-

- From the View menu, click Property Pages.
- In the Property Pages dialog box, make sure Debug is selected in the Configuration box.
- In the folder view on the left, select the C/C++ folder.
- Under the C++ folder, select Optimizer.
- In the properties list on the right, find Optimization. The setting next to it probably says Disable (/Od). Choose one of the other options (Minimum Size (/O1), Maximum Speed (/O2), Full Optimization (/Ox), or Custom).
- If you chose the Custom option for Optimization, you can now set options for any of the other properties shown in the properties list.
- Click Ok.

When debugging optimized code, look at the Disassembly window to see what instructions are actually demonstrated. When setting breakpoints, you need to be aware that the breakpoint may move along with an instruction. For example, consider the following code:

for(x=0; x<10; x++)

Suppose you set a breakpoint at this line. You might expect the breakpoint to be hit 10 times, but if the code is optimized, the breakpoint is only hit once. That's because the first instruction sets the value of x to 0. The compiler recognizes that this only has to be done once and moves it out of the loop. The breakpoint moves with it. The instructions that compare and increment x remain inside the loop. To set a breakpoint on one of these instructions, use the Disassembly Window. Set the step unit to Instruction for greater control when stepping through optimized code.

DebugBreak

The DebugBreak function causes a breakpoint exception to occur in the current process so that the calling thread can signal the debugger and force it to take some action. If the process is not being debugged, the search logic of a standard exception handler is used. In most cases, this causes the calling process to terminate because of an unhandled breakpoint exception. The call is as follows:

VOID DebugBreak(VOID);

I have found this function to be an excellent way to break point in different processes that are put into execution in some asynchronous fashion. Once I am in the particular process I can then set other breakpoints as needed and continue my debugging in that process. This turns out to be a very useful function call when debugging in a multi-process environment.

Assertions

The assertion is one of your best proactive programming debugging constructs. An assertion statement specifies a condition that you expect to hold true at some particular point in your program. If that condition does not hold true, the assertion fails, execution of your program is interrupted, and an Assertion Failed dialog box appears. This dialog box has three buttons:

1. Retry—Debug the assertion or get help on asserts.
2. Ignore—Ignore the assertion and continue running the program.
3. Abort—Halt execution of the program and end the debugging session.

When the debugger halts because of an MFC or C run-time library assertion, it navigates to the point in the source file where the assertion occurred (if the source is available). The assertion message appears in the Output window as well as the Assertion Failed dialog box. You can copy the assertion message from the Output window to a text window if you want to save it for future reference. The Output window may contain other messages as well. Examine these messages carefully, since they provide clues to the cause of the assertion failure. Through the liberal use of assertions in your code, you can catch many errors during development. A good rule is to write an assertion for every assumption you make. If you assume that an argument is not NULL, for example, use an assertion statement to check for that assumption.

Assertion statements compile only when _DEBUG is defined. When _DEBUG is not defined, the compiler treats assertions as null statements. Therefore, assertion statements have zero overhead in your final release program; you can use them liberally in your code without affecting the performance of your release version and without having to use #ifdefs. Visual C++ supports assertion statements based on the following constructs:

- MFC assertions for MFC program.
- ATLASSERT for programs that use ATL.
- CRT assertions for programs that use the C runtime library.
- The ANSI assert function for other C/C++ programs.

You can use assertion to:

- Catch logic errors.
- Check results of an operation.
- Test error conditions that should have been handled.

Caution   When you add assertions to your code, make sure the assertions do not have side effects. For example, consider the following assertion:

ASSERT(nM++ > 0);   — Don't do this!

Because the ASSERT expression is not evaluated in the release version of your program, nM will have different values in the debug and release versions. In MFC, you can use the VERIFY macro instead of ASSERT. VERIFY evaluates the expression but does not check the result in the release version. Be especially careful about using function calls in assertion statements, because evaluating a function can have unexpected side effects.

ASSERT(myFnctn(0) == 1)   — unsafe if myFnctn has side effects
VERIFY(myFnctn(0) == 1)   — safe, VERIFY calls myFnctn in both the debug and release versions, so it is safe to use. You will still have the overhead of an unnecessary function call in the Release version, however.

Detecting and Isolating Memory Leaks

The ability to dynamically allocate and deallocate memory is one of the strongest features of C/C++ programming, but the greatest strength can also be the greatest weakness. This is certainly true of C/C++ applications, where memory-handling problems are among the common bugs. One of the most subtle and hard-to-detect bugs is the memory leak — the failure to properly deallocate memory that was previously allocated. A small memory leak that occurs only once may not be noticed, but programs that leak large amounts of memory, or leak progressively, may display symptoms ranging from poor (and gradually decreasing) performance to running out of memory completely. Worse, a leaking program may use up so much memory that it causes another program to fail, leaving the user with no clue to where the problem truly lies. In addition, even a harmless memory leak may be symptomatic of other problems.

Fortunately, the Visual Studio debugger and CRT libraries provide you with effective means for detecting and identifying memory leaks.

Enabling Memory Leak Detection

The primary tools for detecting memory leaks are the debugger and the CRT debug heap functions. To enable the debug heap functions, include the following statements in your program:

```
#define CRTDBG_MAP_ALLOC
#include <stdlib.h>
#include <crtdbg.h>
```

The #include statements must be in the order shown here. If you change the order, the functions you will use may not work properly. Including crtdbh.h maps the malloc and free functions to their deub versions, _malloc_dbg and _free_dbg, which keep track of memory allocation and deallocation. This mapping occurs only in a debug build (in which _Debug is defined). Release builds use the ordinary malloc and free functions. The #define statement maps the base versions of the CRT heap functions to the corresponding debug versions. You don't absolutely need this statement, but without it, the memory leak dump will contain less useful information.

Once you have added the statements shown above, you can dump memory leak information by including the following statement in your program:

```
_CrtDumpMemoryLeaks();
```

When you run your program under the debugger, _CrtDumpMemoryLeaks displays memory leak information in the Output window. The memory leak information looks like this:

Detected memory leaks!
Dumping objects ->
C:\PROGRAM FILES\VISUAL STUDIO\MyProjects\leaktest\leaktest.cpp(20) :
{18} normal block at 0x00
Data: <   > CD CD CD CD CD CD CD CD CD CD CD CD CD CD CD CD
Object dump complete.

If you do not use #define _CRTDBG_MAP_ALLOC statement, the memory leak dump would look like this:

Detected memory leaks!
Dumping object - >
{18} normal block at 0x00780E80, 64 bytes long.
Data: <   > CD CD CD CD CD CD CD CD CD CD CD CD CD CD CD CD
Object dump complete.

Without _CRTDBG_MAP_ALLOC defined, the display shows:

* The memory allocation number (inside the curly braces).
* The block type (normal, client, or CRT).
* The memory location in hexadecimal form.
* The size of the block in bytes.
* The contents of the first 16 bytes (also in hexadecimal).

With _CRTDBF_MAP_ALLOC defined, the display also shows you the file where the leaked memory was allocated. The number in parentheses following the filename (20, in this example) is the line number within the file. To go to the line in the source file where the memory is allocated:

* Double-click on the line in the Output window that contains the filename and line number.

-or-

* Select the line in the Output window that contains the filename and line number and press F4.

Calling _CrtDumpMemoryLeaks is easy enough if your program always exits in the same place, but what if your program can exit from multiple locations? Instead of putting a call to _CrtDumpMemoryLeaks at each possible exit, you can include the following call at the beginning of your program:

_CrtSetDbgFlag(_CRTDBG_ALLOC_MEM_DF | _CRTDBG_LEAK_CHECK_DF);

This statement automatically calls _CrtDumpMemoryLeaks when your program exits. You must set both bit fields, as shown above.

Event Handling in Visual C

*E*vent handling in Visual C++ uses the Unified Event Model, which allows you to use the same programming model for event handling in all types of classes in Visual C++:

- Native C++ classes (C++ classes that do not implement COM objects)
- COM classes (C++ classes that implement COM objects, typically using ATL classes or coclass attribute)
- Managed classes (C++ classes declared with the __gc keyword or by declaration in a managed context)

Introduction to the Unified Event Model

In the past, various programming environments have provided their own separate ways for components to pass back information about asynchronous "events" to their clients. The C language has function callbacks that work well for this, but C++ has always lacked this kind of callback for an object's methods. You can spend considerable time inventing ways to work around this gap in C++ (using window messages, event interfaces, hardcoded call-back method names, thunks, and so on). COM defines an event model, but it is tedious to implement and maintain, and does not provide event support between two native C++ objects.

The purpose of the Unified Event Model is to allow applications to use events in a way that minimizes the knowledge and dependencies that a component has on its clients and maximizes the component's reusability, and to do this in a consistent way for native (non-COM) C++, COM, and .NET. The model supports single and multithreaded usage and protects data from simultaneous multithread access. It also allows you to derive subclasses from event source or receiver classes and support extended event sourcing/receiving in the derived class.

Event Handling Elements

An event source is an object that defines and contains events. You create an event source using the event_source attribute. An event is a method within an event source that, when called, generates events. You define an event using the keyword __event. To raise an event means to "fire" it, by calling the event method. A delegate is a class that can hold a reference to a method. A delegate class differs from other classes in that it has a signature and can hold references only to methods that match its signature. The .NET Framework has a specific delegate mode. An event receiver (also called an event sink) is an object that receives events. You create an event receiver using the event_receiver attribute. An event handler is a method in an event receiver that receives events. To hook an event means to associate (register) an event with an event handler. You associate a handler method with an event using the intrinsic funct __hook. To unhook an event means to dissociate (deregister) an event from an event handler. You dissociate a handler method from an event using the intrinsic function __unhook.

Attributes and Keywords Supporting Events

Event Source: Use event_source and __event on the event source class, as follows:

```
[event_source(native)]    // optional for native C++ and managed classes
class Csource {
public:
                __event void MyEvent(int nValue);
};
```

Event Receiver: You typically use event_receiver, __hook, and __unhook on the event receiver class, as follows:

```
[event_receiver(native)]      // optional for native C++ and managed classes
class CReceiver {
public:
                void MyHandler1(int nValue) {
                   printf("MyHandler1 was called with value %d.\n", nValue);
                }
                void hookEvent(CSource* pSource) {
                   __hook(&CSource::MyEvent, pSource, &CReceiver::MyHandler1);
                }
                void unhookEvent(CSource* pSource) {
                   __unhook(&CSource::MyEvent, pSource, &CReceiver::MyHandler1);
                }
};
```

Note that the Unified Event Model supports dynamic hooking, that is, hooking/unhooking events in a loop or using conditional logic in a function that receives the source and local methods as parameters.

Event Handling in Native C

In native C++ event handling, you set up an event source and event receiver using the event_source and event_receiver attributes, respectively, specifying type=native. These attributes allow the classes to which they are applied to fire events and handle events in a native, non-COM context.

Declaring Events: In an event source class, use the __event keyword on a method declaration to declare the method as an event. Make sure to declare the method, but do not define it; to do so will generate a compiler error, because the compiler defines the method implicitly when it is made into an event. Native events can be a method with zero or more parameters. The return type can be void or an integral type.

Defining Event Handlers: In an event receiver class, you define event handlers, which are methods with signatures (return types, calling conventions, and arguments) that match the event that they will handle.

Hooking Event Handlers to Events: Also, in an event receiver class, you use the intrinsic function __hook to associate events with event handlers and __unhook to dissociate events from event handlers. You can hook several events to an event handler, or several event handlers to an event.

Firing Events: To fire an event, simply call the method declared as an event in the event source class. If handlers have been hooked to the event, the handlers will be called.

Native C++ Event Code:

```
/*
    File test.cpp
    To execute from the command line:
        CL test.cpp
        Test.exe
*/

#include <stdio.h>

[event_source(native)]
class CSource {
public:
    __event void MyEvent(int nValue);
};
```

```
[event_receiver(native)]
class CReceiver {
public:
    void MyHandler1(int nValue) {
        printf("MyHandler1 was called with value %d.\n", nValue);
    }

    void MyHandler2(int nValue) {
        printf("MyHandler2 was called with value %d.\n", nValue);
    }

    void hookEvent(CSource* pSource) {
        __hook(&CSource::MyEvent, pSource, &CReceiver::MyHandler1);
        __hook(&CSource::MyEvent, pSource, &CReceiver::MyHandler2);
    }

    void unhookEvent(CSource* pSource) {
        __unhook(&CSource::MyEvent, pSource, &CReceiver::MyHandler1);
        __unhook(&CSource::MyEvent, pSource, &CReceiver::MyHandler2);
    }
};

void main() {
    CSource source;
    CReceiver receiver;

    receiver.hookEvent(&source);
    source.MyEvent(123);
    receiver.unhookEvent(&source);
}
```

Event Handling in COM

In COM event handling, you set up an event source and event receiver using the event_source and event_receiver attributes, respectively, specifying type=com. These attributes inject the appropriate code for custom, dispatch, and dual interfaces to allow the classes to which they are applied to fire events and handle events through COM connection points.

Declaring Events: In an event source class, use the __event keyword on an interface declaration to declare that interface's methods as events. The events of that interface are fired when you call them as interface methods. Methods on event interfaces can have zero or more parameters (which should all be in parameters). The return type can be void or any integral type.

Defining Event Handlers: In an event receiver class, you define event handlers, which are methods with signatures (return types, calling conventions, and arguments) that match the event that they will handle. For COM events, calling conventions do not have to match; see "Layout Dependent COM Events" below for details.

Hooking Event Handlers to Events: Also in an event receiver class, you use the intrinsic function __hook to associate events with event handlers and __unhook to dissociate events from event handlers. You can hook several events to an event handler, or several event handlers to an event.

Note: Typically, there are two techniques to allow a COM event receiver to access event source interface definitions. The first, as shown below, is to share a common header file. The second is to use COM #import with the embedded_idl import qualifier, so that the event source type library is dumped with the attribute-generated code preserved.

Firing Events: To fire an event, simply call a method in the interface declared with the __event keyword in the event source class. If handlers have been hooked to the event, the handlers will be called.

COM Common Code:

```
/*
        File server.h (used by the following two files)
*/

#pragma once

[ dual ]
__interface IEvents {
        [id(1)] HRESULT MyEvent([in] int value);
};

[ dual ]
__interface IeventSource {
        [id(1)] HRESULT FireEvent();
};

class DECLSPEC_UUID("530Df3AD-6936-3214-A83B-27B63C7997C4")
CSource;
```

COM Event Source Code:

```
/*
      File server.cpp
      To compile into server.dll and register:
         CL –LD server.cpp
         Regsvr32.exe server.dll
*/

#define _ATL_ATTRIBUTES 1
#include <atlbase.h>
#include <atlcom.h>
#include "server.h"

[ module(DLL, name="EventSource", uuid="6E46B59E-89C3-4c15-A6D8-
B8A1CEC98830") ]

[ coclass, event_source(com) ]
class CSource : public IEventSource {
public:
      __event __interface IEvents;

      HRESULT FireEvent() {
         MyEvent(123);
         Return S_OK;
      }
};
```

COM Event Receiver Code:

```
/*
      File client.cpp
      To compile and run (server.dll must be compiled and registered):
         CL client.cpp
         Client.exe
*/

#define _ATL_ATTRIBUTES 1
#include <atlbase.h>
#include <atlcom.h>
#include <stdio.h>
#include "server.h"

[ module(name="EventReceiver") ];
```

```
[ event_receiver(com) ]
class CReceiver {
public:
    HRESULT MyHandler1(int nValue) {
        printf("MyHandler1 was called with value %d.\n", nValue);
        return S_OK;
    }

    HRESULT MyHandler2(int nValue) {
        printf("MyHandler2 was called with value %d.\n", nValue);
        return S_OK;
    }

    void HookEvent(IEventSource* pSource) {
        __hook(&IEvents::MyEvent, pSource, &CSource::MyHandler1);
        __hook(&IEvents::MyEvent, pSource, &CSource::MyHandler2);
    }

    void UnhookEvent(IEventSource* pSource) {
        __unhook(&IEvents::MyEvent, pSource, &CSource::MyHandler1);
        __unhook(&IEvents::MyEvent, pSource, &CSource::MyHandler2);
    }
};

int main() {
    // Create COM object
    CoInitialize(NULL);
    IEventSource* pSource = 0;
HRESULT hr = CoCreateInstance(__uuidof(CSource, NULL, CLSCTX_ALL,
__uuidof(IEventSource));
if(FAILED(hr)) {
    return -1;
}

// Create receiver and fire event
CReceiver receiver;
receiver.HookEvent(pSource);
    pSource->FireEvent();
    receiver.UnhookEvent(pSource);

    CoUninitialize();
    Return 0;
}
```

Layout Dependent COM Events

Layout dependency is only an issue for COM programming. In native and managed event handling, the signatures (return type, calling convention, and arguments) of the handlers must match their events, but the handler names do not have to match their events. However, in COM event handling, when you set the layout_dependent parameter of event_receiver to true, the name and signature matching is enforced. This means that the names and signatures of the handlers in the event receiver must exactly match the names and signatures of the events to which they are hooked. When layout_dependent is set to false, the calling convention and storage class (virtual, static, and so on) can be mixed and matched between the firing event method and the hooking methods (its delegates). It is slightly more efficient to have layout_dependent=true.

For example, suppose IEventSource is defined to have the following methods:

[id(1)] HRESULT MyEvent1([in] int value);
[id(2)] HRESULT MyEvent2([in] int value);

Assume the event source has the following form:

```
[coclass, event_source(com)]
class CSource : public IEventSource {
public:
        __event __interface IEvents;

        HRESULT FireEvent() {
            MyEvent1(123);
            MyEvent2(123);
            Return S_OK;
        }
};
```

Then, in the event receiver, any handler hooked to a method in IEventSource must match its name and signature, as follows:

```
[coclass, event_receiver(com, true)]
class CReceiver {
public:
        HRESULT MyEvent1(int nValue) {    // name and signature matches
MyEvent1
            ......
        }
        HRESULT MyEvent2(E c, char* pc) {    // signature doesn't match
```

```
MyEvent2
    ......
    }
    HRESULT MyHandler1(int nValue) {    // name doesn't match MyEvent1
(or 2)
    ......
    }
    void HookEvent(IEventsource* pSource) {
    __hook(IFace, pSource);            // Hooks up all name-matched
events
                                      // under layout_dependent = true
    __hook(&IFace::MyEvent1, pSource, &CSink::MyEvent1);    // legal
    __hook(&IFace::MyEvent2, pSource, &CSink::MyEvent2);    // ille-
gal
    __hook(&IFace::MyEvent1, pSource, &CSink::MyHandler1);    //
illegal
    }
};
```

Event Handling in .NET

In managed event handling, you set up an event source and event receiver using the event_source and event_receiver attributes, respectively, specifying type=managed. These attributes inject the appropriate code to allow the classes to which they are applied to fire events and handle events in a managed context.

Declaring Events: In an event source class, use the __event keyword on a method declaration (or a pointer-to-delegate data member) to declare the method as an event. Make sure to declare the method, but do not define it; to do so will generate a compiler error, because the compiler defines the method implicitly when it is made into an event. Managed events can be data members or methods. Managed event methods can have zero or more parameters. If defined with single-cast delegate, the return type of a managed event handler method can be any data type. If defined with a multicast delegate, the return type must be void.

Defining Event Handlers: In an event receiver class, you define event handlers, which are methods with signatures (return types, calling conventions, and arguments) that match the event that they will handle.

Hooking Event Handlers to Events: Also in an event receiver class, you use the intrinsic function __hook to associate events with event handlers and __unhook to dissociate events from event handlers. You can hook several events to an event handler, or several event handlers to an event.

Firing Events: To fire an event, simply call the data member or method declared as an event in the event source class. If handlers have been hooked to the event, the handlers will be called.

Managed Event Source Code:

```
/*
     File cpsource.cpp
     To compile into cpsource.dll:
         CL –LD –CLR cpsource.cpp
*/

#using <mscorlib.dll>
using namespace System

[event_source(managed)]         // optional
public __gc class CPSource {
public:
     __event void MyEvent(Int16 nValue);
};
```

Managed Event Receiver and Main Code:

```
/*
     File cpexecute.cpp
     To compile and run:
         CL –CLR cpexecute.cpp
         execute.exe
*/

#using <mscorlib.dll>
using namespace System;
#using "cpsource.dll"

[ event_receiver(managed) ]      // optional

__gc class CReceiver {
public:
     void MyHandler1(Int16 nValue) {
         Console::Write("MyHandler1 was called with value ");
         Console::WriteLine(nValue);
     }

     void MyHandler2(Int16 nValue) {
```

```
        Console::Write("MyHandler2 was called with value ");
        Console::WriteLine(nValue);
    }

    void HookEvent(CPSource* pSource) {
        __hook(&CPSource::MyEvent, pSource, &CReceiver::MyHandler1);
        __hook(&CPSource::MyEvent, pSource, &CReceiver::MyHandler2);
    }

    void UnhookEvent(CPSource* pSource) {
        __unhook(&CPSource::MyEvent, pSource, &CReceiver::MyHandler1);
        __unhook(&CPSource::MyEvent, pSource, &CReceiver::MyHandler2);
    }
};

void main() {
    CPSource* pSource = new CPSource;
    CReceiver* perceiver = new CReceiver;

    pReceiver->HookEvent(pSource);
    pSource->MyEvent(123);
    pRerceiver->UnhookEvent(pSource);
}
```

Event Handling Keywords

Visual C++ includes attributes and keywords for declaring events and event handlers. The event attributes and keywords can be used in managed programs and in native C++ programs.

1. event_source   Creates an event source.
2. event_receiver   Creates an event receiver (sink).
3. __event   Declares an event.
4. __raise   Emphasizes the call site of an event.
5. __hook   Associates a handler method with an event.
6. __unhook   Dissociates a handler method from an event.

Managed Extensions for C++ Reference

*M*anaged Extensions for C++ include the following reference material:

- Keywords
- Attributes
- Pragmas
- Preprocessor Directives
- Compiler Options
- Linker Options

Keywords

Keyword	Description
__abstract	Declares a class that cannot be instantiated directly.
__box	Creates a copy of a value class.
__delegate	Declares a reference to a unique method within an instance of a managed class.
event	Declares an event.
__finally	Declares a finally block.
__gc	Declares a garbage-collected class.
__identifier	Enables the use of keywords as identifiers.
__interface	Declares a standard interface.
__nogc	Declares a native C++ class that is not garbage-collected.
__pin	Prevents a managed object from being moved by the Common Language Runtime.

__property	Declares a property member for a managed class.
public, private (Accessibility Levels)	Determines the accessibility of specified members.
sealed	Prevents a method or class from being a base class.
try cast	Throws an exception if the cast is illegal.
using	Creates an alias or allows the usage of friendly names.
value	A version of dynamic cast that may throw an exception.

Attributes

Attribute	Description
attribute	Creates a custom attribute.

Pragmas

Pragma	Description
managed, unmanged	Determines if a module compiles functions as managed or unmanaged.

Preprocessor Directives

Directive	Description
#using	Imports metadata into a managed application.

Compiler Options

Option	Description
/CLR	Allows the usage of Managed Extensions for C++.

Linker Options

Option	Description
/ASSEMBLYMODULE	Adds an MSIL module to the assembly of a project.
/ASSEMBLYRESOURCE	Adds a link to a managed resource from a project.
/NOASSEMBLY	Creates an MSIL module without an assembly.

/CLR (Common Language Runtime Compilation)

*T*his appendix covers the details for using the /CLR option in compiling.

/CLR[:noAssembly]

where:
:noAssembly (optional)—Specifies that an assembly manifest should not be inserted into the output file. By default, an assembly manifest is inserted into the output file. You can cause an assembly to not be created with the /NOASSEMBLY linker option.

Remarks:
The /CLR compiler option enables the use of Managed Extensions for C++ and creates an output file that will require the .NET runtime at run time. There may or may not be managed data in the application. /CLR does not imply that classes, interfaces, or structs are managed: use __gc to explicitly specify when you want a construct to be managed. /CLR does imply that all functions will be managed. To make specified functions unmanaged, use the managed pragma. Code compiled with /CLR must also use the #using <mscorlib.dll> statement.

Managed code is code that can be inspected and managed by the .NET runtime. Managed code can access managed objects. By default, the /CLR compiler option is not in effect. When /CLR is in effect, /MT is also in effect. The /COMHEADER DUMPBIN option displays .NET header information for an image that was built with /CLR.

Note the following restrictions on the use of /CLR:

- The use of Run-time Error Checks is not valid with the /CLR compiler option.

- When inline assembly code is found in a managed function, the compiler will try to complete the compilation by compiling the function as unmanaged native code. Inline assembly will not appear in a managed function.
- When /CLR is used to compile a program that does not use Managed Extensions for C++, the following guidelines apply to the use of inline assembly:

  1. Inline assembly code that assumes knowledge of the native stack layout, calling conventions outside of the current function, or other low-level information about the computer may fail if that knowledge is applied to the stack frame for a managed function. Functions containing inline assembly code are generated as unmanaged functions, as if they were placed in a separate module that was compiled without /CLR.

  2. Inline assembly code in module-static functions is not supported:
     Static void TestInlineAsmInStaticFunc(void) {
     __asm { nop }
     }

  3. Inline assembly code in functions that pass copy-constructed function parameters is not supported:

     class CMyClass {
     public:
         int a, b, c;
         CMyClass() {
         a = b = c = 1;
         }
         CMyClass(const CMyClass& mSrc) {
         a = b = c = mSrc.a + 1;
         }
     };

         void TestCopyCtors(void) {
             CMyClass m;
             f(e, m, 4);
             __asm { nop }
         }

- The vprintf Functions cannot be called from a program compiled with /CLR.
- The naked __declspec modifier is ignored under /CLR.
- The use of dllexport or dllimport on classes is not permitted under /CLR.

- The use of C++ Exception Handling is not permitted under /CLR. The translator function set by _set_se_translator will affect only catches in unmanaged code.
- The comparison of function pointers is not permitted under /CLR.
- The use of setjmp and longjmp is not permitted under /CLR.
- The use of functions that are not fully prototyped is not permitted under /CLR.
- /GL compiler option is not supported with /CLR.
- /Zd compiler option is not supported with /CLR.
- /ZI compiler option is not supported with /CLR.
- /ML and MLD compiler options are not supported with /CLR.
- Passing a wide character to a .NET Frameworks output routine without also specifying /Zc:wchar_t or without casting the character to __wchar_t will cause the output to appear as an unsigned short int. For example, Console::WriteLine(L' ') will output 32. Console::Writeline((__wchar_t)L' ') will output a space.

To set this compiler option in the Visual Studio development environment:

1. Open the project's Property Pages dialog box.
2. Click the Configuration Properties folder.
3. Click the General property page.
4. Modify the Compile as manage property.

C# Compiler Options

Listed Alphabetically

Option	Purpose
@	Specify a response file.
/?	List compiler options to stdout.
/addmodule	Specify one or more modules to be part of this assembly.
/baseaddress	Specify the preferred base address at which to load a DLL.
/bugreport	Create a file that contains information that makes it easy to report a bug.
/checked	Specify whether integer arithmetic that overflows the bounds of the data type will cause an exception at run time.
/codepage	Specify the code page to use for all source code files in the compilation.
/debug	Emit debugging information.
/define	Define preprocessor symbols.
/doc	Process documentation comments to an XML file.
/fullpaths	Specify the absolute path to the file in compiler output.
/help	List compiler options to stdout.
/incremental	Enable incremental compilation of source code files.
/linkresource	Link a .NET resource to an assembly.

/main	Specify the location of the Main method.
/nologo	Suppress compiler banner information.
/nooutput	Compile but do not create an output file.
/nostdlib	Do not import standard library (mscorlib.dll).
/nowarn	Suppress the compiler's ability to generate specified warnings.
/optimize	Enable/disable optimizations.
/out	Specify output file.
/recurse	Search subdirectories for source files to compile.
/reference	Import metadata from a file that contains an assembly.
/resource	Embed a .NET resource into the output file.
/target	Specify the format of the output file using one of four options: /target:exe /target:library /target:module /target:winexe
/unsafe	Compile code that uses the unsafe keyword.
/warn	Set warning level.
/warnaserror	Promote warnings to errors.
/win32icon	Insert a .ico file into the output file.
/win32res	Insert a win32 resource into the output file.

Listed by Category

Optimization

Option	Purpose
/optimize	Enable/disable optimizations.

Output Files

Option	Purpose
/doc	Process documentation comments to XML file.
/out	Specify output file.
/nooutput	Compile but do not create output file.
/target	Specify the format of the output file using one of four options: /target:exe /target:library /target:module /target:winexe

.NET Assemblies

Option	Purpose
/addmodule	Specify one or more modules to be part of this assembly.
/nostdlib	Do not import standard library (mscorlib.dll).
/reference	Import metadata from a file that contains an assembly.

Debugging/Error Checking

Option	Purpose
/bugreport	Create a file that contains information that makes it easy to report a bug.
/checked	Specify whether integer arithmetic that overflows the bounds of the data type will cause an exception at run time.
/debug	Emit debugging information.
/fullpaths	Specify the absolute path to the file in compiler output.
/nowarn	Suppress the compiler's ability to generate specified warnings.
/warn	Set warning level.
/warnaserror	Promote warnings to errors.

Preprocessor

Option	Purpose
/define	Define preprocessor symbols.

Resources

Option	Purpose
/linkresource	Link a .NET resource to an assembly.
/resource	Embed a .NET resource into the output file.
/win32icon	Insert a .ico file into the output file.
/win32res	Insert a Win32 resource into the output file.

Miscellaneous

Option	Purpose
@	Specify a response file.
/?	List compiler options to stdout.
/baseaddress	Specify the preferred base address at which to load a DLL.
/codepage	Specify the code page to use for all source code files in the compilation.
/help	List compiler options to stdout.
/incremental	Enable incremental compilation of source code files.
/main	Specify the location of the Main method.
/nologo	Suppress compiler banner information.
/recurse	Search subdirectories for source files to compile.
/unsafe	Compile code that uses the unsafe keyword.

Building from the Command Line

The compiler can be invoked at the command line by typing the name of its executable (csc.exe) on the command line. You may need to adjust your path if you want csc.exe to be invoked from any subdirectory on your computer. The batch file vcvars32.bat sets the appropriate environment variables to enable command line builds. To run vcvars32.bat:

1. At the command prompt, change to the \bin subdirectory of your Visual C++ installation.

2. Run vcvars32.bat by typing vcvars32.

    Caution: vcvars32.bat can vary from machine to machine. Do not replace a missing or damaged vcvars32.bat file with vcvars32.bat from another machine. Rerun setup to replace the missing file.

Sample Command Lines

- Compiles File.cs product File.exe:
  cscFile.cs
- Compiles File.cs producing File.dll:
  csc /target:library File.cs
- Compiles File.cs but no executable is created (useful for simply checking syntax):
  csc /nooutput File.cs
- Compiles File.cs and creates My.exe:
  csc /out:My.exe File.cs
- Compiles all of the C# files in the current directory, with optimization on and defines the DEBUG symbol. The output is File2.exe:
  csc /define:DEBG /optimize /out:File2.exe *.cs
- Compiles all of the C# files in the current directory producing a debug version of File2.dll. No logo and no warnings are displayed:
  csc /target:library /out:File2.dll /warn:0 /nologo /debug *.cs
- Compiles all of the C# files in the current directory to Something.xyz (a DLL):
  csc /target:library /out:Something.xyz *.cs

C# Keywords

Keywords are predefined reserved identifiers that have special meanings to the compiler. They cannot be used as identifiers in your program unless they include @ as a prefix. For example, *@if* is a legal identifier but *if* is not because it is a keyword.

abstract	enum	long	stackalloc
as	event	namespace	static
base	explicit	new	string
bool	extern	null	struct
break	false	object	switch
byte	finally	operator	this
case	fixed	out	throw
catch	float	override	true
char	for	params	try
checked	foreach	private	typeof
class	goto	protected	uint
const	if	public	ulong
continue	implicit	readonly	unchecked
decimal	in	ref	unsafe
default	int	return	ushort
delegate	interface	sbyte	using
do	internal	sealed	virtual
double	is	short	void
else	lock	sizeof	while

Built-in Types Table

The following table shows the keywords for built-in C# types, which are aliases of predefined types in the **System** namespace.

C# Type	.NET Type
bool	System.Boolean
byte	System.Byte
sbyte	System.Sbyte
char	System.Char
decimal	System.Decimal
double	System.Double
float	System.Single
int	System.Int32
uint	System.Uint32
long	System.Int64
ulong	System.Uint64
object	System.Object
short	System.Int16
ushort	System.Uint16
string	System.String

All the types in the table, except object and string, are referred to as simple types. The # type keywords and their aliases are interchangeable. For example, you can declare an integer variable by using either of the following declarations:

```
int x = 123;
System.Int32 x = 123;
```

To display the actual type for any C# type use the system method GetType(). For example, the following statement displays the system alias that represents the type of myVariable:

```
Console.WriteLine(myVariable.GetType());
```

C# Operators

C# provides a large set of operators, which are symbols that specify which operations to perform in an expression. C# predefines the usual arithmetic and logical operators, as well as a variety of others as shown in the following table. In addition, many operators can be overloaded by the user, thus changing their meaning when applied to a user-defined type.

Operator Category	Operators
Arithmetic	+ - * / %
Logical(Boolean and bitwise)	& | ^ ! ~ && | | true false
String concatenation	+
Increment, decrement	++ —
Shift	<< >>
Relational	== != < > <= >=
Assignment	= += -= *= /= %= &= |= ^= <<= >>=
Member access	.
Indexing	[]
Cast	()
Conditional	?:
Delegate concatenation and removal	+ -
Object creation	new
Type information	is sizeof typeof
Overflow exception control	checked unchecked
Indirection and address	* -> {} &

C# Preprocessor Directives

The following are the C# language's preprocessor directives:

- #if
- #else
- #elif
- #endif
- #define
- #undef
- #warning
- #error
- #line
- #region
- #endregion

While the C# compiler does not have a separate preprocessor, the directives described in the above list are processed as if there was one; these directive are used in a conditional compilation. Unlike C and C++ directives, you cannot use these directives to create macros. A preprocessor directive must be the only instruction on a line.

C# Libraries Tutorial

This tutorial demonstrates how to create a managed DLL file by using the necessary compiler options, and how to use the library by a client program. The second part of this appendix covers creating and using C# DLLs. Also the C# Compiler Options have been covered in Appendix M. The DLL library is built from the following two C# source files:

- Factorial.cs: Calculates and returns the factorial of a number.
- DigitCounter.cs: Counts the number of digits in the passed string.

To build the library, type the following at the command prompt:

csc /target:library /out:Functions.dll Factorial.cs DigitCounter.cs

where:

/target:library	Specifies that the output is a DLL and not an executable file. (This also stops the compiler from looking for a default entry point.)
/out:Functions.dll	Specifies that the output file name is Functions.dll. Normally, the output name is the same name as the first C# source file on the command line (in this example, Factorial).
Factorial.cs DigitCounter.cs	The files to compile and place in the DLL.

The client program that uses the DLL is compiled from the source file:

- FunctionClient.cs: Displays the factorial of the input arguments.

To compile the program, type the following at the command prompt:

csc /out:FunctionTest.exe /R:Functions.DLL FunctionClient.cs

where:

/out:FunctionTest.exe	Specifies that the output file name is FunctionTest.exe.
/R:Functions.DLL	Include Functions.DLL when resolving references. This DLL must be located in the current directory or have a fully qualified path.
FunctionClient.cs	The client source code.

This creates the executable file FunctionTest.exe. Following are the listing of the three source files used in this program followed by code discussion for each file.

File 1—Factorial.cs
The following code calculates the factorial of the integer passed to the method.

```
000:    // Libraries\Factorial.cs
001:    using System;
002:
003:    namespace Functions
004:    {
005:            public class Factorial
006:            {
007:                    public static int Calc(int i)
008:                    {
009:                            return((i <= 1) ? 1 : (i  * Calc(i – 1)));
010:                    }
011:            }
012:    }
```

Code Discussion:
- Line 003 declares a namespace. Nearly all C# code will be organized into namespaces. You need to package your libraries according to their namespace so the .NET runtime can correctly load the classes.
- Lines 005–011 declare the Factorial class that has one static method.
- The Calc static method calculates the factorial value for the specified integer passed in.

File 2—DigitCounter.cs
The following code is used to count the number of digit characters in the passed string:

```
000:    // Libraries\DigitCounter.cs
001:    using System;
002:
003:    namespace Functions
004:    {
005:            public class DigitCount
006:            {
007:                    public static int NumberofDigits(string theString)
008:                    {
009:                            int count = 0;
010:                            for ( int i = 0; i < theString.Length; i++)
011:                            {
012:                                    if ( Char.IsDigit(theString[i]) )
013:                                    {
014:                                            count++;
015:                                    }
016:                            }
017:
018:                            return count;
019:                    }
020:            }
021:    }
```

Code Discussion:

- Line 003 declares a namespace. Note that this second file declares the same namespace as the one in Factorial.cs. This simply allows types to be added to the same namespace.
- Lines 005–020 declare the DigitCount class that has one static method.
- The NumberofDigits static method calculates the number of digit characters in the passed string.

File 3—FunctionClient.cs
Once you build a library it can be used by other programs. The following client program uses the classes defined in the library. The basic function of the program is to take each command-line parameter and attempt to compute the factorial value for each argument.

```
000:    // Libraries\FunctionClient.cs
001:    using System;
002:    using Functions;
003:    class FunctionClient
004:    {
005:            public static void Main(string[] args)
006:            {
007:                    Console.WriteLine("Function Client");
008:
009:                    if ( args.Length == 0 )
010:                    {
011:                            Console.WriteLine("Usage: FunctionTest ");
012:                            return;
013:                    }
014:
015:                    for ( int i = 0; i < args.Length; i++ )
016:                    {
017:                            int num = Int32.Parse(args[i]);
018:                            Console.WriteLine(
019:                                "The Digit Count for String [{0}] is [{1}]",
020:                                args[i],
021:                                DigitCount.NumberofDigits(args[i]));
022:                            Console.WriteLine(
023:                                "The Factorial for [{0} is [{1}]",
024:                                num,
025:                                Factorial.Calc(num);
026:                    }
027:            }
028:    }
```

Code Discussion:
- Line 002: the using directive makes the types defined in the Functions namespace available in this compilation unit.
- Line 025: invokes the Calc static method in the Factorial class.
- Line 021: invokes the NumberofDigits static method in the DigitCount class.

Sample Run:
The following command line uses the program FunctionTest to calculate the factorial of the three integers 3, 5, and 10. It also displays the number of digits for each argument.

FunctionTest 3 5 10

This run give the output:

Function Client

The Digit Count for String [3] is [1]

The Factorial for [3] is [6]

The Digit Count for String [5] is [1]

The Factorial for [5] is [120]

The Digit Count for String [10] is [2]

The Factorial for [10] is [3628800]

Note   To run the client executable (FunctionTest.exe), the file Functions.DLL must be in the current directory, a child directory, or in a directory specified by the CORPATH environment variable. If you change the name of the DLL, the program will not be able to load the class. CORPATH is an environment variable that the .NET runtime uses to look for classes.

Creating and Using C# DLLs

A dynamic linking library (DLL) is linked to your program at run time. To demonstrate building and using a DLL, consider the following scenario:

- MyLibrary.DLL: The library file that contains the methods to be called at run time. In this example, the DLL contains two methods, Add and Multiply.
- Add.cs: The source file that contains the method Add(long i, long j). It returns the sum of its parameters. The class AddClass that contains the method Add is a member of the namespace MyMethods.
- Mult.cs: The source code that contains the method Multiply(long x, long y). It returns the product of its parameters. The class MultiplyClass that contains the method Multiply is also a member of the namespace MyMethods.
- MyClient.cs: The file that contains the Main method. It uses the methods in the DLL file to calculate the sum and the product of the run-time arguments.

File: Add.cs

```
//      Add two numbers
using System:
namespace MyMethods
{
        public class AddClass
        {
                public static long Add(long i, long j)
                {
                        return(i + j);
                }
        }
}
```

File: Mult.cs

```
//      Multiply two numbers
using System;
namespace MyMethods
{
        public class MultiplyClass
        {
                public static long Multiply(long x, long y)
                {
                        return (x * y);
                }
        }
}
```

File: MyClient.cs

```
//      Calling methods from a DLL file
using System;
using MyMethods;
class MyClient
{
        public static void Main(string[] args)
        {
                Console.WriteLine("Calling methods form MyLibrary.DLL:");
                if (args.Length != 2)
                {
                        Console.WriteLine("Usage:  MyClient  <num1>
<num2>");
```

```
                    return;
            }
            long num1 = long.Parse(args[0]);
            long num2 = long.Parse(args[1]);
            long sum = AddClass.Add(num1, num2);
            long product = MultiplyClass.Multiply(num1, num2);
            Console.WriteLine("The sum of {0} and {1} is {2}",
            num1, num2, sum);
            Console.WriteLine("The product of {0} and {1} is {2},
            num1, num2, product);
        }
}
```

The above are the algorithm that uses the DLL methods, Add and Multiply. It starts with parsing the arguments entered from the command line, num1 and num2. Then it calculates the sum by using the Add method on the AddClass class, and the product by using the Multiply method on the MultiplyClass class. Notice that the using directive at the beginning of the section allows you to used the unqualified class name to reference the DLL methods at compile time. For example:

MultiplyClass. Multiply(num1, num2);

Otherwise, you have to use the fully qualified names. For example:

MyMethods.MultiplyClass.Multiply(num1, num2);

Compilation:
To build the file MyLibrary.DLL, compile the two files Add.cs and Mult.cs using the following command line:
csc /target:library /out:MyLibrary.DLL add.cs Mult.cs

The /target:library compiler option tells the compiler to output a DLL instead of an EXE file. The /out compiler option followed by a file name is used to specify the DLL file name. Otherwise, the compiler uses the first file (Add.cs) as the name of the DLL. To build the executable file MyClient.exe, use the following command line:

csc /out:MyClient.exe /reference:MyLibrary.DLL MyClient.cs

The /out compiler option tells the compiler to output an EXE file and specifies the name of the output file (MyClient.exe). This compiler option is optional. The reference compiler option specifies the DLL file(s) that this program uses.

Execution:

To run the program, enter the name of the EXE file, followed by two numbers. For example:

MyClient 1234 5678

Output:

Calling methods from MyLibrary.DLL

The sum of 1234 and 5678 is 6912

The product of 1234 and 5678 is 7006652

ABOUT THE AUTHOR

Contacting the Author

Dr. Reeves is founder and president of Computer Engineering, Inc. (CEI), a computer systems and software development company based in Howell, Michigan. Dr. Reeves has some forty years experience in designing and developing computer hardware and software applications. He holds degrees in Engineering and Computer Science, and is a nationally recognized author, consultant, and teacher.

If you have questions, comments, or suggestions for improving this book, we would like to hear from you. You can contact the author by U.S. mail or by email at the following addresses:

Dr. Ronald D. Reeves
P.O. Box 315
Howell, MI 48844
Email: ce@ismi.net

About UCI Software Technical Training

The evolution of UCI Software Technical Training mirrors the rapid rate of change in the software industry.

In 1984, UCI began providing consulting and training services to professional programmers and systems engineers on Digital Equipment Corporation's VMS operating system.

In the late 1980s, UCI's business grew to include training for programmers and systems engineers in the UNIX environment, open systems, and distributed computing. In fact, working for the Open Software Foundation we taught one of the very first OSF/DCE courses in the world!

With the emergence of Microsoft as an industry leader, in 1992 UCI became one of the first Microsoft Training Partners.

Today UCI provides onsite and public training for software and systems engineers, with a focus on programming and web developer curriculum.

UCI has maintained a leadership role in training IT professionals on leading-edge technology since the company was founded. With this background, UCI instructors possess a clear understanding of the issues faced by IT organizations in an industry where the only constant is change. This experience translates to effective, real-life training experience for UCI's clients.

Our instructors—including the president and owner—possess real-world experience. Most are authors of leading-edge books, and all have earned multiple industry-recognized certifications.

The founder of UCI, Andrew Scoppa, serves as advisor for a book series on Microsoft technologies published by Prentice Hall PTR. He is nationally recognized as a leader in the programmer-training field. The series consists of 11 books written by UCI's instructors, including topics in distributed application programming, E-commerce, SQL Server, and Windows 2000 device drivers. These books provide valuable technical information for programmers and software engineers.

Index

S

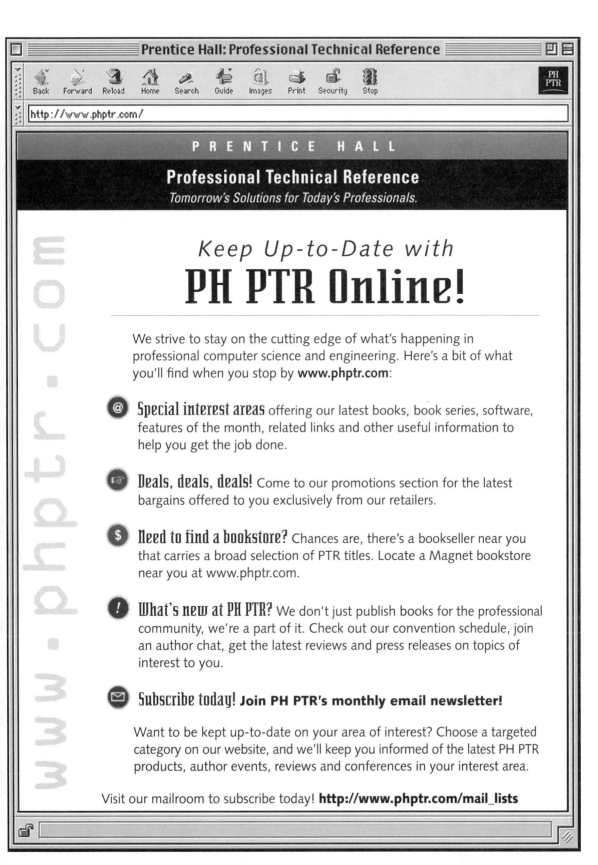

Prentice Hall: Professional Technical Reference

http://www.phptr.com/

PRENTICE HALL

Professional Technical Reference
Tomorrow's Solutions for Today's Professionals.

Keep Up-to-Date with
PH PTR Online!

We strive to stay on the cutting edge of what's happening in professional computer science and engineering. Here's a bit of what you'll find when you stop by **www.phptr.com**:

@ **Special interest areas** offering our latest books, book series, software, features of the month, related links and other useful information to help you get the job done.

✉ **Deals, deals, deals!** Come to our promotions section for the latest bargains offered to you exclusively from our retailers.

$ **Need to find a bookstore?** Chances are, there's a bookseller near you that carries a broad selection of PTR titles. Locate a Magnet bookstore near you at www.phptr.com.

! **What's new at PH PTR?** We don't just publish books for the professional community, we're a part of it. Check out our convention schedule, join an author chat, get the latest reviews and press releases on topics of interest to you.

✉ **Subscribe today! Join PH PTR's monthly email newsletter!**

Want to be kept up-to-date on your area of interest? Choose a targeted category on our website, and we'll keep you informed of the latest PH PTR products, author events, reviews and conferences in your interest area.

Visit our mailroom to subscribe today! **http://www.phptr.com/mail_lists**

InformIT

Solutions from experts you know and trust.

Articles | Free Library | eBooks | Expert Q & A | Training | Career Center | Downloads | MyInformIT

Login   Register   About InformIT

Topics
Operating Systems
Web Development
Programming
Networking
Certification
and more...

Expert Access

Free Content

www.informit.com

- Free, in-depth articles and supplements

- Master the skills you need, when you need them

- Choose from industry leading books, ebooks, and training products

- Get answers when you need them - from live experts or InformIT's comprehensive library

- Achieve industry certification and advance your career

Visit InformIT today and get great content from PH PTR

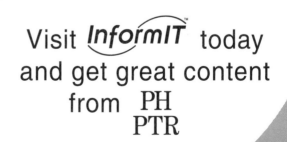

Prentice Hall and InformIT are trademarks of Pearson plc /
Copyright © 2000 Pearson

LICENSE AGREEMENT AND LIMITED WARRANTY

READ THE FOLLOWING TERMS AND CONDITIONS CAREFULLY BEFORE OPENING THIS DISK PACKAGE. THIS LEGAL DOCUMENT IS AN AGREEMENT BETWEEN YOU AND PRENTICE-HALL, INC. (THE "COMPANY"). BY OPENING THIS SEALED DISK PACKAGE, YOU ARE AGREEING TO BE BOUND BY THESE TERMS AND CONDITIONS. IF YOU DO NOT AGREE WITH THESE TERMS AND CONDITIONS, DO NOT OPEN THE DISK PACKAGE. PROMPTLY RETURN THE UNOPENED DISK PACKAGE AND ALL ACCOMPANYING ITEMS TO THE PLACE YOU OBTAINED THEM FOR A FULL REFUND OF ANY SUMS YOU HAVE PAID.

1. **GRANT OF LICENSE:** In consideration of your payment of the license fee, which is part of the price you paid for this product, and your agreement to abide by the terms and conditions of this Agreement, the Company grants to you a nonexclusive right to use and display the copy of the enclosed software program (hereinafter the "SOFTWARE") on a single computer (i.e., with a single CPU) at a single location so long as you comply with the terms of this Agreement. The Company reserves all rights not expressly granted to you under this Agreement.

2. **OWNERSHIP OF SOFTWARE:** You own only the magnetic or physical media (the enclosed disks) on which the SOFTWARE is recorded or fixed, but the Company retains all the rights, title, and ownership to the SOFTWARE recorded on the original disk copy(ies) and all subsequent copies of the SOFTWARE, regardless of the form or media on which the original or other copies may exist. This license is not a sale of the original SOFTWARE or any copy to you.

3. **COPY RESTRICTIONS:** This SOFTWARE and the accompanying printed materials and user manual (the "Documentation") are the subject of copyright. You may not copy the Documentation or the SOFTWARE, except that you may make a single copy of the SOFTWARE for backup or archival purposes only. You may be held legally responsible for any copying or copyright infringement which is caused or encouraged by your failure to abide by the terms of this restriction.

4. **USE RESTRICTIONS:** You may not network the SOFTWARE or otherwise use it on more than one computer or computer terminal at the same time. You may physically transfer the SOFTWARE from one computer to another provided that the SOFTWARE is used on only one computer at a time. You may not distribute copies of the SOFTWARE or Documentation to others. You may not reverse engineer, disassemble, decompile, modify, adapt, translate, or create derivative works based on the SOFTWARE or the Documentation without the prior written consent of the Company.

5. **TRANSFER RESTRICTIONS:** The enclosed SOFTWARE is licensed only to you and may not be transferred to any one else without the prior written consent of the Company. Any unauthorized transfer of the SOFTWARE shall result in the immediate termination of this Agreement.

6. **TERMINATION:** This license is effective until terminated. This license will terminate automatically without notice from the Company and become null and void if you fail to comply with any provisions or limitations of this license. Upon termination, you shall destroy the Documentation and all copies of the SOFTWARE. All provisions of this Agreement as to warranties, limitation of liability, remedies or damages, and our ownership rights shall survive termination.

7. **MISCELLANEOUS:** This Agreement shall be construed in accordance with the laws of the United States of America and the State of New York and shall benefit the Company, its affiliates, and assignees.

8. **LIMITED WARRANTY AND DISCLAIMER OF WARRANTY:** The Company warrants that the SOFTWARE, when properly used in accordance with the Documentation, will operate in substantial conformity with the description of the SOFTWARE set forth in the Documentation. The Company does not warrant that the SOFTWARE will meet your requirements or that the operation of the SOFTWARE will be uninterrupted or error-free. The Company warrants that the media on which the SOFTWARE is delivered shall be free from defects in materials and workmanship under normal use for a period of thirty (30) days from the date of your purchase. Your only remedy and the Company's only obligation under these limited warranties is, at the Company's option, return of the warranted item for a refund of any amounts paid by you or replacement of the item. Any replacement of SOFTWARE or media under the warranties shall not extend the original warranty period. The limited warranty set forth above shall not apply to any SOFTWARE which the Company determines in good faith has been subject to misuse, neglect, improper installation, repair, alteration, or damage by you. EXCEPT FOR THE EXPRESSED WARRANTIES SET FORTH ABOVE, THE COMPANY DISCLAIMS ALL WARRANTIES, EXPRESS OR IMPLIED, INCLUDING WITHOUT LIMITATION, THE IMPLIED WARRANTIES OF MERCHANTABILITY AND FITNESS FOR A PARTICULAR PURPOSE. EXCEPT FOR THE EXPRESS WARRANTY SET FORTH ABOVE, THE COMPANY DOES NOT WARRANT, GUARANTEE, OR MAKE ANY REPRESENTATION REGARDING THE USE OR THE RESULTS OF THE USE OF THE SOFTWARE IN TERMS OF ITS CORRECTNESS, ACCURACY, RELIABILITY, CURRENTNESS, OR OTHERWISE.

IN NO EVENT, SHALL THE COMPANY OR ITS EMPLOYEES, AGENTS, SUPPLIERS, OR CONTRACTORS BE LIABLE FOR ANY INCIDENTAL, INDIRECT, SPECIAL, OR CONSEQUENTIAL DAMAGES ARISING OUT OF OR IN CONNECTION WITH THE LICENSE GRANTED UNDER THIS AGREEMENT, OR FOR LOSS OF USE, LOSS OF DATA, LOSS OF INCOME OR PROFIT, OR OTHER LOSSES, SUSTAINED AS A RESULT OF INJURY TO ANY PERSON, OR LOSS OF OR DAMAGE TO PROPERTY, OR CLAIMS OF THIRD PARTIES, EVEN IF THE COMPANY OR AN AUTHORIZED REPRESENTATIVE OF THE COMPANY HAS BEEN ADVISED OF THE POSSIBILITY OF SUCH DAMAGES. IN NO EVENT SHALL LIABILITY OF THE COMPANY FOR DAMAGES WITH RESPECT TO THE SOFTWARE EXCEED THE AMOUNTS ACTUALLY PAID BY YOU, IF ANY, FOR THE SOFTWARE.

SOME JURISDICTIONS DO NOT ALLOW THE LIMITATION OF IMPLIED WARRANTIES OR LIABILITY FOR INCIDENTAL, INDIRECT, SPECIAL, OR CONSEQUENTIAL DAMAGES, SO THE ABOVE LIMITATIONS MAY NOT ALWAYS APPLY. THE WARRANTIES IN THIS AGREEMENT GIVE YOU SPECIFIC LEGAL RIGHTS AND YOU MAY ALSO HAVE OTHER RIGHTS WHICH VARY IN ACCORDANCE WITH LOCAL LAW.

ACKNOWLEDGMENT

YOU ACKNOWLEDGE THAT YOU HAVE READ THIS AGREEMENT, UNDERSTAND IT, AND AGREE TO BE BOUND BY ITS TERMS AND CONDITIONS. YOU ALSO AGREE THAT THIS AGREEMENT IS THE COMPLETE AND EXCLUSIVE STATEMENT OF THE AGREEMENT BETWEEN YOU AND THE COMPANY AND SUPERSEDES ALL PROPOSALS OR PRIOR AGREEMENTS, ORAL, OR WRITTEN, AND ANY OTHER COMMUNICATIONS BETWEEN YOU AND THE COMPANY OR ANY REPRESENTATIVE OF THE COMPANY RELATING TO THE SUBJECT MATTER OF THIS AGREEMENT.

Should you have any questions concerning this Agreement or if you wish to contact the Company for any reason, please contact in writing at the address below.

Robin Short
Prentice Hall PTR
One Lake Street, Upper Saddle River, New Jersey 07458

CARROLL COLLEGE LIBRARY

2 5052 00664860 6

About the CD
Before You Begin

Prerequisites

The exercise labs on the CD assume you have access to Visual Studio.NET. However, the code can be compiled and run using the C# compiler that is installed with the Runtime SDK.

Exercises

The exercises give you practice with the concepts and techniques covered in the lab.

The code is in the Arrays and Collections Folder.

Exercise 1: Simple Arrays

In this exercise, you will learn how to use single dimensional arrays in C#.

Exercise 2: Multidimensional Arrays

In this exercise, you will learn how to use multidimensional arrays and jagged arrays in C#.

Exercise 3: Arrays and Collection Classes

In this exercise, you will learn how to use the array-like collection classes in the Framework, and the difference between the collection classes and built-in arrays.

Exercise 4: A User-Defined Collection

In this exercise, you will learn how to define a collection so that it can be indexed and iterated using the C# for each statement.

System Requirements

Platforms

Windows 2000

See the platform support page, which is kept up to date with all the system requirements and can be found at:

http://edocs.bea.com/wls/platforms/index.html

Use of the *J2EE Applications and BEA WebLogic Server* CD-ROM is subject to the terms of the License Agreement following the index of this book.

Technical Support

Prentice Hall does not offer technical support for this software. If there is a problem with the CD, however, you may obtain a replacement CD by emailing a description of the problem. Send your email to:

```
disc_exchange@prenhall.com
```

WITHDRAWN
CARROLL UNIVERSITY LIBRARY